THE PRENTICE HALL
ATLAS
of
WORLD HISTORY
SECOND EDITION

Produced in Collaboration with Dorling Kindersley

DORLING KINDERSLEY
LONDON · NEW YORK · MUNICH
MELBOURNE · DELHI
www.dk.com

PEARSON
Prentice
Hall

UPPER SADDLE RIVER, NJ 07458

Library of Congress Cataloging-in-Publication Data

Pearson/Prentice Hall.
    The Prentice Hall atlas of world history / Pearson Prentice Hall;
produced in collaboration with Dorling Kindersley.-- 2nd ed.
    p. cm.
    Includes index.
    ISBN-13: 978-0-13-604247-1
    ISBN-10: 0-13-604247-3
    1. Historical geography – Maps. 2. World history – Maps.
    I. Title: Atlas of world history. II. Dorling Kindersley, Inc. III. Title.
G1030.P23 2008
911--dc22

                                                    2007052305

THE TEAM AT PRENTICE HALL:

EXECUTIVE EDITOR Charles Cavaliere
EDITORIAL ASSISTANTS Lauren Aylward and Maureen Diana
MARKETING MANAGER Laura Lee Manley
SENIOR MANAGING EDITOR Mary Carnis
PRODUCTION EDITOR Denise Brown
OPERATIONS SUPERVISOR Mary Ann Gloriande

MAP CONSULTANTS:

Tom Angle, Metropolitan Community College
Chris Bierwirth, Murray State University
Robert Bond, San Diego Mesa College

THE TEAM AT DK:

CARTOGRAPHIC MANAGER David Roberts
CARTOGRAPHER Paul Antonio
PROJECT ART EDITOR Clive Savage
PROJECT MANAGER Richard Czapnik
ASSOCIATE PUBLISHER Nigel Duffield
CARTOGRAPHY Selected maps taken from the *DK Atlas of World History* (ISBN: 0-7566-0967-4)

Maps designed and produced by DK Education, a division of Dorling Kindersley Limited, 80 Strand London WC2R 0RL. DK and the DK logo are registered trademarks of Dorling Kindersley Limited.

Pearson Education LTD.
Pearson Education Singapore, Pte. Ltd
Pearson Education, Canada, Ltd
Pearson Education–Japan
Pearson Education Malaysia, Pte. Ltd

Pearson Educación de Mexico, S.A. de C.V.
Pearson Education North Asia Ltd
Pearson Education Australia PTY, Limited
Pearson Education, Upper Saddle River, NJ

10 9 8 7 6 5 4 3 2 1
ISBN-13: 978-0-13-604247-1
ISBN-10: 0-13-604247-3

CONTENTS

CONTENTS

CHANGES TO THE SECOND EDITION

• **Enhanced Maps** Every map has been improved by enhancing or refining the clarity of its presentation, or by removing extraneous or unnecessary information

• **Improved Introductions** The introductions to many of the maps have been revised, simplified, or updated.

• **Revised Focus Questions** Many of the Focus Questions have been rewritten so that they more directly ask students to relate conceptual problems to the map at hand.

• **New Section on Historical Maps** A two-page section, entitled "About the Maps on the Front and Back Covers," provides fascinating details and background context on five historical maps.

NEW MAPS IN THE SECOND EDITION

Civilizations and Cultures of North America and Central America, 100-1500CE

Civilizations of Mesoamerica and Central America

The Empires of the Andes

Global Economies and Technologies, ca. 1500

African Slave-Exporting Regions, ca. 1750

The Enlightenment in Europe: Subscriptions to the Encyclopedia

Qing China, 1644-1800

The Decolonization of Africa

Palestine and Israel, 1947-2007

The United States in the 1960s: Protests and Urban Unrest

Global Warming, 1976-2006

HOW TO USE THIS ATLAS

MAPS USE A UNIQUE VISUAL language to convey a great deal of detailed information in a relatively simple form. The maps in this atlas use a variety of different projections – a technique used to show the Earth's curved surface on a flat map – to trace the geographical, physical, and social development of humans, from over 4 million years ago to the present. This page explains how to look for different features on the maps and how to unravel the different layers of information you can find on them.

Projection

Projections, which show the world at global, continental, or country scale, vary with each map. The projections for this atlas have been carefully chosen, ensuring that there is as little distortion as possible.

Scalebar

When using a map to work out what distances are in reality, it is necessary to refer to the scale of that particular map. The maps in this atlas use a linear scale. This only works on equal-area maps (where distances are true); on all other maps the scalebar is omitted.

Map Key

Maps use symbols to both show the location of a feature, and to give information about that feature. The symbols used in this atlas are explained in the key that accompanies each map.

Timeline

Many of the maps featured in this atlas are accompanied by timelines. Various important events and developments are plotted along a historical line, which shows the order in which they occured during a certain period in history. Where a place or event shown on the map and colored in the key is also named on the timeline, the corresponding section on the timeline is given the same color as that on the key, to allow for cross-referencing.

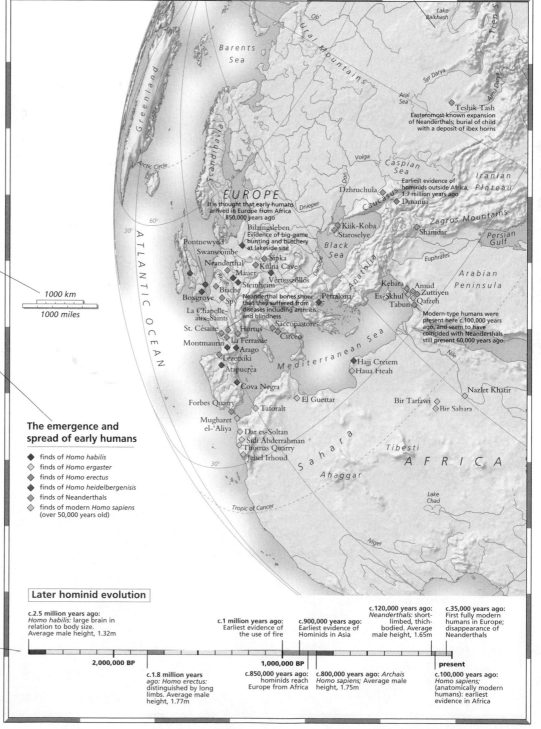

1000 km
1000 miles

The emergence and spread of early humans

- ◆ finds of *Homo habilis*
- ◇ finds of *Homo ergaster*
- ◇ finds of *Homo erectus*
- ◆ finds of *Homo heidelbergenisis*
- ◇ finds of Neanderthals
- ◇ finds of modern *Homo sapiens* (over 50,000 years old)

Later hominid evolution

c.2.5 million years ago: *Homo habilis:* large brain in relation to body size. Average male height, 1.32m.

c.1 million years ago: Earliest evidence of the use of fire

c.900,000 years ago: Earliest evidence of Hominids in Asia

c.120,000 years ago: *Neanderthals:* short-limbed, thich-bodied. Average male height, 1.65m

c.35,000 years ago: First fully modern humans in Europe; disappearance of Neanderthals

2,000,000 BP

1,000,000 BP

present

c.1.8 million years ago: *Homo erectus:* distinguished by long limbs. Average male height, 1.77m.

c.850,000 years ago: hominids reach Europe from Africa

c.800,000 years ago: *Archais Homo sapiens;* Average male height, 1.75m

c.100,000 years ago: *Homo sapiens;* (anatomically modern humans): earliest evidence in Africa

EARLY HOMINIDS

THE EARLIEST IDENTIFIABLE human ancestors date to over 4.5 million years ago, and were upright walking hominids with many apelike characteristics. *Australopithecus afarensis*, represented by an adult female known as "Lucy," flourished in the Hadar region of Ethiopia 3.4 million years ago. This Australopithecine, or "southern ape," evolved into several forms by 2.5 million years ago, among them a larger brained *Homo*, the ancestor of all later humans. Until about 1.8 million years ago, these humans were confined to their continent of origin, tropical Africa.

What environmental factors influenced the development of early hominids?

Aramis

S a h a r a

Lake Chad

Recent discoveries of a new australopithecine (*A.bahrelchazali*) stretch the geographical range 3800 km west of Great Rift Valley

Equator

Congo Basin

Congo

A F R I C A

Cunene

Kalahari Desert

Tropic of Capricorn

Swartkrans

Taung

ATLANTIC OCEAN

Orange River

Drakensbe

Elevation

- 100 meters (330ft)
- 250 meters (820ft)
- 500 meters (1,640ft)
- 1000 meters (3,280ft)
- 2000 meters (6,560ft)
- 3000 meters (9,840ft)
- 4000 meters (13,123ft)
- 6000 meters (19,685ft)
- 7000 meters (22,965ft)

500 km

500 miles

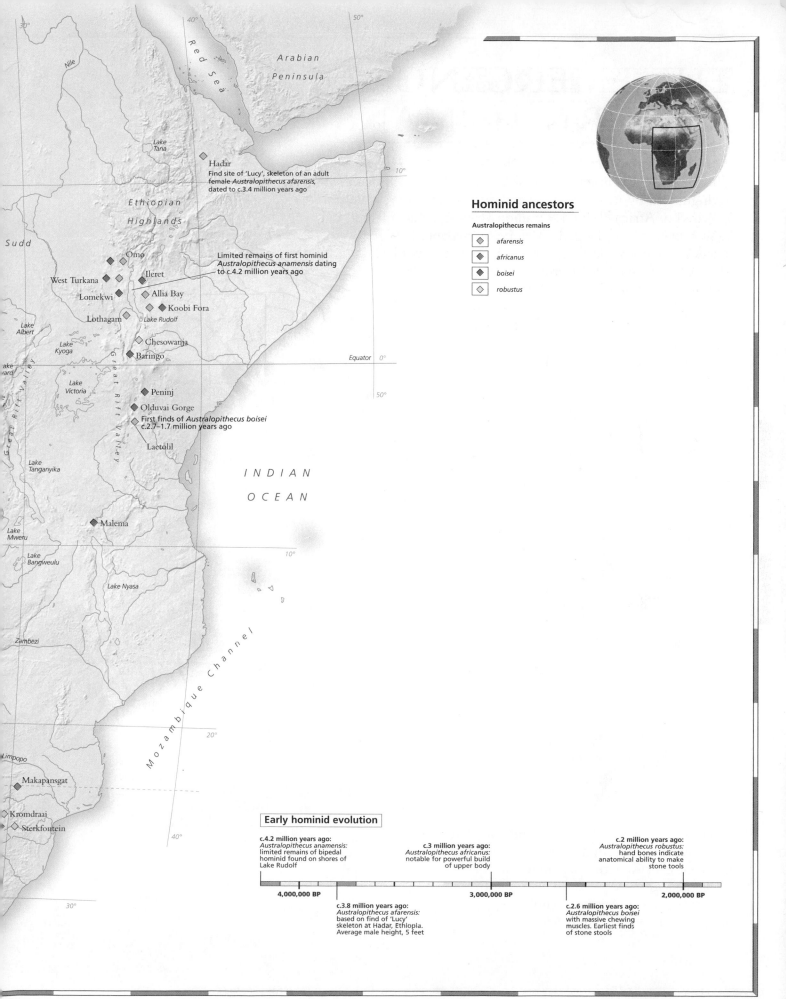

Hominid ancestors

Australopithecus remains

◇ *afarensis*

◆ *africanus*

◆ *boisei*

◇ *robustus*

Hadar
Find site of 'Lucy', skeleton of an adult female *Australopithecus afarensis*, dated to c.3.4 million years ago

Omo

Ileret

Limited remains of first hominid *Australopithecus anamensis* dating to c.4.2 million years ago

West Turkana

Allia Bay

Lomekwi

Koobi Fora

Lothagam

Lake Rudolf

Chesowanja

Baringo

Peninj

Olduvai Gorge

First finds of *Australopithecus boisei* c.2.7–1.7 million years ago

Laetolil

INDIAN OCEAN

Malema

Makapansgat

Kromdraai

Sterkfontein

Early hominid evolution

c.4.2 million years ago:
Australopithecus anamensis: limited remains of bipedal hominid found on shores of Lake Rudolf

c.3 million years ago:
Australopithecus africanus: notable for powerful build of upper body

c.2 million years ago:
Australopithecus robustus: hand bones indicate anatomical ability to make stone tools

4,000,000 BP

3,000,000 BP

2,000,000 BP

c.3.8 million years ago:
Australopithecus afarensis: based on find of 'Lucy' skeleton at Hadar, Ethiopia. Average male height, 5 feet

c.2.6 million years ago:
Australopithecus boisei with massive chewing muscles. Earliest finds of stone stools

THE EMERGENCE OF MODERN HUMANS

THE FIRST REPRESENTATIVE of the *Homo* genus, *Homo habilis* ("handy person"), emerged about 2.5 million years ago and was distinguished by its toolmaking abilities. *Homo erectus*, which appeared in Africa about 1.9 million years ago, had a larger brain capacity, long-legged physique, and adapted successfully to a wide range of environments, spreading from Africa to Asia and Europe over the next 1.25 million years. The earliest fossil remains of fully modern humans, *Homo sapiens*, found in Africa, date to c.150,000 years ago. Resourceful and inventive, modern humans colonized all kinds of environments, and became the sole surviving human species.

Why did several hominid species coexist for millions of years in the past, but since about 37,000 years ago there has been just one?

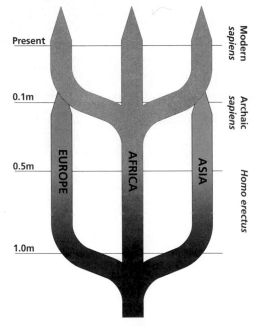

Present		Modern sapiens
0.1m		Archaic sapiens
0.5m	EUROPE · AFRICA · ASIA	*Homo erectus*
1.0m		

OUT OF AFRICA. This model suggests that *Homo erectus* emigrated from Africa, but then died out everywhere else. The evolution to *Homo sapiens* took place only among those that remained in Africa — who later emigrated to Europe and Asia.

Teshik-Tash
Easternmost known expansion of Neanderthals; burial of child with a deposit of ibex horns

Earliest evidence of hominids outside Africa, 1.7 million years ago
Dmanisi

Dzhruchula
Kiik-Koba
Staroselye
Shanidar

Bilzingsleben
Evidence of big-game hunting and butchery at lakeside site
Pontnewydd
Swanscombe
Sipka
Kůlna Cave
Neanderthal
Mauer
Vértesszöllös
Steinheim
Neanderthal bones show that they suffered from diseases including arthritis and blindness
Biache
Boxgrove
Spy
Petralona
La Chapelle-aux-Saints
Kebara
Amud
Zuttiyen
Es-Skhul
Qafzeh
Tabun
St. Césaire
Hortus
Saccopastore
Modern-type humans were present here c.100,000 years ago, and seem to have coincided with Neanderthals still present 60,000 years a...
Montmaurin
La Ferrassie
Circeo
Lezetxiki
Arago
Atapuerca
Cova Negra
Hajj Creiem
Haua Fteah
Forbes Quarry
El Guettar
Bir Tarfawi
Nazlet K...
Taforalt
Bir Sahara
Mugharet el-'Aliya
Dar es-Soltan
Sidi Abderrahman
Thomas Quarry
Jebel Irhoud

ARCTIC OCEAN
Lena
Lake Baikal
Yenisey
Siberia
Altai Mountains
Ob'
Lake Balkhash
Barents Sea
Ural Mountains
Syr Darya
Amu Darya
Aral Sea
Greenland
Volga
Caspian Sea
Iran Plateau
Scandinavia
EUROPE
Dnieper
Don
Caucasus
Zagros Mountains
Arctic Circle
Black Sea
Anatolia
Euphrates
Arabian Peninsula
ATLANTIC OCEAN
Rhine
Danube
Mediterranean Sea
Nile
Sahara
Tibesti
AFRICA
Ahaggar
Tropic of Cancer
Niger
Lake Chad
ATLANTIC OCEAN
Equator

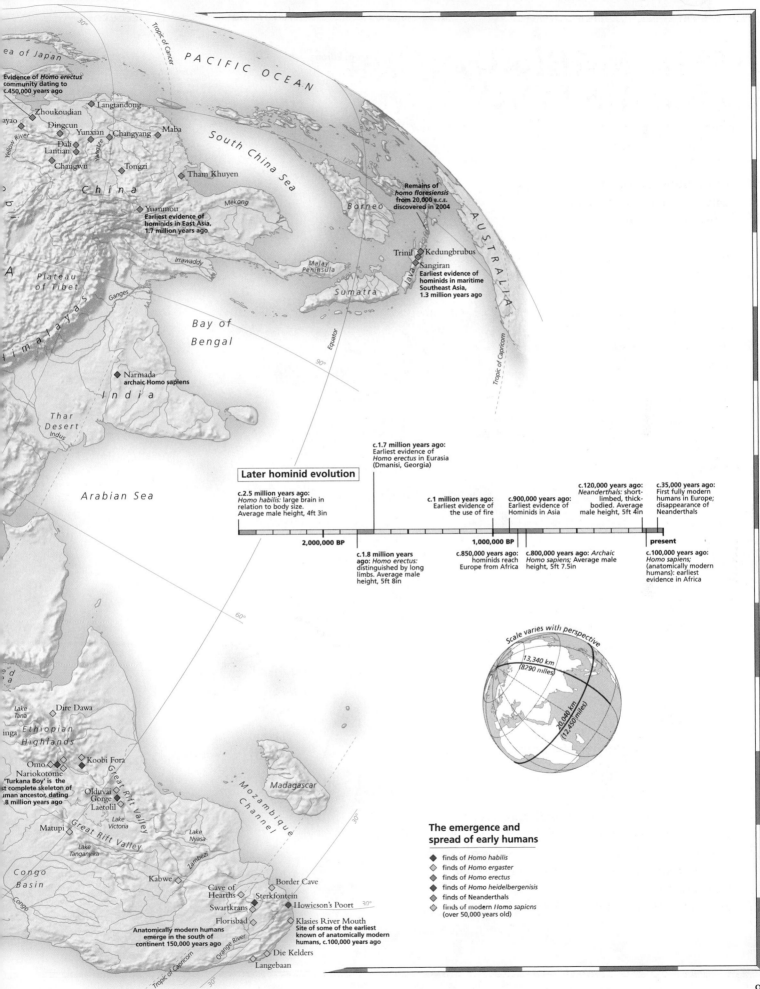

Evidence of *Homo erectus* community dating to c.450,000 years ago

PACIFIC OCEAN

Sea of Japan

ayao
Zhoukoudian   Langtandong
Dingcun
Yunxian   Changyang   Maba
Dali
Lantian
Changwu
Tongzi

Yellow River
Yangtze

China

South China Sea

Tham Khuyen

Yuanmou
Earliest evidence of hominids in East Asia, 1.7 million years ago

Mekong

Irrawaddy

Plateau of Tibet

Ganges

Himalayas

Borneo

AUSTRALIA

Remains of *homo floresiensis* from 20,000 B.C.E. discovered in 2004

Trinil   Kedungbrubus
Sangiran
Earliest evidence of hominids in maritime Southeast Asia, 1.3 million years ago

Malay Peninsula

Sumatra

Java

Bay of Bengal

Narmada
archaic Homo sapiens

India

Thar Desert

Indus

Arabian Sea

Equator

90°

60°

Later hominid evolution

c.1.7 million years ago:
Earliest evidence of *Homo erectus* in Eurasia (Dmanisi, Georgia)

c.2.5 million years ago:
Homo habilis: large brain in relation to body size. Average male height, 4ft 3in

c.1 million years ago:
Earliest evidence of the use of fire

c.900,000 years ago:
Earliest evidence of Hominids in Asia

c.120,000 years ago:
Neanderthals: short-limbed, thick-bodied. Average male height, 5ft 4in

c.35,000 years ago:
First fully modern humans in Europe; disappearance of Neanderthals

2,000,000 BP   1,000,000 BP   present

c.1.8 million years ago: *Homo erectus*: distinguished by long limbs. Average male height, 5ft 8in

c.850,000 years ago: hominids reach Europe from Africa

c.800,000 years ago: *Archaic Homo sapiens*; Average male height, 5ft 7.5in

c.100,000 years ago: *Homo sapiens*; (anatomically modern humans): earliest evidence in Africa

Scale varies with perspective

13,340 km (8290 miles)

20,040 km (12,450 miles)

Lake Tana
Dire Dawa

Ethiopian Highlands

inga

Omo
Nariokotome
Turkana Boy' is the st complete skeleton of man ancestor, dating .8 million years ago

Koobi Fora

Great Rift Valley

Olduvai Gorge
Laetolil

Lake Victoria

Matupi

Great Rift Valley

Lake Nyasa

Lake Tanganyika

Zambezi

Congo Basin

Congo

Madagascar

Mozambique Channel

30°

Kabwe

Cave of Hearths
Swartkrans
Florisbad

Border Cave
Sterkfontein
Howieson's Poort   30°

Klasies River Mouth
Site of some of the earliest known of anatomically modern humans, c.100,000 years ago

Anatomically modern humans emerge in the south of continent 150,000 years ago

Die Kelders
Langebaan

Tropic of Capricorn   30°

Orange River

The emergence and spread of early humans

◆ finds of *Homo habilis*
◇ finds of *Homo ergaster*
◇ finds of *Homo erectus*
◆ finds of *Homo heidelbergenisis*
◇ finds of Neanderthals
◇ finds of modern *Homo sapiens* (over 50,000 years old)

9

THE WORLD: PREHISTORY TO 10,000 BCE

BY 30,000 YEARS AGO, humans had colonized much of the globe. When the last Ice Age reached its peak 20,000 years ago, they were forced to adapt to survive the harsh conditions. As the temperatures rose and ice sheets retreated, the spread of modern humans contributed to the extinction of megafauna.

How did climate change affect the spread of modern humans?

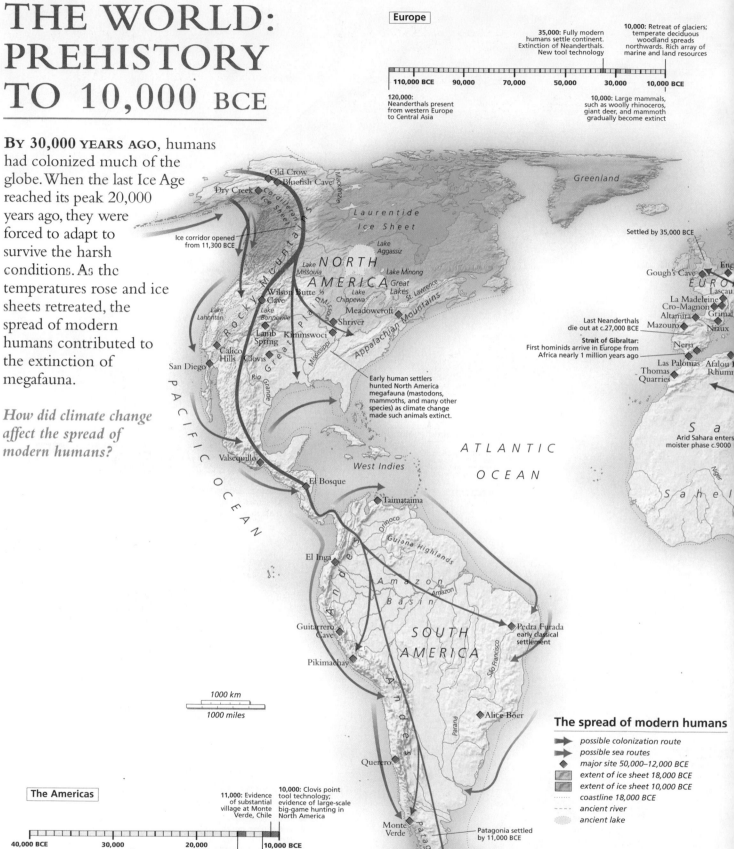

Europe

35,000: Fully modern humans settle continent. Extinction of Neanderthals. New tool technology

10,000: Retreat of glaciers; temperate deciduous woodland spreads northwards. Rich array of marine and land resources

110,000 BCE 90,000 70,000 50,000 30,000 10,000 BCE

120,000: Neanderthals present from western Europe to Central Asia

10,000: Large mammals, such as woolly rhinoceros, giant deer, and mammoth gradually become extinct

Settled by 35,000 BCE

Last Neanderthals die out at c.27,000 BCE

Strait of Gibraltar: First hominids arrive in Europe from Africa nearly 1 million years ago

Arid Sahara enters moister phase c.9000

Early human settlers hunted North America megafauna (mastodons, mammoths, and many other species) as climate change made such animals extinct.

Ice corridor opened from 11,300 BCE

ATLANTIC OCEAN

Pedra Furada early classical settlement

Patagonia settled by 11,000 BCE

1000 km
1000 miles

The spread of modern humans

- ➤ *possible colonization route*
- ➤ *possible sea routes*
- ◆ *major site 50,000–12,000 BCE*
- *extent of ice sheet 18,000 BCE*
- *extent of ice sheet 10,000 BCE*
- *coastline 18,000 BCE*
- *ancient river*
- *ancient lake*

The Americas

11,000: Evidence of substantial village at Monte Verde, Chile

10,000: Clovis point tool technology; evidence of large-scale big-game hunting in North America

40,000 BCE 30,000 20,000 10,000 BCE

15,000: Meadowcroft rock shelter, Pennsylvania

13,000: Evidence of human settlement at Bluefish Cave, Yukon

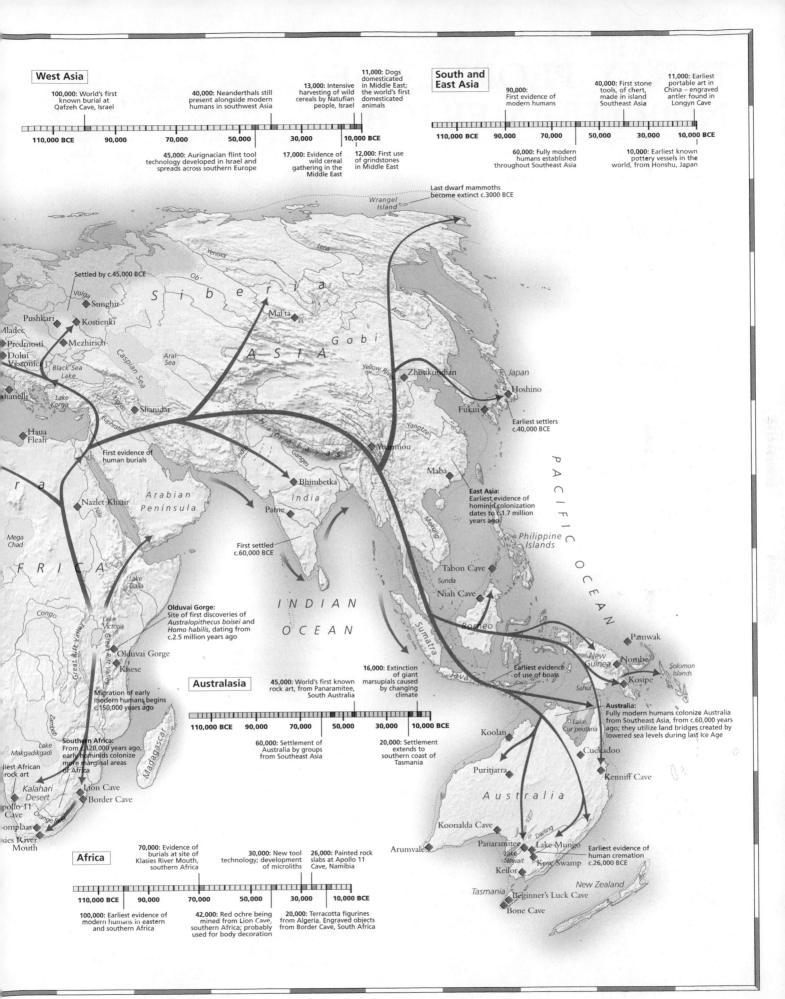

West Asia

100,000: World's first known burial at Qafzeh Cave, Israel

40,000: Neanderthals still present alongside modern humans in southwest Asia

13,000: Intensive harvesting of wild cereals by Natufian people, Israel

11,000: Dogs domesticated in Middle East; the world's first domesticated animals

110,000 BCE — 90,000 — 70,000 — 50,000 — 30,000 — 10,000 BCE

45,000: Aurignacian flint tool technology developed in Israel and spreads across southern Europe

17,000: Evidence of wild cereal gathering in the Middle East

12,000: First use of grindstones in Middle East

South and East Asia

90,000: First evidence of modern humans

40,000: First stone tools, of chert, made in island Southeast Asia

11,000: Earliest portable art in China – engraved antler found in Longyn Cave

110,000 BCE — 90,000 — 70,000 — 50,000 — 30,000 — 10,000 BCE

60,000: Fully modern humans established throughout Southeast Asia

10,000: Earliest known pottery vessels in the world, from Honshu, Japan

Last dwarf mammoths become extinct c.3000 BCE

Wrangel Island

Yenisey

Lena

Ob

S i b e r i a

Settled by c.45,000 BCE

Volga

Sunghir

Pushkari • Kostienki

Mladec

Predmostí • Mezhirich

Dolní Věstonice

Black Sea Lake

anelli

Lake Konya

A S I A

Caspian Sea

Aral Sea

Mal'ta

G o b i

Zhoukoudian

Yellow River

Japan

Hoshino

Fukui

Earliest settlers c.40,000 BCE

Shanidar

Tigris

Euphrates

First evidence of human burials

H i m a l a y a s

Indus

Ganges

Yuanmou

Yangtze

Maba

East Asia: Earliest evidence of hominid colonization dates to c.1.7 million years ago

Haua Fleah

ra

Nazlet Khatir

Nile

A r a b i a n   P e n i n s u l a

India

Bhimbetka

Patne

First settled c.60,000 BCE

Mekong

Philippine Islands

P A C I F I C   O C E A N

Mega Chad

A F R I C A

I N D I A N

O C E A N

Tabon Cave

Sunda

Niah Cave

Lake Galla

Olduvai Gorge: Site of first discoveries of *Australopithecus boisei* and *Homo habilis*, dating from c.2.5 million years ago

Congo

Lake Victoria

Great Rift Valley

Olduvai Gorge

Kisese

Sumatra

Borneo

Pamwak

New Guinea

Nombe

Solomon Islands

Kosipe

Migration of early modern humans begins c.150,000 years ago

Zambezi

Australasia

45,000: World's first known rock art, from Panaramitee, South Australia

16,000: Extinction of giant marsupials caused by changing climate

110,000 BCE — 90,000 — 70,000 — 50,000 — 30,000 — 10,000 BCE

60,000: Settlement of Australia by groups from Southeast Asia

20,000: Settlement extends to southern coast of Tasmania

Earliest evidence of use of boats

Java

Sahul

Lake Curpeutaria

Australia: Fully modern humans colonize Australia from Southeast Asia, from c.60,000 years ago; they utilize land bridges created by lowered sea levels during last Ice Age

Koolan

Cuckadoo

Lake Makgadikgadi

Southern Africa: From c.120,000 years ago, early hominids colonize more marginal areas of Africa

liest African rock art

Kalahari Desert

Lion Cave

Border Cave

Orange River

pollo 11 Cave

omplaas

sies River Mouth

Puritjarra

Kenniff Cave

A u s t r a l i a

Koonalda Cave

Darling

Arumvale

Panaramitee

Lake-Mungo

Earliest evidence of human cremation c.26,000 BCE

Lake Nawait

Kow Swamp

Keilor

New Zealand

Tasmania

Beginner's Luck Cave

Bone Cave

Africa

70,000: Evidence of burials at site of Klasies River Mouth, southern Africa

30,000: New tool technology; development of microliths

26,000: Painted rock slabs at Apollo 11 Cave, Namibia

110,000 BCE — 90,000 — 70,000 — 50,000 — 30,000 — 10,000 BCE

100,000: Earliest evidence of modern humans in eastern and southern Africa

42,000: Red ochre being mined from Lion Cave, southern Africa; probably used for body decoration

20,000: Terracotta figurines from Algeria. Engraved objects from Border Cave, South Africa

EARLY PEOPLES OF NORTH AMERICA

THE FIRST HUMAN SETTLERS of North America crossed from Siberia into Alaska around 15,000 years ago—the date is uncertain. They traveled south along the Pacific continental shelf as Ice Age glaciers melted, settling throughout the Americas. Over the millennia, their descendants adapted to every environment imaginable, from deserts to tropical rainforest. By 2,500 BCE, sedentary villages flourished in Mesoamerica, where maize and bean cultivation developed.

Why did complex societies first appear in Mesoamerica before other areas of North America?

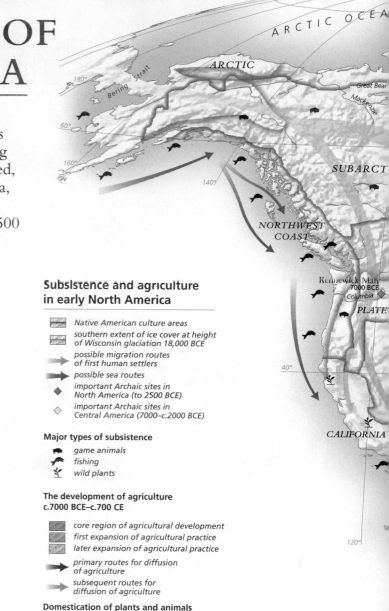

Subsistence and agriculture in early North America

- Native American culture areas
- southern extent of ice cover at height of Wisconsin glaciation 18,000 BCE
- → possible migration routes of first human settlers
- → possible sea routes
- ◆ important Archaic sites in North America (to 2500 BCE)
- ◇ important Archaic sites in Central America (7000–c.2000 BCE)

Major types of subsistence

- game animals
- fishing
- wild plants

The development of agriculture c.7000 BCE–c.700 CE

- core region of agricultural development
- first expansion of agricultural practice
- later expansion of agricultural practice
- → primary routes for diffusion of agriculture
- → subsequent routes for diffusion of agriculture

Domestication of plants and animals

○	beans	pumpkin
	turkey	squash
	chili pepper	sunflower
	tobacco	dog
	avocado	bottle gourd
	maize	peanut
	cotton	sweet potato
	amaranth	tomato

Symbols in red denote core areas of plant and animal domestication; symbols in green denote dispersal of domesticated plants and animals

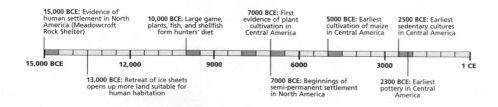

Early human settlement of North and Central America

15,000 BCE: Evidence of human settlement in North America (Meadowcroft Rock Shelter)

10,000 BCE: Large game, plants, fish, and shellfish form hunters' diet

7000 BCE: First evidence of plant cultivation in Central America

5000 BCE: Earliest cultivation of maize in Central America

2500 BCE: Earliest sedentary cultures in Central America

15,000 BCE	12,000	9000	6000	3000	1 CE

13,000 BCE: Retreat of ice sheets opens up more land suitable for human habitation

7000 BCE: Beginnings of semi-permanent settlement in North America

2300 BCE: Earliest pottery in Central America

Greenland

ARCTIC

ARCTIC

Great Slave
Lake

Lake Athabasca

Hudson Bay

SUBARCTIC

NORTH AMERICA

Lake Superior

Lake
Michigan

Lake
Huron

Lake
Ontario

GREAT PLAINS

ROCKY Mountains

Missouri

Lake Erie

NORTHEAST

Meadowcroft
Rock Shelter
c.15,000 BCE

Koster
c.6000–8000 BCE

Ohio

Appalachian Mountains

GREAT
BASIN

Red River

Mississippi

Russell Cave
c.7000–8000 BCE

Stallings Island
2500 BCE: Earliest pottery
in North America

Watson Brake Mounds
c.3500 BCE

SOUTHEAST

500 km

500 miles

SOUTHWEST

Rio Grande

Lower California

Gulf of Mexico

ATLANTIC
OCEAN

Armadillo

Ocampo

Cueva Humida

Cuba

Hispaniola

PACIFIC
OCEAN

Coxcatlan Cave

Yanhuitlan

Santa Marta

MESOAMERICA

Comitan

CIRCUM-CARIBBEAN

Caribbean Sea

Islona de
Chantuto

El Chayal

Isthmus of
Panama

SOUTH
AMERICA

Equator

EARLY PEOPLES OF SOUTH AMERICA

SOUTH AMERICA was settled from the north, possibly more than 13,000 years ago. By 10,000 BCE, hunter-gatherers had colonized the entire subcontinent. Cereal and root cultivation developed before 3000 BCE. Successful agriculture led to growing populations and increasingly stratified societies. By 1800 BCE, large temples appeared on the Peruvian coast, and a distinctive religious iconography spread from Chavín de Huantar after 900 BCE.

How did the environment of South America affect the spread of agriculture?

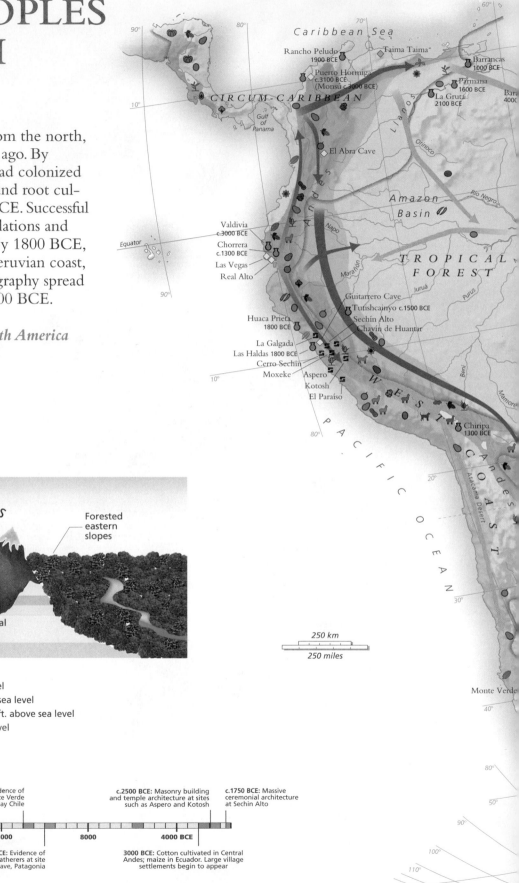

The Andean Environment

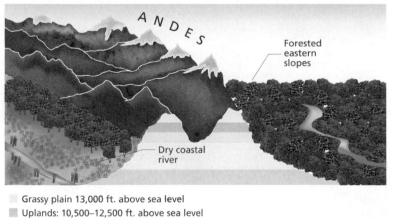

Forested eastern slopes

Dry coastal river

Grassy plain 13,000 ft. above sea level
Uplands: 10,500–12,500 ft. above sea level
Frost-free valleys 7,500–10,000 ft. above sea level
Lower slopes of mountains: 2,400–7,000 ft. above sea level
Dry coastal region: 2,400 ft. above sea level

250 km
250 miles

Earliest settlements in South America

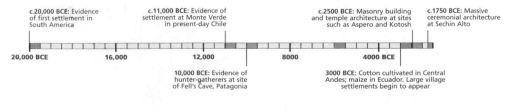

c.20,000 BCE: Evidence of first settlement in South America

c.11,000 BCE: Evidence of settlement at Monte Verde in present-day Chile

c.2500 BCE: Masonry building and temple architecture at sites such as Aspero and Kotosh

c.1750 BCE: Massive ceremonial architecture at Sechín Alto

20,000 BCE   16,000   12,000   8000   4000 BCE

10,000 BCE: Evidence of hunter-gatherers at site of Fell's Cave, Patagonia

3000 BCE: Cotton cultivated in Central Andes; maize in Ecuador. Large village settlements begin to appear

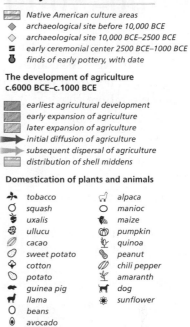

Settlement and agriculture in early South America

- Native American culture areas
- ◆ archaeological site before 10,000 BCE
- ◇ archaeological site 10,000 BCE–2500 BCE
- ⛉ early ceremonial center 2500 BCE–1000 BCE
- 🝩 finds of early pottery, with date

The development of agriculture c.6000 BCE–c.1000 BCE

- earliest agricultural development
- early expansion of agriculture
- later expansion of agriculture
- → initial diffusion of agriculture
- ⇒ subsequent dispersal of agriculture
- distribution of shell middens

Domestication of plants and animals

🌿 tobacco	🦙 alpaca
🜂 squash	○ manioc
🌿 uxalis	🥔 maize
🥬 ullucu	🎃 pumpkin
🫘 cacao	🌱 quinoa
🥜 sweet potato	🥜 peanut
🍠 cotton	🌶 chili pepper
◯ potato	🌾 amaranth
🐀 guinea pig	🐕 dog
🦙 llama	✳ sunflower
○ beans	
◉ avocado	

Symbols in red denote core areas of plant and animal domestication; symbols in green denote dispersal of domesticated plants and animals

Scale varies with perspective

3560 km (1816 miles)

6224km (3864 miles)

15

THE WORLD: 10,000–5000 BCE

By 7000 BCE, farming was the main means of subsistence in West Asia, although hunter-gathering remained the most common form of subsistence elsewhere. Over the next 5,000 years farming became established independently in other areas.

How might changing ecological conditions have contributed to the shift from hunting and gathering to agriculture?

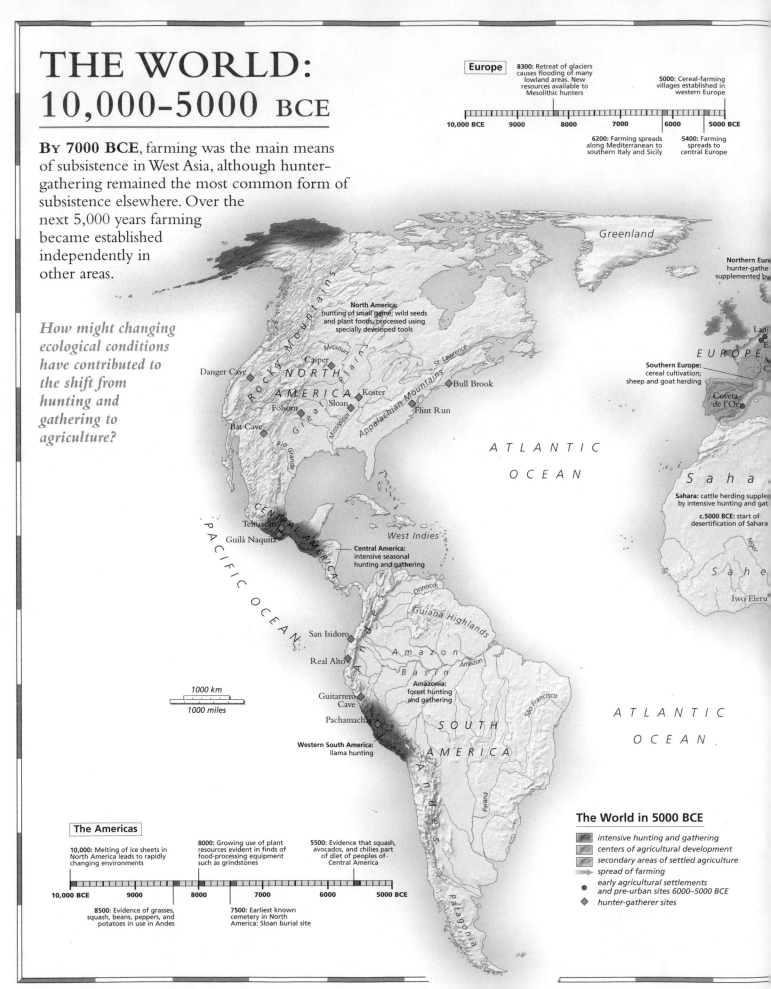

Europe

8300: Retreat of glaciers causes flooding of many lowland areas. New resources available to Mesolithic hunters

5000: Cereal-farming villages established in western Europe

10,000 BCE   9000   8000   7000   6000   5000 BCE

6200: Farming spreads along Mediterranean to southern Italy and Sicily

5400: Farming spreads to central Europe

Greenland

North America: hunting of small game; wild seeds and plant foods, processed using specially developed tools

Rocky Mountains

Missouri

Casper

Danger Cave

NORTH

AMERICA

Great Plains

St. Lawrence

Koster

Sloan

Folsom

Mississippi

Appalachian Mountains

Bull Brook

Flint Run

Bat Cave

Rio Grande

ATLANTIC

OCEAN

Northern Eur[o]pe hunter-gathe[rers] supplemented by

Lang[...]

EUROPE

Southern Europe: cereal cultivation; sheep and goat herding

Coveta de l'Or

CENTRAL AMERICA

Tehuacán

Guilá Naquitz

West Indies

Central America: intensive seasonal hunting and gathering

Saha[ra]

Sahara: cattle herding supplem[ented] by intensive hunting and gat[hering]

c.5000 BCE: start of desertification of Sahara

Niger

Sahe[l]

Iwo Eleru

PACIFIC OCEAN

Orinoco

Guiana Highlands

Amazon

Basin

Amazon

San Isidoro

Andes

Real Alto

Amazonia: forest hunting and gathering

1000 km

1000 miles

Guitarrero Cave

Pachamachay

Western South America: llama hunting

SOUTH

AMERICA

São Francisco

ATLANTIC

OCEAN

Andes

Paraná

Patagonia

The Americas

10,000: Melting of ice sheets in North America leads to rapidly changing environments

8000: Growing use of plant resources evident in finds of food-processing equipment such as grindstones

5500: Evidence that squash, avocados, and chilies part of diet of peoples of Central America

10,000 BCE   9000   8000   7000   6000   5000 BCE

8500: Evidence of grasses, squash, beans, peppers, and potatoes in use in Andes

7500: Earliest known cemetery in North America: Sloan burial site

The World in 5000 BCE

- intensive hunting and gathering
- centers of agricultural development
- secondary areas of settled agriculture
- → spread of farming
- ● early agricultural settlements and pre-urban sites 6000–5000 BCE
- ◆ hunter-gatherer sites

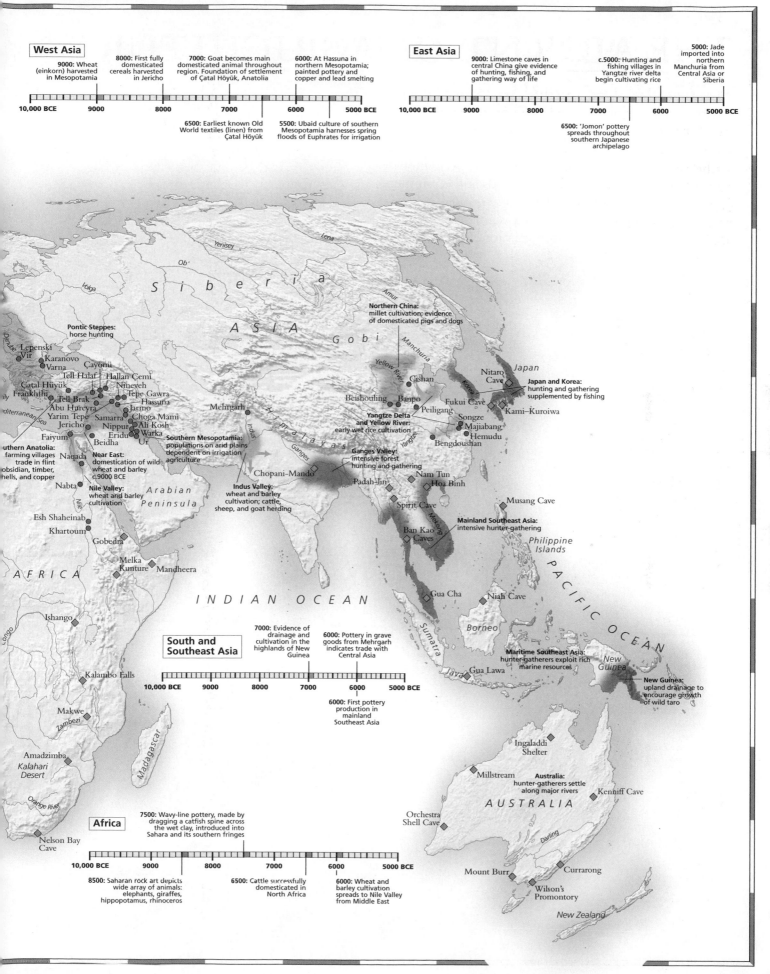

West Asia

9000: Wheat (einkorn) harvested in Mesopotamia

8000: First fully domesticated cereals harvested in Jericho

7000: Goat becomes main domesticated animal throughout region. Foundation of settlement of Çatal Höyük, Anatolia

6000: At Hassuna in northern Mesopotamia; painted pottery and copper and lead smelting

10,000 BCE   9000   8000   7000   6000   5000 BCE

6500: Earliest known Old World textiles (linen) from Çatal Höyük

5500: Ubaid culture of southern Mesopotamia harnesses spring floods of Euphrates for irrigation

East Asia

9000: Limestone caves in central China give evidence of hunting, fishing, and gathering way of life

c.5000: Hunting and fishing villages in Yangtze river delta begin cultivating rice

5000: Jade imported into northern Manchuria from Central Asia or Siberia

10,000 BCE   9000   8000   7000   6000   5000 BCE

6500: 'Jomon' pottery spreads throughout southern Japanese archipelago

Map labels:

Yenisey
Lena
Ob'
Volga
SIBERIA
ASIA
Gobi
Amur
Manchuria

Northern China: millet cultivation; evidence of domesticated pigs and dogs

Pontic Steppes: horse hunting

Lepenski Vir
Karanovo
Varna
Çayönü
Tell Halaf
Hallan Çemi
Nineveh
Çatal Hüyük
Frankhthi
Tepe Gawra
Tell Brak
Hassuna
Abu Hureyra
Jarmo
Yarim Tepe
Samarra
Choga Mami
Jericho
Nippur
Ali Kosh
Faiyum
Eridu
Warka
Beidha
Ur

Mehrgarh
Yellow River
Cishan
Beishouling
Banpo
Peiligang
Nitaro Cave
Japan
Fukui Cave
Kami–Kuroiwa
Songze
Majiabang
Hemudu
Bengdoushan
Korea

Yangtze Delta and Yellow River: early wet rice cultivation

Japan and Korea: hunting and gathering supplemented by fishing

Southern Anatolia: farming villages trade in flint, obsidian, timber, shells, and copper

Near East: domestication of wild wheat and barley c.9000 BCE

Southern Mesopotamia: populations on arid plains dependent on irrigation agriculture

Indus
Ganges
Himalayas

Ganges Valley: intensive forest hunting and gathering

Nabta
Nile Valley: wheat and barley cultivation

Arabian Peninsula

Indus Valley: wheat and barley cultivation; cattle, sheep, and goat herding

Chopani-Mando
Padah-lin
Nam Tun
Hoa Binh
Spirit Cave
Musang Cave

Esh Shaheinab
Khartoum
Gobedra

Melka Kunture
Mandheera

Ban Kao Caves

Mainland Southeast Asia: intensive hunter-gathering

Philippine Islands

AFRICA

INDIAN OCEAN

Gua Cha
Niah Cave
Sumatra
Borneo
PACIFIC OCEAN

South and Southeast Asia

7000: Evidence of drainage and cultivation in the highlands of New Guinea

6000: Pottery in grave goods from Mehrgarh indicates trade with Central Asia

10,000 BCE   9000   8000   7000   6000   5000 BCE

6000: First pottery production in mainland Southeast Asia

Ishango
Kalambo Falls
Congo
Makwe
Zambezi
Amadzimba
Kalahari Desert
Madagascar
Orange River

Gua Lawa
Java
Mekong

Maritime Southeast Asia: hunter-gatherers exploit rich marine resources

New Guinea

New Guinea: upland drainage to encourage growth of wild taro

Ingaladdi Shelter
Millstream
Kenniff Cave

Australia: hunter-gatherers settle along major rivers

AUSTRALIA
Darling

Africa

7500: Wavy-line pottery, made by dragging a catfish spine across the wet clay, introduced into Sahara and its southern fringes

Orchestra Shell Cave

10,000 BCE   9000   8000   7000   6000   5000 BCE

8500: Saharan rock art depicts wide array of animals: elephants, giraffes, hippopotamus, rhinoceros

6500: Cattle successfully domesticated in North Africa

6000: Wheat and barley cultivation spreads to Nile Valley from Middle East

Nelson Bay Cave

Mount Burr
Currarong
Wilson's Promontory

New Zealand

THE ADVENT OF AGRICULTURE

THE APPEARANCE OF FARMING transformed the face of the Earth. It was not merely a change in subsistence – it also transformed the way in which our ancestors lived. Agriculture, and the vastly greater crop yields it produced, enabled large groups of people to live in permanent villages, surrounded by material goods and equipment. Specialized craftsmen produced these goods, supported by the community as a whole – the beginnings of social differentiation.

What common features characterize the areas where agriculture first appeared?

The spread of agriculture

areas of early agriculture, with dates of first domestication of plants and animals

diffusion of agricultural skills

Staple crops under cultivation by c.4000 BCE

- wheat
- barley
- millet
- maize
- rice

Wild ancestors of domesticated animals

- aurochs (wild cattle)
- pig
- sheep
- ass
- dromedary camel
- horse
- bactrian camel
- gaur (wild ox)
- buffalo
- chicken
- goat
- yak
- turkey
- guanaco (llama)
- guinea pig
- alpaca
- banteng

Eastern North America:
sunflower
sumpweed
tepary bean

Central America:
maize
sweet potato
manioc
squash
bottle gourd
tomato
avocado
cotton

South America:
manioc
potato
cotton
peanut
squash
bottle gourd
chili pepper
lima bean
tomato

c.4500 BCE
c.4750 BCE
1000 BCE
c.3000 BCE
c.4500 BCE
c.4500 BCE

Greenland
Iceland
Brit Isl

NORTH AMERICA
Rocky Mountains
Great Plains
Great Lakes
St. Lawrence
Missouri
Mississippi
Rio Grande
Appalachian Mountains
Gulf of Mexico
Caribbean Sea
ATLANTIC OCEAN
PACIFIC OCEAN

SOUTH AMERICA
Orinoco
Guiana Highlands
Amazon Basin
Amazon
Andes
São Francisco
Paraná
Patagonia
ATLANTIC OCEAN

1000 km
1000 miles

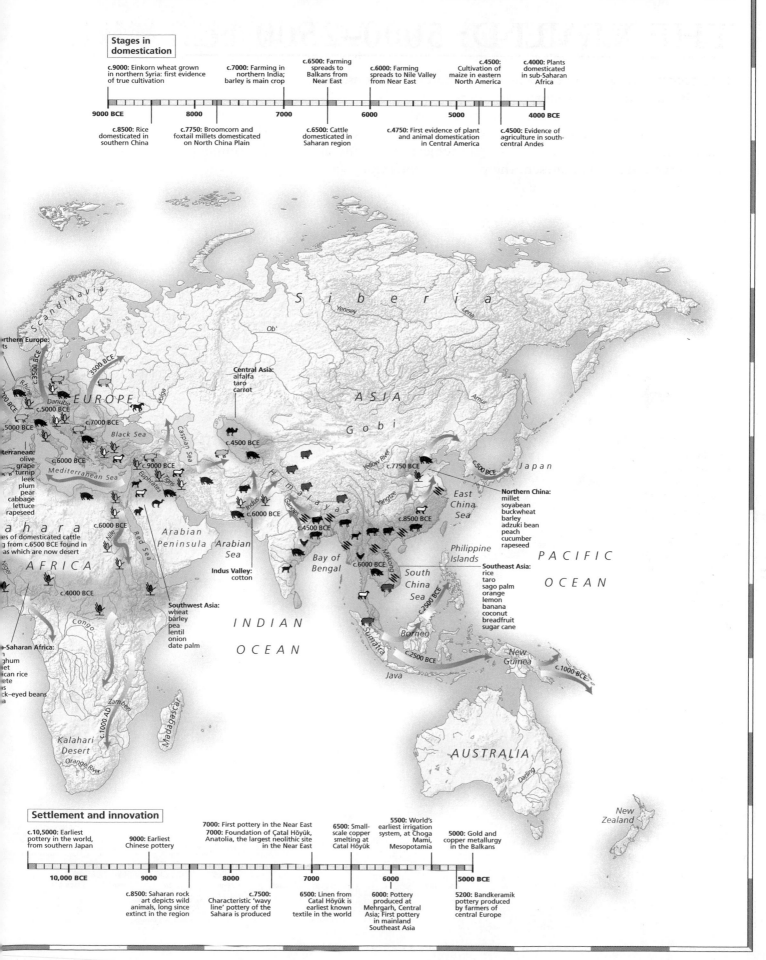

Stages in domestication

c.9000: Einkorn wheat grown in northern Syria: first evidence of true cultivation

c.7000: Farming in northern India; barley is main crop

c.6500: Farming spreads to Balkans from Near East

c.6000: Farming spreads to Nile Valley from Near East

c.4500: Cultivation of maize in eastern North America

c.4000: Plants domesticated in sub-Saharan Africa

c.8500: Rice domesticated in southern China

c.7750: Broomcorn and foxtail millets domesticated on North China Plain

c.6500: Cattle domesticated in Saharan region

c.4750: First evidence of plant and animal domestication in Central America

c.4500: Evidence of agriculture in south-central Andes

9000 BCE   8000   7000   6000   5000   4000 BCE

Map labels:

Scandinavia · Siberia · Yenisey · Lena · Ob' · EUROPE · Rhine · Danube · Volga · ASIA · Gobi · Amur · Black Sea · Caspian Sea · Mediterranean Sea · Euphrates · Tigris · Yellow River · Japan · East China Sea · Yangtze · Mekong · Himalayas · Indus · Ganges · Bay of Bengal · Arabian Peninsula · Arabian Sea · Red Sea · Nile · Sahara · AFRICA · Niger · Congo · INDIAN OCEAN · South China Sea · Philippine Islands · PACIFIC OCEAN · Borneo · Sumatra · Java · New Guinea · Madagascar · Zambezi · Kalahari Desert · Orange River · AUSTRALIA · Darling · New Zealand

Central Asia:
alfalfa
taro
carrot

Northern China:
millet
soyabean
buckwheat
barley
adzuki bean
peach
cucumber
rapeseed

Southeast Asia:
rice
taro
sago palm
orange
lemon
banana
coconut
breadfruit
sugar cane

Indus Valley:
cotton

Southwest Asia:
wheat
barley
pea
lentil
onion
date palm

Mediterranean:
olive
grape
turnip
leek
plum
pear
cabbage
lettuce
rapeseed

sub-Saharan Africa:
...ghum
...et
...ite
...s
...ck-eyed beans
...a

Dates on map: c.3500 BCE · c.3500 BCE · c.5000 BCE · c.7000 BCE · c.5000 BCE · c.6000 BCE · c.9000 BCE · c.6000 BCE · c.6000 BCE · c.4000 BCE · c.4500 BCE · c.6000 BCE · c.4500 BCE · c.7750 BCE · c.500 BCE · c.8500 BCE · c.6000 BCE · c.2500 BCE · c.2500 BCE · c.1000 BCE · c.1000 AD

ies of domesticated cattle
g from c.6500 BCE found in
as which are now desert

Settlement and innovation

c.10,5000: Earliest pottery in the world, from southern Japan

9000: Earliest Chinese pottery

7000: First pottery in the Near East
7000: Foundation of Çatal Höyük, Anatolia, the largest neolithic site in the Near East

6500: Small-scale copper smelting at Çatal Höyük

5500: World's earliest irrigation system, at Choga Mami, Mesopotamia

5000: Gold and copper metallurgy in the Balkans

c.8500: Saharan rock art depicts wild animals, long since extinct in the region

c.7500: Characteristic 'wavy line' pottery of the Sahara is produced

6500: Linen from Çatal Höyük is earliest known textile in the world

6000: Pottery produced at Mehrgarh, Central Asia; First pottery in mainland Southeast Asia

5200: Bandkeramik pottery produced by farmers of central Europe

10,000 BCE   9000   8000   7000   6000   5000 BCE

THE WORLD: 5000–2500 BCE

THE FERTILE VALLEYS of the Nile, Tigris, Euphrates, Indus, and Yellow rivers were able to support very large populations, and it was here that the great urban civilizations of the ancient world emerged. Urban societies were hierarchical, with complex labor divisions. They were administered, economically and spiritually, by an elite literate class, and in some cases, were subject to a divine monarch. Monuments came to symbolize and represent the powers of the ruling elite.

Eastern Europe:
Agriculture well established.
Advanced copper technology

Scandinavia:
Seasonal fishing
communities

CORDED
WARE
BURILS

Stonehenge
Carnac **BEAKER
BURIALS**

Western Europe:
Agriculture well established.
Burial in megalithic tombs

*Livest
herdin*

PIT GR

Danube
Black
Hattush

Mediterranean Sea

Gizq
Memphis
Saqq
OLD
KINGDC
OF EGY

Sahara:
Gradual desiccation.
Inhabitants move
to the periphery

Sahara

Sudan

Southwest North America:
Nomadic hunter-gatherers
mainly dependent on
wild plant foods

Mississippi Valley:
Sedentary hunter-gatherers
dependent on year-round
supply of wild food resources
and occasional cultivation

*MISSISSIPPI
VALLEY*

*Great
Lakes*

Hunter-gatherers

Hunter-gatherers

CENTRAL AMERICA

West Indies

ATLANTIC
OCEAN

Central America:
Permanent settlements; slow
transition from hunting and
gathering to farming

**River Orinoco and
River Amazon basin:**
Slow transition from hunting and
gathering to horticultural villages

Guiana Highlands

*Amazon
Basin*

Hunter-gatherers

Tropical Africa:
Intensive use of forest
resources

Congo

Sudan:
Intensive use of wild
finger millet and sorghum

*Hunter
gathere*

*What geographical,
ecological, and economic
factors led to the
development of early urban
civilizations?*

PACIFIC OCEAN

Andes:
Coastal groups lived
in large fishing camps

1000 km

1000 miles

*Kalahari
Desert*

Orange River

The Americas

4000: First pottery in
the Americas from
Amazon Basin

3400: Farming
villages established
in Tehuacan Valley

2500: Evidence of long
distance trade throughout
South America, mainly
of valuables

Africa

3400: First walled towns
appear in Egypt

3000: First evidence
of hieroglyphic
writing system

2530: Construction
of Great Pyramid of
Khufu, the largest of
the Egyptian
pyramids, at Giza

| 5000 BCE | 4500 | 4000 | 3500 | 3000 | 2500 BCE |

| 5000 BCE | 4500 | 4000 | 3500 | 3000 | 2500 BCE |

c.4750: First agriculture in
Americas: maize grown in
Central America's
Tehuacan valley

3500: Cotton
cultivated in Central
America; used to
make fishing nets
and textiles

2600: Large
temple complexes
built in villages
along the
Andean coast

3100: King Narmer unifies
Upper and Lower Egypt, and
becomes first pharaoh. City of
Memphis is founded

2650: The step
pyramid of Djoser, the
first Egyptian pyramid,
is built at Saqqara

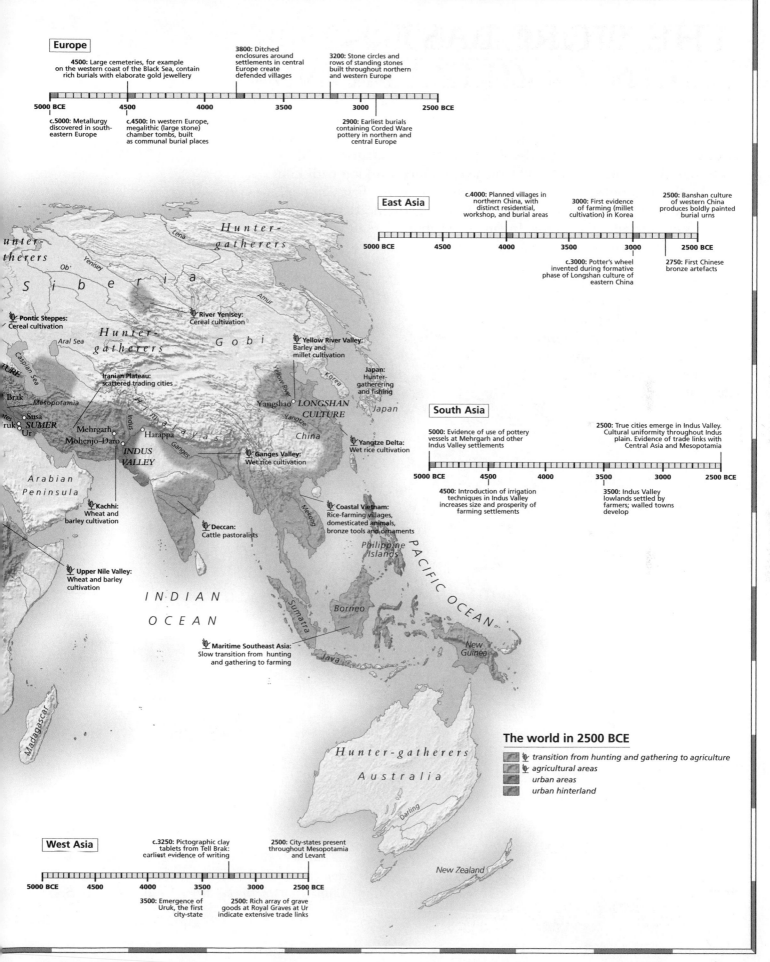

Europe

4500: Large cemeteries, for example on the western coast of the Black Sea, contain rich burials with elaborate gold jewellery

3800: Ditched enclosures around settlements in central Europe create defended villages

3200: Stone circles and rows of standing stones built throughout northern and western Europe

5000 BCE   4500   4000   3500   3000   2500 BCE

c.5000: Metallurgy discovered in south-eastern Europe

c.4500: In western Europe, megalithic (large stone) chamber tombs, built as communal burial places

2900: Earliest burials containing Corded Ware pottery in northern and central Europe

East Asia

c.4000: Planned villages in northern China, with distinct residential, workshop, and burial areas

3000: First evidence of farming (millet cultivation) in Korea

2500: Banshan culture of western China produces boldly painted burial urns

5000 BCE   4500   4000   3500   3000   2500 BCE

c.3000: Potter's wheel invented during formative phase of Longshan culture of eastern China

2750: First Chinese bronze artefacts

South Asia

5000: Evidence of use of pottery vessels at Mehrgarh and other Indus Valley settlements

2500: True cities emerge in Indus Valley. Cultural uniformity throughout Indus plain. Evidence of trade links with Central Asia and Mesopotamia

5000 BCE   4500   4000   3500   3000   2500 BCE

4500: Introduction of irrigation techniques in Indus Valley increases size and prosperity of farming settlements

3500: Indus Valley lowlands settled by farmers; walled towns develop

West Asia

c.3250: Pictographic clay tablets from Tell Brak: carliest evidence of writing

2500: City-states present throughout Mesopotamia and Levant

5000 BCE   4500   4000   3500   3000   2500 BCE

3500: Emergence of Uruk, the first city-state

2500: Rich array of grave goods at Royal Graves at Ur indicate extensive trade links

Hunter-gatherers

Siberia

unter-therers

Pontic Steppes: Cereal cultivation

Hunter-gatherers

River Yenisey: Cereal cultivation

Gobi

Yellow River Valley: Barley and millet cultivation

Japan: Hunter-gathering and fishing

Iranian Plateau: scattered trading cities

Brak

Susa
SUMER
ruk
Ur

Mehrgarh
Mohenjo-Daro   Harappa
INDUS VALLEY

Yangshao   LONGSHAN CULTURE

China

Yangtze Delta: Wet rice cultivation

Ganges Valley: Wet rice cultivation

Arabian Peninsula

Kachhi: Wheat and barley cultivation

Deccan: Cattle pastoralists

Coastal Vietnam: Rice-farming villages, domesticated animals, bronze tools and ornaments

Upper Nile Valley: Wheat and barley cultivation

INDIAN OCEAN

Philippine Islands

PACIFIC OCEAN

Borneo

Sumatra

New Guinea

Java

Maritime Southeast Asia: Slow transition from hunting and gathering to farming

Madagascar

The world in 2500 BCE

transition from hunting and gathering to agriculture
agricultural areas
urban areas
urban hinterland

Hunter-gatherers
Australia

New Zealand

THE FIRST EAST ASIAN CIVILIZATIONS

THE EMERGENCE OF ORGANIZED CULTURES in East Asia took a variety of forms. The fertile soils of the Yellow River basin and the Yangtze valley provided the potential for the development of the first agricultural communities in the region 8000 years ago. Pottery working with kilns and bronze technology developed, accompanied by the first Chinese states and empires; the region remains to this day the heartland of China's culture and population. In Japan, the abundance of natural resources, especially fish and seafood, meant that hunter-gathering persisted, alongside features normally associated with sedentary agriculture – the world's earliest pottery is found here. Across the steppe grasslands of Central Asia, communities developed a mobile culture now revealed through elaborate burials and decorated grave goods.

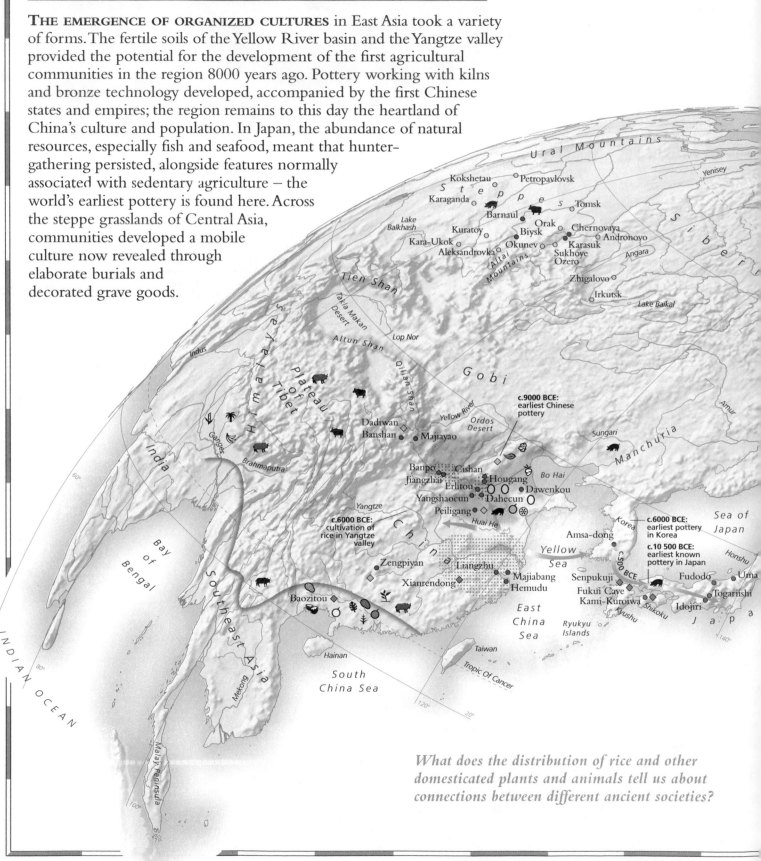

What does the distribution of rice and other domesticated plants and animals tell us about connections between different ancient societies?

The agricultural revolution
6000–2000 BCE

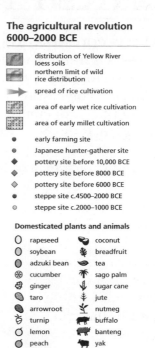

distribution of Yellow River loess soils

northern limit of wild rice distribution

spread of rice cultivation

area of early wet rice cultivation

area of early millet cultivation

● early farming site

● Japanese hunter-gatherer site

◆ pottery site before 10,000 BCE

◆ pottery site before 8000 BCE

◇ pottery site before 6000 BCE

● steppe site c.4500–2000 BCE

○ steppe site c.2000–1000 BCE

Domesticated plants and animals

◯	rapeseed		coconut
◯	soybean		breadfruit
◯	adzuki bean		tea
✳	cucumber		sago palm
	ginger		sugar cane
	taro		jute
	arrowroot		nutmeg
	turnip		buffalo
	lemon		banteng
	peach		yak
	grapefruit		pig
	banana		

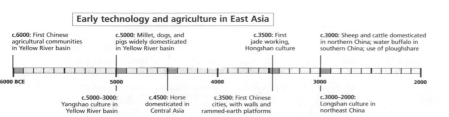

Early technology and agriculture in East Asia

c.6000: First Chinese agricultural communities in Yellow River basin

c.5000: Millet, dogs, and pigs widely domesticated in Yellow River basin

c.3500: First jade working, Hongshan culture

c.3000: Sheep and cattle domesticated in northern China; water buffalo in southern China; use of ploughshare

c.5000–3000: Yangshao culture in Yellow River basin

c.4500: Horse domesticated in Central Asia

c.3500: First Chinese cities, with walls and rammed-earth platforms

c.3000–2000: Longshan culture in northeast China

6000 BCE 5000 4000 3000 2000

POLYNESIAN MIGRATIONS

THE FIRST WAVE OF COLONIZATION of the Pacific, between 2000 and 1500 BCE, took settlers from New Guinea and neighbouring islands as far as the Fiji Islands. From there, they sailed on to Tonga and Samoa. In about 200 BCE, the Polynesians embarked on a series of far longer voyages, crossing vast tracts of empty ocean to settle the Marquesas, the Society Islands, Hawaii, Rapa Nui (Easter Island), and New Zealand.

What environmental factors allowed the Polynesians to colonize the Pacific?

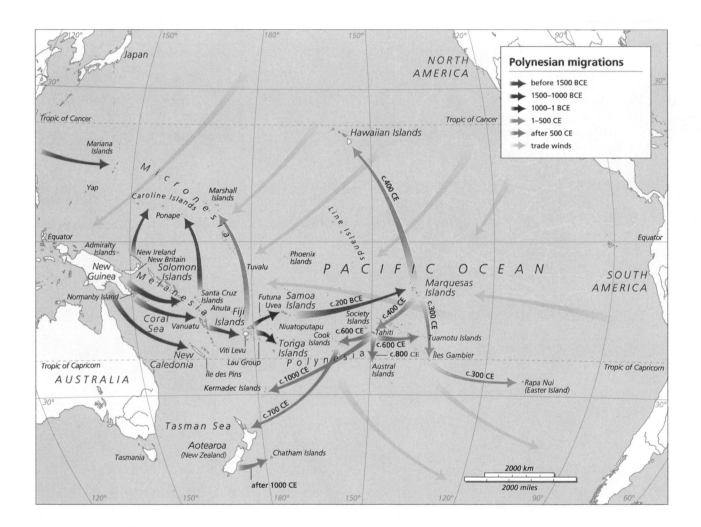

Polynesian migrations

→ before 1500 BCE
→ 1500–1000 BCE
→ 1000–1 BCE
→ 1–500 CE
→ after 500 CE
→ trade winds

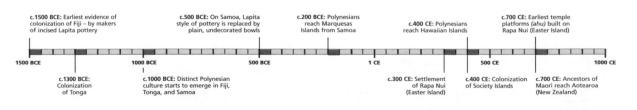

Polynesian voyages 1500 BCE–1000 CE

c.1500 BCE: Earliest evidence of colonization of Fiji – by makers of incised Lapita pottery

c.500 BCE: On Samoa, Lapita style of pottery is replaced by plain, undecorated bowls

c.200 BCE: Polynesians reach Marquesas Islands from Samoa

c.400 CE: Polynesians reach Hawaiian Islands

c.700 CE: Earliest temple platforms (*ahu*) built on Rapa Nui (Easter Island)

| 1500 BCE | 1000 BCE | 500 BCE | 1 CE | 500 CE | 1000 CE |

c.1300 BCE: Colonization of Tonga

c.1000 BCE: Distinct Polynesian culture starts to emerge in Fiji, Tonga, and Samoa

c.300 CE: Settlement of Rapa Nui (Easter Island)

c.400 CE: Colonization of Society Islands

c.700 CE: Ancestors of Maori reach Aotearoa (New Zealand)

THE FERTILE CRESCENT

THE "FERTILE CRESCENT" is traditionally seen as the cradle of civilization. Here the first farming settlements were established, expanding into fortified walled towns. By 3500 BCE the first city-states, centers of population and trade, had grown up in Mesopotamia. Each had at its heart a mud-brick temple raised on a high platform. These structures later became ziggurats.

How was irrigation central to the development of civilization in the Fertile Crescent?

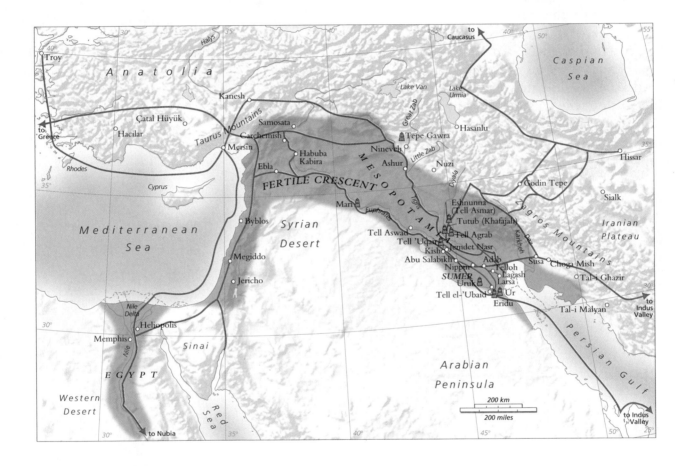

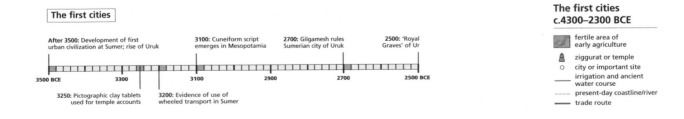

The first cities

After 3500: Development of first urban civilization at Sumer; rise of Uruk

3100: Cuneiform script emerges in Mesopotamia

2700: Gilgamesh rules Sumerian city of Uruk

2500: 'Royal Graves' of Ur

3500 BCE — 3300 — 3100 — 2900 — 2700 — 2500 BCE

3250: Pictographic clay tablets used for temple accounts

3200: Evidence of use of wheeled transport in Sumer

The first cities
c.4300–2300 BCE

- fertile area of early agriculture
- ziggurat or temple
- city or important site
- irrigation and ancient water course
- present-day coastline/river
- trade route

URBAN CENTERS AND TRADE ROUTES

By 2500 BCE cities were established in three major centers: the Nile Valley, Mesopotamia, and the Indus Valley, with a scattering of other cities across the intervening terrain. The culmination of a long process of settlement and expansion – some early cities had populations tens of thousands strong – the first urban civilizations all relied on rich agricultural lands to support their growth. In each case, lack of the most important natural resources – timber, metal, and stone – forced these urban civilizations to establish trading networks which ultimately extended from the Hindu Kush to the Mediterranean.

What impact did trade have on the development of early cities and civilizations?

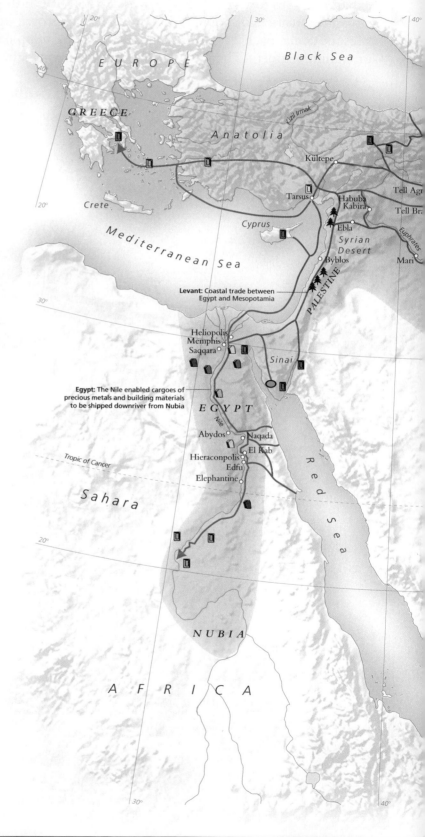

Black Sea

EUROPE

GREECE

Anatolia

Kızıl Irmak

Kültepe

Tarsus

Habuba Kabira

Tell Agr

Tell Bra

Crete

Cyprus

Ebla

Syrian Desert

Euphrates

Mari

Mediterranean Sea

Byblos

PALESTINE

Levant: Coastal trade between Egypt and Mesopotamia

Heliopolis
Memphis
Saqqara

Sinai

Egypt: The Nile enabled cargoes of precious metals and building materials to be shipped downriver from Nubia

EGYPT

Nile

Abydos

Naqada

El Kab

Hieraconpolis

Edfu

Elephantine

Red Sea

Tropic of Cancer

Sahara

20°

NUBIA

AFRICA

250 km

250 miles

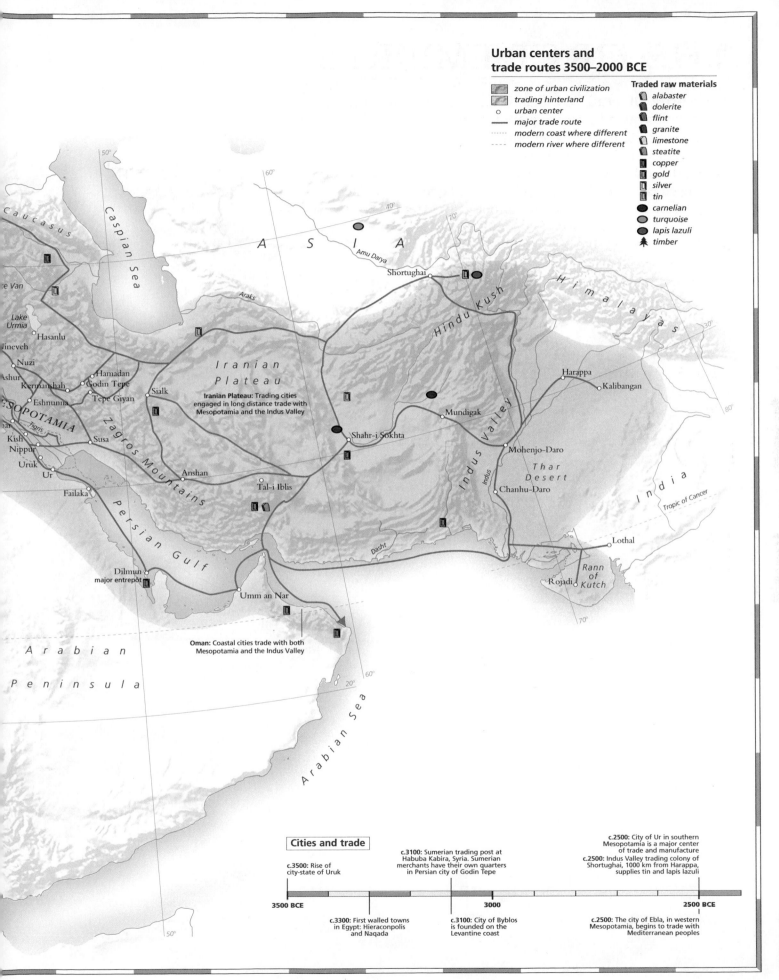

Urban centers and trade routes 3500–2000 BCE

zone of urban civilization
trading hinterland
○ urban center
— major trade route
⋯ modern coast where different
--- modern river where different

Traded raw materials
alabaster
dolerite
flint
granite
limestone
steatite
copper
gold
silver
tin
carnelian
turquoise
lapis lazuli
timber

Iranian Plateau: Trading cities
engaged in long distance trade with
Mesopotamia and the Indus Valley

Oman: Coastal cities trade with both
Mesopotamia and the Indus Valley

Caucasus
Caspian Sea
ASIA
Amu Darya
Shortughai
Lake Van
Araks
Hindu Kush
Himalayas
Lake Urmia
Hasanlu
Nineveh
Iranian Plateau
Nuzi
Ashur
Hamadan
Godin Tepe
Harappa
Kermanshah
Tepe Giyan
Sialk
Kalibangan
ESHNUNNA
Mundigak
Indus Valley
MESOPOTAMIA
Kish
Shahr-i Sokhta
Susa
Nippur
Anshan
Uruk
Mohenjo-Daro
Ur
Tal-i Iblis
Thar Desert
Failaka
Chanhu-Daro
India
Zagros Mountains
Tigris
Tropic of Cancer
Persian Gulf
Indus
Dasht
Lothal
Dilmun
major entrepôt
Rann of Kutch
Umm an Nar
Rojadi
Arabian Peninsula
Arabian Sea

Cities and trade

c.3500: Rise of
city-state of Uruk

c.3100: Sumerian trading post at
Habuba Kabira, Syria. Sumerian
merchants have their own quarters
in Persian city of Godin Tepe

c.2500: City of Ur in southern
Mesopotamia is a major center
of trade and manufacture

c.2500: Indus Valley trading colony of
Shortughai, 1000 km from Harappa,
supplies tin and lapis lazuli

3500 BCE	3000	2500 BCE

c.3300: First walled towns
in Egypt: Hieraconpolis
and Naqada

c.3100: City of Byblos
is founded on the
Levantine coast

c.2500: The city of Ebla, in western
Mesopotamia, begins to trade with
Mediterranean peoples

THE FIRST EMPIRES

IN ABOUT 2300 BCE, Akkadian King Sargon I came to power at Kish. Subsequently, he conquered the independent city-states of the south, and created an empire by conquering Elam and parts of Syria and Anatolia. However, Sargon's empire soon collapsed. Ur became the dominant power, followed by the short-lived empires of Shamshi-Adad and Hammurabi. The Hittites rose to prominence in Anatolia after 1650 BCE, extending their empire into Syria and competing with the Egyptians and Mitanni.

Why did ancient Mesopotamian empires rise and fall in such rapid succession?

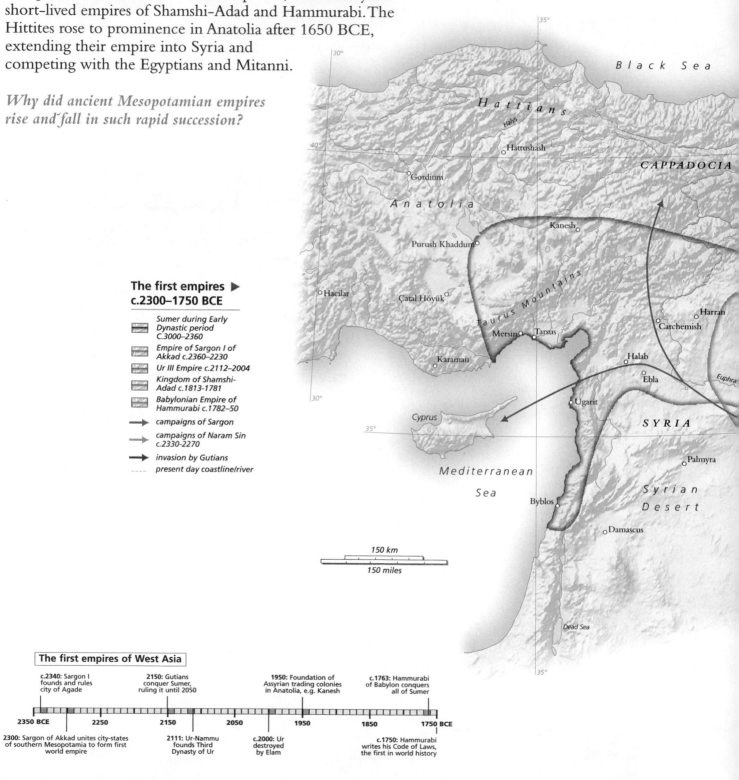

The first empires ▶ c.2300–1750 BCE

▨	*Sumer during Early Dynastic period C.3000–2360*
▨	*Empire of Sargon I of Akkad c.2360–2230*
▨	*Ur III Empire c.2112–2004*
▨	*Kingdom of Shamshi-Adad c.1813-1781*
▨	*Babylonian Empire of Hammurabi c.1782–50*
→	*campaigns of Sargon*
→	*campaigns of Naram Sin c.2330-2270*
→	*invasion by Gutians*
----	*present day coastline/river*

150 km
150 miles

The first empires of West Asia

c.2340: Sargon I founds and rules city of Agade

2150: Gutians conquer Sumer, ruling it until 2050

1950: Foundation of Assyrian trading colonies in Anatolia, e.g. Kanesh

c.1763: Hammurabi of Babylon conquers all of Sumer

| 2350 BCE | 2250 | 2150 | 2050 | 1950 | 1850 | 1750 BCE |

2300: Sargon of Akkad unites city-states of southern Mesopotamia to form first world empire

2111: Ur-Nammu founds Third Dynasty of Ur

c.2000: Ur destroyed by Elam

c.1750: Hammurabi writes his Code of Laws, the first in world history

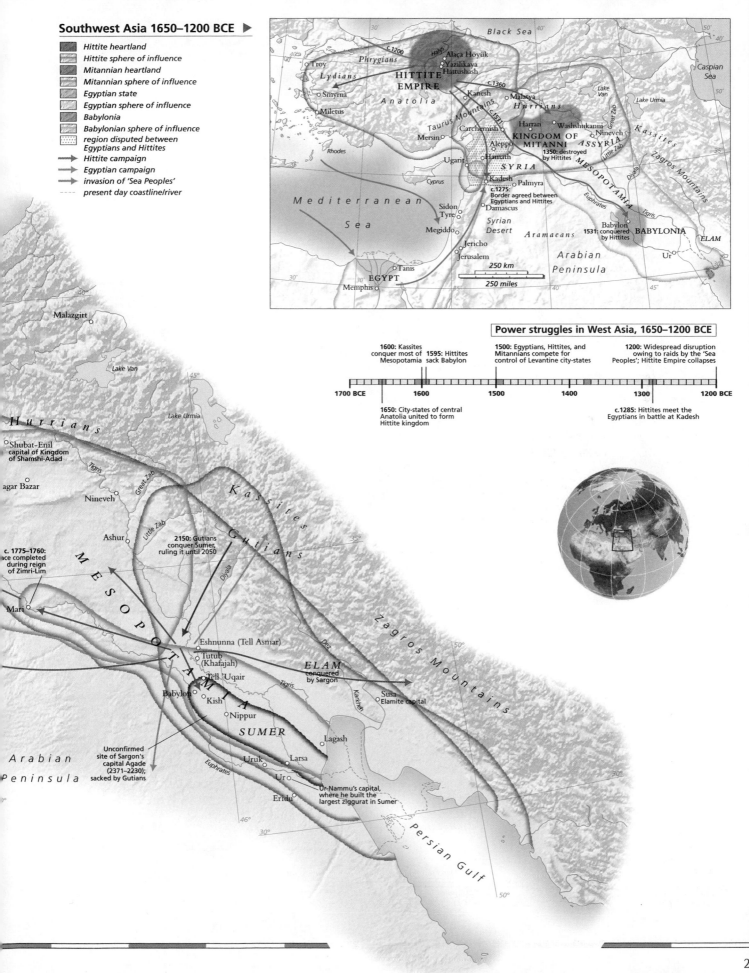

Southwest Asia 1650–1200 BCE ▶

- ▨ Hittite heartland
- ▨ Hittite sphere of influence
- ▨ Mitannian heartland
- ▨ Mitannian sphere of influence
- ▨ Egyptian state
- ▨ Egyptian sphere of influence
- ▨ Babylonia
- ▨ Babylonian sphere of influence
- ▨ region disputed between Egyptians and Hittites
- → Hittite campaign
- → Egyptian campaign
- → invasion of 'Sea Peoples'
- --- present day coastline/river

Map labels (upper inset)

Black Sea · c.1200 · Alaça Höyük · Yazilikaya · Hattushash · Troy · Phrygians · Lydians · Smyrna · HITTITE EMPIRE · Kanesh · c.1360 · Malatya · Halys · Hurrians · Lake Van · Caspian Sea · Anatolia · Taurus Mountains · Miletus · Carchemish · Harran · Washshukanni · Nineveh · Kassites · Mersin · Aleppo · KINGDOM OF MITANNI · ASSYRIA · Rhodes · Ugarit · Hamath · 1350: destroyed by Hittites · SYRIA · Little Zab · MESOPOTAMIA · Zagros Mountains · Mediterranean Sea · Cyprus · Kadesh · c.1275: Border agreed between Egyptians and Hittites · Palmyra · Euphrates · Sidon · Tyre · Damascus · Syrian Desert · Aramaeans · Tigris · Babylon · 1531: conquered by Hittites · BABYLONIA · ELAM · Megiddo · Jericho · Arabian Peninsula · Ur · Jerusalem · 250 km · 250 miles · Tanis · EGYPT · Memphis

Power struggles in West Asia, 1650–1200 BCE

1600: Kassites conquer most of Mesopotamia
1595: Hittites sack Babylon
1500: Egyptians, Hittites, and Mitannians compete for control of Levantine city-states
1200: Widespread disruption owing to raids by the 'Sea Peoples'; Hittite Empire collapses

1700 BCE — 1600 — 1500 — 1400 — 1300 — 1200 BCE

1650: City-states of central Anatolia united to form Hittite kingdom
c.1285: Hittites meet the Egyptians in battle at Kadesh

Map labels (lower relief map)

Malazgirt · Lake Van · Hurrians · Shubat-Enil capital of Kingdom of Shamshi-Adad · ˙agar Bazar · Tigris · Lake Urmia · Great Zab · Kassites · Gutians · Nineveh · Little Zab · 2150: Gutians conquer Sumer, ruling it until 2050 · Ashur · c. 1775–1760: ...ace completed during reign of Zimri-Lim · MESOPOTAMIA · Diyala · Zagros Mountains · Mari · Eshnunna (Tell Asmar) · Tutub (Khafajah) · Des · ELAM conquered by Sargon · Tell Uqair · Tigris · Susa Elamite capital · Babylon · Kish · Karkheh · Nippur · Arabian Peninsula · SUMER · Lagash · Unconfirmed site of Sargon's capital Agade (2371–2230); sacked by Gutians · Uruk · Larsa · Euphrates · Ur · Eridu · Ur-Nammu's capital, where he built the largest ziggurat in Sumer · Persian Gulf

THE GROWTH OF THE CITY

ALL CITIES THAT DEVELOPED during the two thousand years after 3500 BCE symbolized a social chasm between the ruler and the ruled, the sacred and the secular. The early expansion of urban civilization in southern Mesopotamia created a swathe of cities, from Ur to Mycenae, which thrived on trade and contact, supplemented by taxes, tolls, and tributes. Major urban areas flourished in southern and eastern Asia, and were developing in the southeast.

Where are most cities at this time located?
Why?

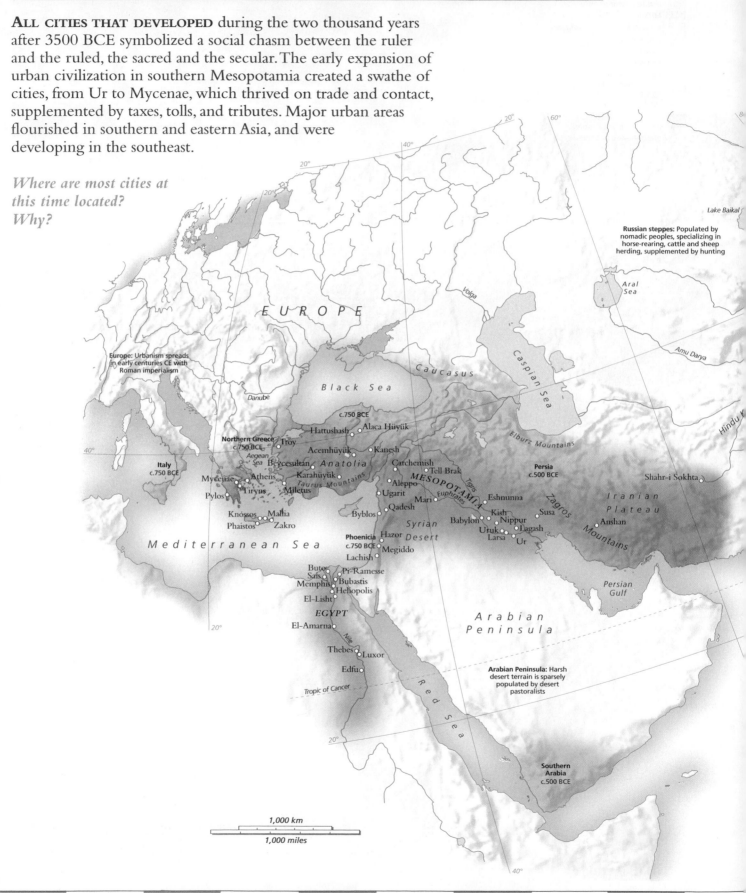

Lake Baikal

Russian steppes: Populated by nomadic peoples, specializing in horse-rearing, cattle and sheep herding, supplemented by hunting

Aral Sea

Amu Darya

Volga

EUROPE

Europe: Urbanism spreads in early centuries CE with Roman imperialism

Caucasus

Caspian Sea

Black Sea

Danube

Hindu K

c.750 BCE

Hattushash   Alaca Hüyük

Northern Greece Troy
c.750 BCE
Aegean   Acemhüyük   Kanesh
Sea   Beycesultan   *Anatolia*   Carchemish
Italy   Karahüyük   Tell Brak   **Persia**   Shahr-i Sokhta
c.750 BCE   Aleppo   MESOPOTAMIA   c.500 BCE
Mycenae   Athens   Miletus   *Taurus Mountains*   Ugarit   Mari   Euphrates   Eshnunna   Zagros   *Iranian Plateau*
Pylos   Tiryns   Qadesh   Kish   Susa   Anshan
Knossos   Mallia   Byblos   *Syrian*   Babylon   Nippur   Mountains
Phaistos   Zakro   Hazor   *Desert*   Uruk   Lagash
Megiddo   Larsa   Ur
Phoenicia
c.750 BCE
Mediterranean Sea   Lachish
   Buto   Pi-Ramesse
   Sais   Bubastis   *Arabian*
Memphis   Heliopolis   *Peninsula*
El-Lisht
EGYPT
El-Amarna

Elburz Mountains

Persian Gulf

Arabian Peninsula: Harsh desert terrain is sparsely populated by desert pastoralists

Thebes   Luxor

Edfu

Nile

Red Sea

Tropic of Cancer

Southern Arabia
c.500 BCE

1,000 km

1,000 miles

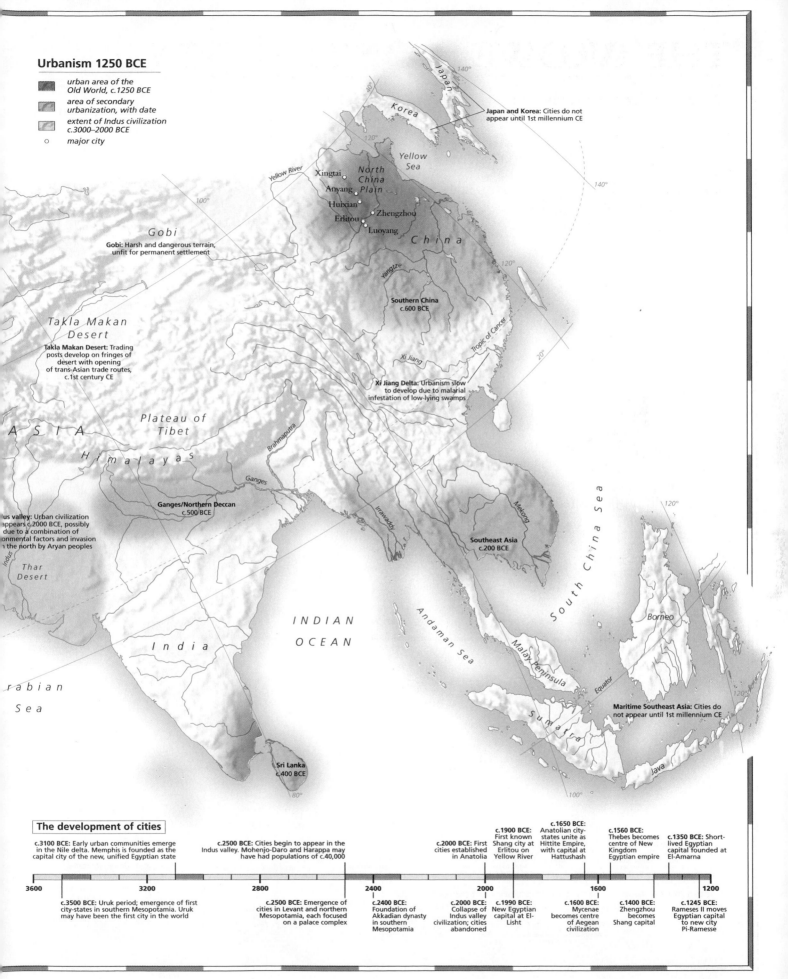

Urbanism 1250 BCE

- urban area of the Old World, c.1250 BCE
- area of secondary urbanization, with date
- extent of Indus civilization c.3000–2000 BCE
- ○ major city

Japan and Korea: Cities do not appear until 1st millennium CE

Gobi: Harsh and dangerous terrain, unfit for permanent settlement

Takla Makan Desert: Trading posts develop on fringes of desert with opening of trans-Asian trade routes, c.1st century CE

Xingtai
Anyang
Huixian
Erlitou
Zhengzhou
Luoyang

North China Plain

China

Southern China c.600 BCE

Xi Jiang Delta: Urbanism slow to develop due to malarial infestation of low-lying swamps

Gobi

Yellow River

Yellow Sea

Japan

Korea

ASIA

Plateau of Tibet

Himalayas

Takla Makan Desert

Brahmaputra

Ganges

Ganges/Northern Deccan c.500 BCE

us valley: Urban civilization appears c.2000 BCE, possibly due to a combination of ...onmental factors and invasion ...n the north by Aryan peoples

Thar Desert

India

Irrawaddy

Mekong

Southeast Asia c.200 BCE

INDIAN OCEAN

Andaman Sea

South China Sea

Malay Peninsula

Borneo

Sumatra

Java

Equator

Maritime Southeast Asia: Cities do not appear until 1st millennium CE

rabian Sea

Sri Lanka c.400 BCE

The development of cities

c.3100 BCE: Early urban communities emerge in the Nile delta. Memphis is founded as the capital city of the new, unified Egyptian state

c.2500 BCE: Cities begin to appear in the Indus valley. Mohenjo-Daro and Harappa may have had populations of c.40,000

c.2000 BCE: First cities established in Anatolia

c.1900 BCE: First known Shang city at Erlitou on Yellow River

c.1650 BCE: Anatolian city-states unite as Hittite Empire, with capital at Hattushash

c.1560 BCE: Thebes becomes centre of New Kingdom Egyptian empire

c.1350 BCE: Short-lived Egyptian capital founded at El-Amarna

3600   3200   2800   2400   2000   1600   1200

c.3500 BCE: Uruk period; emergence of first city-states in southern Mesopotamia. Uruk may have been the first city in the world

c.2500 BCE: Emergence of cities in Levant and northern Mesopotamia, each focused on a palace complex

c.2400 BCE: Foundation of Akkadian dynasty in southern Mesopotamia

c.2000 BCE: Collapse of Indus valley civilization; cities abandoned

c.1990 BCE: New Egyptian capital at El-Lisht

c.1600 BCE: Mycenae becomes centre of Aegean civilization

c.1400 BCE: Zhengzhou becomes Shang capital

c.1245 BCE: Rameses II moves Egyptian capital to new city Pi-Ramesse

THE WORLD: 750–500 BCE

CIVILIZATIONS OF EURASIA now lay in a more or less continuous belt from the Mediterranean to China. Both trade and cultural contact were well-established; understanding of iron metallurgy had spread from the Middle East as far as China and sub-Saharan Africa, and by the 6th century BCE Chinese silk was beginning to appear in Europe. All these civilizations, however, were increasingly subjected to incursions by tribes of nomadic pastoralists who were rapidly spreading across Central Asia, eastern Europe, and Siberia. In the Americas, the Olmec, Zapotec, and Chavin cultures flourished.

What factors favored expansion of empires and states worldwide? What factors limited expansion?

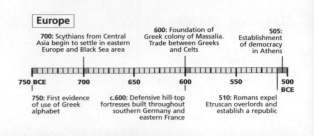

Europe

700: Scythians from Central Asia begin to settle in eastern Europe and Black Sea area

600: Foundation of Greek colony of Massalia. Trade between Greeks and Celts

505: Establishment of democracy in Athens

750 BCE — 700 — 650 — 600 — 550 — 500 BCE

750: First evidence of use of Greek alphabet

c.600: Defensive hill-top fortresses built throughout southern Germany and eastern France

510: Romans expel Etruscan overlords and establish a republic

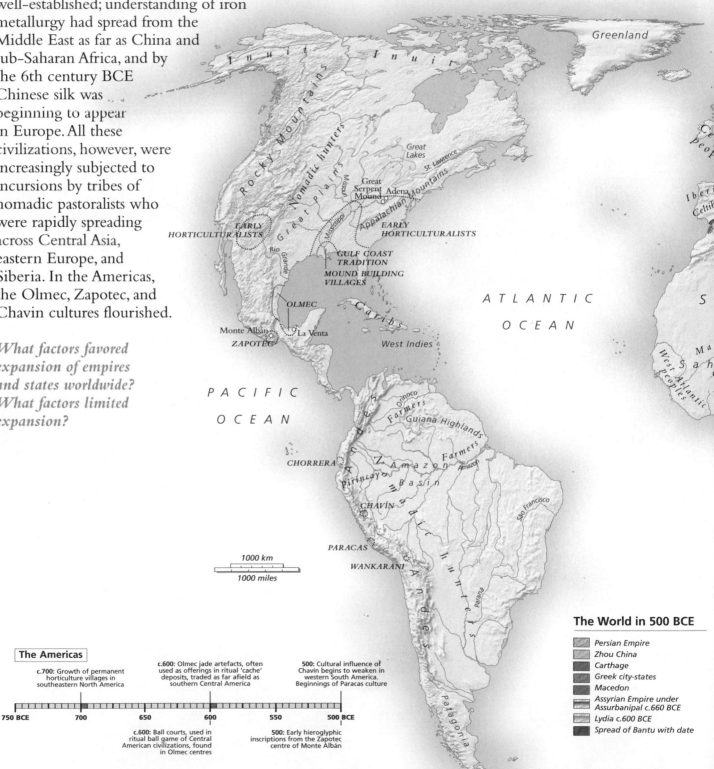

1000 km

1000 miles

The Americas

c.700: Growth of permanent horticulture villages in southeastern North America

c.600: Olmec jade artefacts, often used as offerings in ritual 'cache' deposits, traded as far afield as southern Central America

500: Cultural influence of Chavín begins to weaken in western South America. Beginnings of Paracas culture

750 BCE — 700 — 650 — 600 — 550 — 500 BCE

c.600: Ball courts, used in ritual ball game of Central American civilizations, found in Olmec centres

500: Early hieroglyphic inscriptions from the Zapotec centre of Monte Albán

The World in 500 BCE

- Persian Empire
- Zhou China
- Carthage
- Greek city-states
- Macedon
- Assyrian Empire under Assurbanipal c.660 BCE
- Lydia c.600 BCE
- Spread of Bantu with date

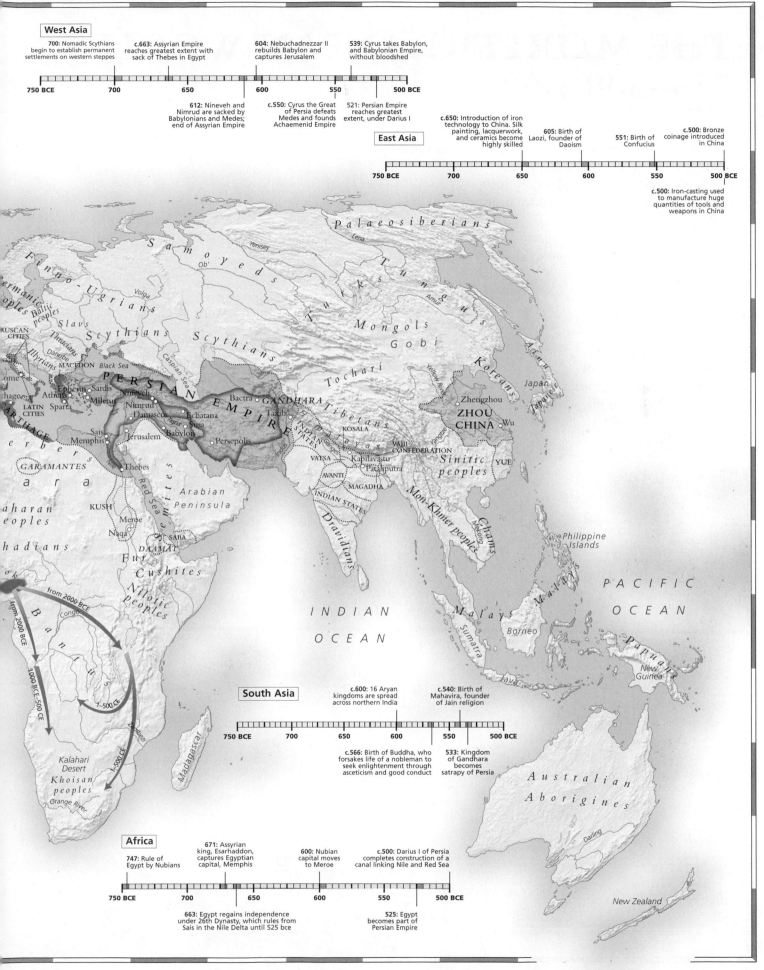

700: Nomadic Scythians begin to establish permanent settlements on western steppes

c.663: Assyrian Empire reaches greatest extent with sack of Thebes in Egypt

604: Nebuchadnezzar II rebuilds Babylon and captures Jerusalem

539: Cyrus takes Babylon, and Babylonian Empire, without bloodshed

750 BCE — 700 — 650 — 600 — 550 — 500 BCE

612: Nineveh and Nimrud are sacked by Babylonians and Medes; end of Assyrian Empire

c.550: Cyrus the Great of Persia defeats Medes and founds Achaemenid Empire

521: Persian Empire reaches greatest extent, under Darius I

East Asia

c.650: Introduction of iron technology to China. Silk painting, lacquerwork, and ceramics become highly skilled

605: Birth of Laozi, founder of Daoism

551: Birth of Confucius

c.500: Bronze coinage introduced in China

750 BCE — 700 — 650 — 600 — 550 — 500 BCE

c.500: Iron-casting used to manufacture huge quantities of tools and weapons in China

South Asia

c.600: 16 Aryan kingdoms are spread across northern India

c.540: Birth of Mahavira, founder of Jain religion

750 BCE — 700 — 650 — 600 — 550 — 500 BCE

c.566: Birth of Buddha, who forsakes life of a nobleman to seek enlightenment through asceticism and good conduct

533: Kingdom of Gandhara becomes satrapy of Persia

Africa

747: Rule of Egypt by Nubians

671: Assyrian king, Esarhaddon, captures Egyptian capital, Memphis

600: Nubian capital moves to Meroe

c.500: Darius I of Persia completes construction of a canal linking Nile and Red Sea

750 BCE — 700 — 650 — 600 — 550 — 500 BCE

663: Egypt regains independence under 26th Dynasty, which rules from Sais in the Nile Delta until 525 bce

525: Egypt becomes part of Persian Empire

THE MEDITERRANEAN WORLD: 700–300 BCE

Between 700 and 300 BCE the Mediterranean world shaped
Western civilization. Though the Phoenicians were active in
maritime trade and colonization, the impact
of Classical Greek ideas on art, philosophy,
science, and politics was far more profound.

*How were colonies and colonization central
to the ancient Mediterranean world?*

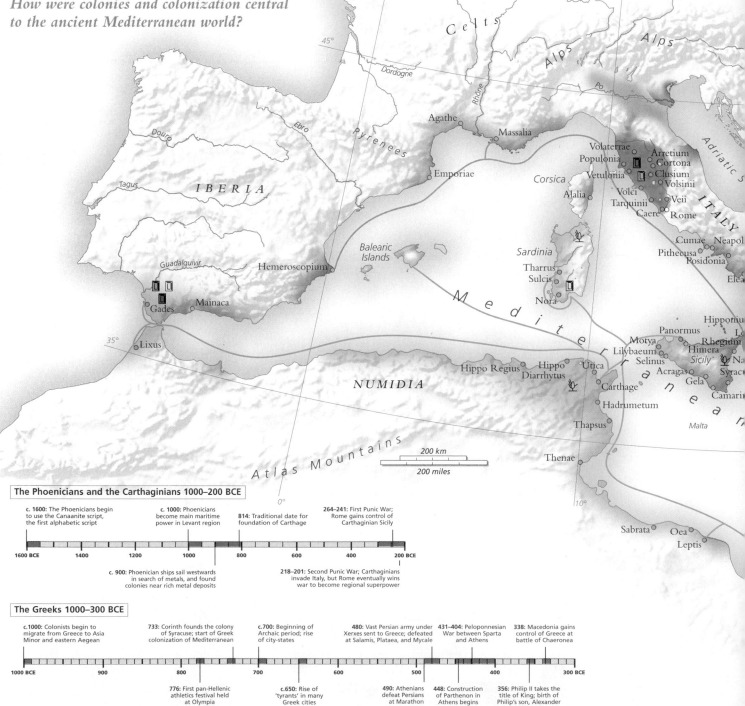

The Phoenicians and the Carthaginians 1000–200 BCE

c. 1600: The Phoenicians begin
to use the Canaanite script,
the first alphabetic script

c. 1000: Phoenicians
become main maritime
power in Levant region

814: Traditional date for
foundation of Carthage

264–241: First Punic War;
Rome gains control of
Carthaginian Sicily

| 1600 BCE | 1400 | 1200 | 1000 | 800 | 600 | 400 | 200 BCE |

c. 900: Phoenician ships sail westwards
in search of metals, and found
colonies near rich metal deposits

218–201: Second Punic War; Carthaginians
invade Italy, but Rome eventually wins
war to become regional superpower

The Greeks 1000–300 BCE

c.1000: Colonists begin to
migrate from Greece to Asia
Minor and eastern Aegean

733: Corinth founds the colony
of Syracuse; start of Greek
colonization of Mediterranean

c.700: Beginning of
Archaic period; rise
of city-states

480: Vast Persian army under
Xerxes sent to Greece; defeated
at Salamis, Plataea, and Mycale

431–404: Peloponnesian
War between Sparta
and Athens

338: Macedonia gains
control of Greece at
battle of Chaeronea

| 1000 BCE | 900 | 800 | 700 | 600 | 500 | 400 | 300 BCE |

776: First pan-Hellenic
athletics festival held
at Olympia

c.650: Rise of
'tyrants' in many
Greek cities

490: Athenians
defeat Persians
at Marathon

448: Construction
of Parthenon in
Athens begins

356: Philip II takes the
title of King; birth of
Philip's son, Alexander

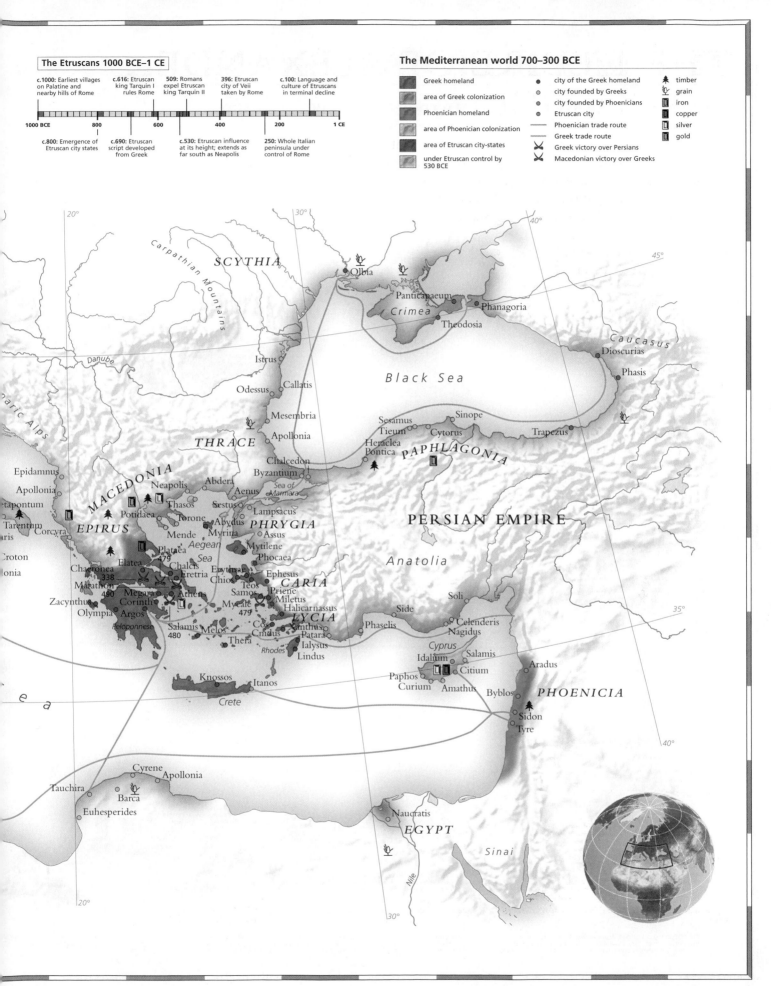

The Etruscans 1000 BCE–1 CE

c.1000: Earliest villages on Palatine and nearby hills of Rome
c.616: Etruscan king Tarquin I rules Rome
509: Romans expel Etruscan king Tarquin II
396: Etruscan city of Veii taken by Rome
c.100: Language and culture of Etruscans in terminal decline

1000 BCE — 800 — 600 — 400 — 200 — 1 CE

c.800: Emergence of Etruscan city states
c.690: Etruscan script developed from Greek
c.530: Etruscan influence at its height; extends as far south as Neapolis
250: Whole Italian peninsula under control of Rome

The Mediterranean world 700–300 BCE

- Greek homeland
- area of Greek colonization
- Phoenician homeland
- area of Phoenician colonization
- area of Etruscan city-states
- under Etruscan control by 530 BCE

- ● city of the Greek homeland
- ○ city founded by Greeks
- ◐ city founded by Phoenicians
- ● Etruscan city
- —— Phoenician trade route
- —— Greek trade route
- ✕ Greek victory over Persians
- ✕ Macedonian victory over Greeks

- ♣ timber
- grain
- iron
- copper
- silver
- gold

SCYTHIA

Carpathian Mountains

Olbia
Panticapaeum
Crimea
Phanagoria
Theodosia
Caucasus
Dioscurias
Phasis

Danube
Istrus
Odessus
Callatis
Mesembria
Apollonia

Black Sea

Sesamus
Tieum
Heraclea Pontica
Cytorus
Sinope
Trapezus

THRACE

Chalcedon
Byzantium
PAPHLAGONIA

Epidamnus
Apollonia
Metapontum
Tarentum
Corcyra
Croton
olonia

MACEDONIA
EPIRUS

Neapolis
Abdera
Aenus
Sea of Marmara

PERSIAN EMPIRE

Thasos
Sestus
Lampsacus
Potidaea
Torone
Abydus
Mende
Myrina
Assus
PHRYGIA

Anatolia

Plataea
479
Elatea
Aegean Sea
Mytilene
Phocaea

Chaeronea
338
Chalcis
Erythrae
Ephesus
CARIA

Marathon
490
Eretria
Chios
Teos
Priene
Miletus
Soli

Zacynthus
Megara
Athens
Samos
Halicarnassus
Side
Celenderis
Nagidus

Olympia
Corinth
Mycale
479
LYCIA
Phaselis

Argos
Peloponnese
Cos
Xanthus
Cyprus

Salamis
480
Melos
Cnidus
Patara
Idalium
Salamis
Aradus

Thera
Rhodes
Ialysus
Lindus
Paphos
Citium
PHOENICIA

Knossos
Itanos
Curium
Amathus
Byblos

Crete
Sidon
Tyre

Tauchira
Cyrene
Apollonia

Barca
Euhesperides

Naucratis

EGYPT

Sinai

Nile

35

THE EMPIRE OF ALEXANDER

THE CONQUESTS OF ALEXANDER OF MACEDON (356–323 BCE) took Greek armies as far east as India, and forced Persia, the most powerful empire in the world, into submission. This audacious military feat, accomplished in just ten years, created a truly cosmopolitan civilization, known as Hellenism, which spread Greek culture from Egypt to the Hindu Kush. In turn, Egyptian and Asian cultures also influenced the development of Hellenistic civilization.

Why is the Empire of Alexander considered a global empire?

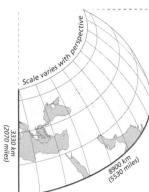

Scale varies with perspective

3330 km (2070 miles)

8900 km (5530 miles)

The Empire of Alexander

- Empire of Alexander
- dependent regions
- independent states
- → route of Alexander the Great
- → route of Nearchus
- → return route of Craterus
- ✗ major battle
- — Persian Royal Road

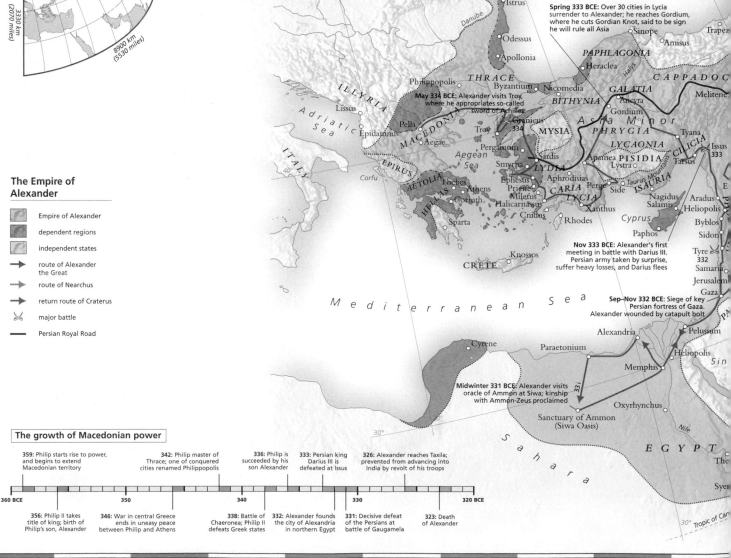

Spring 333 BCE: Over 30 cities in Lycia surrender to Alexander; he reaches Gordium, where he cuts Gordian Knot, said to be sign he will rule all Asia

May 334 BCE: Alexander visits Troy, where he appropriates so-called sword of Achilles

Nov 333 BCE: Alexander's first meeting in battle with Darius III. Persian army taken by surprise, suffer heavy losses, and Darius flees

Sep–Nov 332 BCE: Siege of key Persian fortress of Gaza. Alexander wounded by catapult bolt

Midwinter 331 BCE: Alexander visits oracle of Ammon at Siwa; kinship with Ammon-Zeus proclaimed

The growth of Macedonian power

359: Philip starts rise to power, and begins to extend Macedonian territory

356: Philip II takes title of king; birth of Philip's son, Alexander

346: War in central Greece ends in uneasy peace between Philip and Athens

342: Philip master of Thrace; one of conquered cities renamed Philippopolis

338: Battle of Chaeronea; Philip II defeats Greek states

336: Philip is succeeded by his son Alexander

333: Persian king Darius III is defeated at Issus

332: Alexander founds the city of Alexandria in northern Egypt

331: Decisive defeat of the Persians at battle of Gaugamela

326: Alexander reaches Taxila; prevented from advancing into India by revolt of his troops

323: Death of Alexander

360 BCE   350   340   330   320 BCE

Takla Makan Desert

Plateau of Tibet

Brahmaputra

Aral Sea

CHORASMIA

steppes

Ural

Autumn 329 BCE: Greeks use Maracanda as forward base for raids into surrounding regions. Revolt by conquered peoples harshly repressed

Tashkent

Jaxartes

Alexandria Eschate (Kokand)

Spring 328 BCE: Capture of Sogdian Rock

Maracanda (Samarkand)

Sogdian Rock

Spring 327 BCE: Alexander marries Roxanne, daughter of Sogdian baron, Oxyartes

Himalayas

90°

Bukhara

Nautaca

Oxus

SOGDIANA

Aornos 327

Drapsaca

Indus

Hydaspes

Taxila

Bucephala

Winter 327 BCE: Campaigns in Swat valley

Spring 326 BCE: Leading army of some 80,000 troops and 30,000 camp-followers, Alexander crosses Indus and marches on Taxila

Kara Kum

Alexandria ad Oxum (Ai Khanoum)

Bactra

PARAPAMISUS

BACTRIA

Caspian Sea

Alexandria (Merv)

Spring 329 BCE: Alexander crosses Hindu Kush

Hindu Kush

Hydaspes

326

Sep 326 BCE: At Hyphasis River, Greek troops refuse to go any further. Army turns back

Hydraotes

Zaradros

May 326 BCE: Death of Alexander's horse, Bucephalus. City founded in his memory

ucasus

LCHIS

Cyrus

Meshed

330

Susia

ARIA

MALAVA

Bojnurd

Artacoana

Alexandria Areion (Herat)

RMENIA

Araxes

MARDI

Elburz Mountains

HYRCANIA

Hecatompylos

PARTHIA

DRANGIANA

Alexandria Arachoton (Kandahar)

ARACHOSIA

Opiana

Nov 326 BCE: Army passes through Punjab and Sind, ruthlessly crushing all resistance

Thar Desert

INDIA

80°

1 Oct 331 BCE: Alexander's second battle with Darius III, whose army includes elephants and scythe-wheeled chariots. Victory for Alexander signals effective end of Persian Empire

Amol

Caspian Gates

Rhagae

Great Salt Desert

Summer 330 BCE: In pursuit of retreating Darius, Alexander passes through Caspian Gates (rocky defile guarded by Persian fortress). Discovers Darius dying, murdered by conspiring Persian commanders

Quetta

Nad-i-Ali

Indus

Gaugamela

Nineveh

Arbela

331

MEDIA

Ecbatana

PARAETACENE

Gabae

Iranian Plateau

CARMANIA

Pattala

ESOPOTAMIA

Carrhae

Nicephorium

sacus

Feb 324 BCE: Returns to Susa. Mass marriage of Greek soldiers to Persian brides

Tigris

Susa

331

SUSIANA

324

Persian Gates

PERSIS

Zagros Mountains

330

Pasargadae

Persepolis

Alexandria (Gulashkird)

325

Pura

GEDROSIA

Kokala

Autumn 325 BCE: Alexander leads troops through Makran desert, where heat and thirst cause terrible loss of life. Rest of the army makes wide detour around the desert, under the leadership of Craterus

70°

Palmyra

Euphrates

RIA

Syrian Desert

BABYLONIA

Babylon

331

Harmozia

Gwadar

Arabian Sea

30 Jan 330 BCE: Alexander reaches Persepolis; army sacks city. Royal palace later put to torch by Alexander and troops

Gulf of Oman

Nov 331 BCE: Following surrender of Babylon, Alexander enters city in triumph

10 Jun 323 BCE: Alexander dies in Babylon

Persian Gulf

Jan 330 BCE: Alexander attempts to go through Persian Gates (a pass through Zagros Mountains). When ambushed by Persians, Alexander leads army up steep, narrow track to surprise enemy from the rear

325 BCE: Alexander's fleet, built to descend the Indus, is brought back to the Persian Gulf by Nearchus

60°

Arabian Peninsula

Red Sea

20°

40°

50°

THE WORLD: 500–250 BCE

THE 5TH CENTURY BCE was an age of enlightened and innovative thought. It was the climax of the Classical Age in Greece. At the same time, the Buddhist religion, based on the precepts of Siddhartha Gautama (c. 566–486 BCE), was spreading throughout the Indian subcontinent. In China, the teachings of Confucius (551–479 BCE) were concerned with ethical conduct and propriety in human relations. Yet the ensuing centuries would be a time of conflict and conquest.

What is the connection between political developments and philosophical and religious thinking during this period?

The World in 250 BCE

- Qin Empire
- Carthage
- Massalia
- Greek city-states
- Macedon
- Mauryan Empire
- Seleucid Empire
- ◆ Ptolemaic Empire
- Empire of Alexander the Great 323 BCE

Europe

490: Greeks defeat Persians at Marathon

443–429: Athens flourishes under rule of Pericles

390: Celts sack Rome

336: Alexander embarks on conquest of Persian Empire

323: Death of Alexander the Great

264: Rome leads single Italian confederacy

500 BCE — 450 — 400 — 350 — 300 — 250 BCE

c.450: Celts expand into British Isles and to east and south

431–404: Peloponnesian Wars between Athens and Sparta

338: Philip II of Macedon defeats Greek states

260: Start of Roman conflict with Carthage

The Americas

c.500: Paracas culture of southern Peru, famed for brightly colored textiles, emerges

c.350: Beginnings of Nazca culture in southern Peru

500 BCE — 450 — 400 — 350 — 300 — 250 BCE

c.400: Early Zapotec culture flourishing around city of Monte Albán

c.300: Hopewell culture in eastern North America develops traditions of earlier Adena culture

Africa

c.500: First iron-working in sub-Saharan Africa. Beginning of period of Nok culture in Niger Delta

332: Alexander the Great conquers Egypt. He lays the foundations of Alexandria

302: Ptolemy I declares himself king of Egypt. The Ptolemies took pharaonic titles and worshipped Egyptian deities

500 BCE — 450 — 400 — 350 — 300 — 250 BCE

c.500: Iron-using Bantus begin to spread from Niger to East African lakes region and down west coast of Africa

c.250: Settlement of Jenne-jeno is founded on inland Niger Delta

East Asia

c.450: Burials at Pazyryk and Noin Ula in Siberia give insight into life of steppe nomads

500 BCE — 450

c.480: Death of Confucius, who developed humanistic ethical system

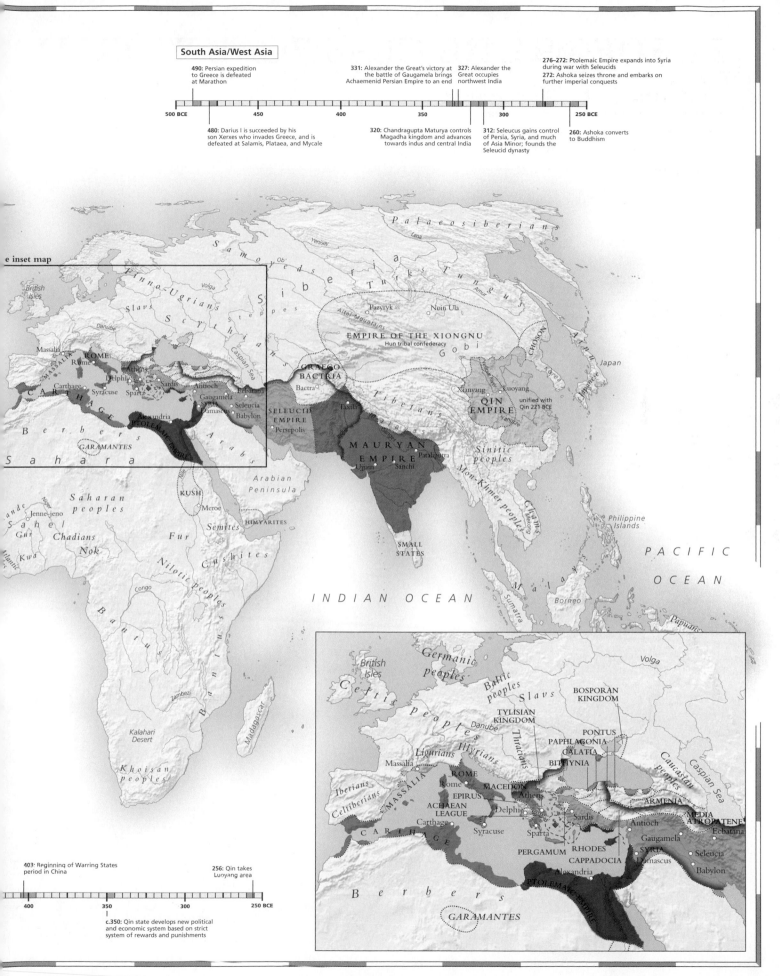

490: Persian expedition to Greece is defeated at Marathon

331: Alexander the Great's victory at the battle of Gaugamela brings Achaemenid Persian Empire to an end

327: Alexander the Great occupies northwest India

276–272: Ptolemaic Empire expands into Syria during war with Seleucids

272: Ashoka seizes throne and embarks on further imperial conquests

480: Darius I is succeeded by his son Xerxes who invades Greece, and is defeated at Salamis, Plataea, and Mycale

320: Chandragupta Maturya controls Magadha kingdom and advances towards indus and central India

312: Seleucus gains control of Persia, Syria, and much of Asia Minor; founds the Seleucid dynasty

260: Ashoka converts to Buddhism

500 BCE — 450 — 400 — 350 — 300 — 250 BCE

403: Beginning of Warring States period in China

256: Qin takes Luoyang area

400 — 350 — 300 — 250 BCE

c.350: Qin state develops new political and economic system based on strict system of rewards and punishments

39

TRADE IN THE CLASSICAL WORLD

BY THE BEGINNING of the 1st millennium CE, a series of commercial and political networks had evolved which combined to form a nexus of trade linking the eastern shores of the Atlantic Ocean, the Indian Ocean, and the western shores of the Pacific.

Trade is important for the movement of goods and services, but what else can move along trade routes?

Eurasian and African trade c.1 CE

| Roman Empire and client states |
| Han Empire |
| Sinkiang (Han protectorate 73–94 CE) |

Trade routes
- Roman
- Trans–Saharan (rudimentary route)
- Indian Ocean
- Silk Road
- Scythian (rudimentary route)
- China
- East Africa
- amber
- incense
- other (rudimentary route)

Goods traded
- amber
- animals
- clothing
- gold
- silver
- grain
- horses
- incense
- ivory
- olive oil
- precious stones
- silk
- slaves
- spices
- timber
- tin
- tortoiseshell
- wine

Scale varies with perspective

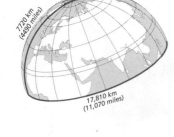

7720 km (4430 miles)

17,810 km (11,070 miles)

Sea of Okhotsk · Kurile Islands

Amur

Lake Baikal

S i b e r i a

A S I A

DZUNGARIA

Altai Mountains

Lake Balkhash · Kitai

Kuldja

Aksu · Tien Shan · Turfan

SINKIANG · Jiaohei

Yarkand · Dunhuang

Kashgar · Khotan

Takla Makan Desert

FERGHANA

Pamirs

Marakanda

SOGDIANA

Amu Darya

Aral Sea · Syr Darya

Tocharians

Iranians

TRANSOXIANA

KUSHAN EMPIRE

Merv · Bactra

BACTRIA · Begram

Hindu Kush

Taxila

PARTHIA

Alexandria · Areion

Iranian Plateau

atompylos

P e r s i a

Zagros Mountains

Kandahar

PAHLAVAS

Indus

Thar Desert

Mathura

SHAKAS

I n d i a

Ganges

Pataliputra · Nalanda · MAGADHA

Brahmaputra

Tamluk

Barygaza (Broach)

Mandagora

SATAVAHANAS

Masulipatam

MAHA-MEGHAVAHANAS

Poduca

CHOLA

Muziris · Colchi

PANDYA · Taprobane

Arabian Sea

Asabon · Barbaricon

Omana

sian f

Zenobia

MEN

Cana · Gulf of Aden · Socotra

Etriporion

Aromata

Horn of Africa

Sarapion

INDIAN OCEAN

Plateau of Tibet

Tibetans

T i b e t

Himalayas

Xiongnu

Gobi

Awui

Wuwei

Chang'an

Chengdu

Kunming

Yangtze

Yellow River

KOREA

Yellow Sea

Kaifeng · Luoyang

Hankou · Ningbo

HAN EMPIRE

China

Fuzhou · Quanzhou

Nanhai (Guangzhou)

Hangzhou · East China Sea

Taiwan

Hainan

Cattigara

Chams

Mekong

Mon-Khmer peoples

Irrawaddy

Thaton

Oc Eo

Trang

J A P A N

Sea of Japan

Tropic of Cancer

PACIFIC OCEAN

Philippine Islands

Luzon

Moluccas

South China Sea

M a l a y s

Borneo · Celebes

Sumatra · E a s t

Java Sea

Java · I n d i e s

Bay of Bengal

Andaman Islands

Nicobar Islands

Equator

The Classical World

141: Wudi expands Han power into Central Asia

60: Establishment of Kushan Empire

c.150: Ptolemy publishes first World Atlas

200: Han dynasty collapses

396: Roman Empire divided into eastern and western halves

200 BCE — 100 BCE — 1 CE — 100 — 200 — 300 — 400

31: Roman victory at Actium consolidates control of eastern Mediterranean

117: Roman Empire at greatest extent

224: Beginning of Sassanian control in Persia

238: First Germanic incursions into Roman Empire

370: Huns enter Europe

THE ROMAN EMPIRE

AT THE HEIGHT OF ITS POWER in the 2nd century, Rome ruled over some 50 million people scattered in over 5000 administrative units. For the most part, the subjects of the Empire accepted Roman rule, and, at least in the west, many adopted Roman culture and the Latin language. After 212 CE, all free inhabitants of the Empire had the status of Roman citizens.

What were the limitations on the expansion of the Roman Empire?

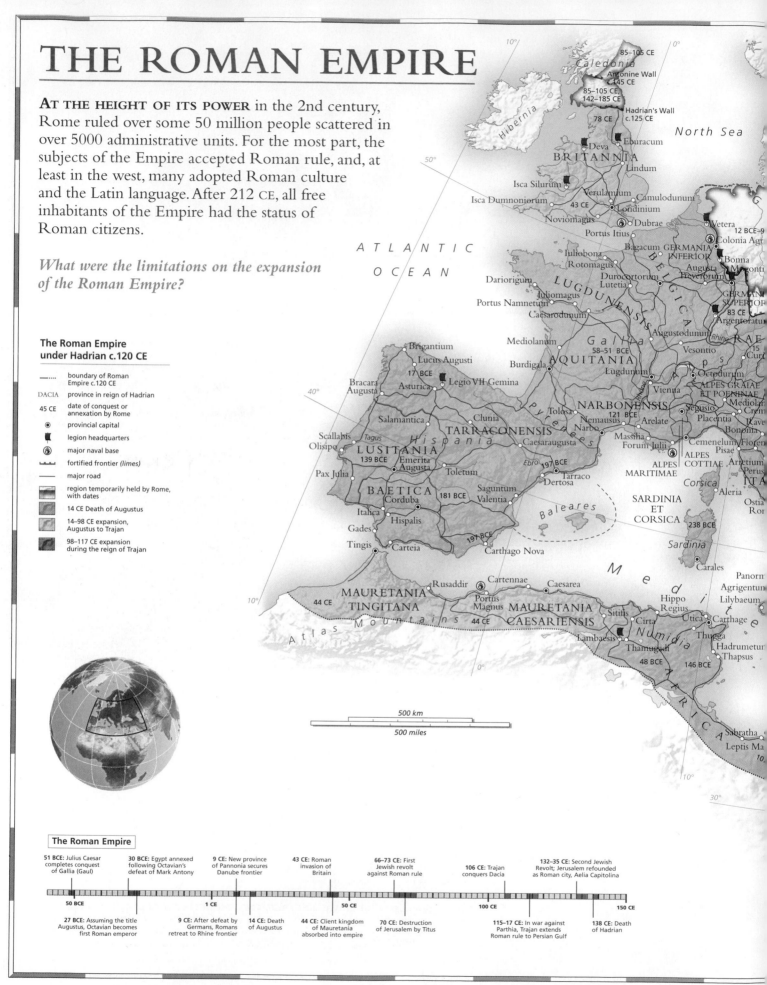

The Roman Empire under Hadrian c.120 CE

.....	boundary of Roman Empire c.120 CE
DACIA	province in reign of Hadrian
45 CE	date of conquest or annexation by Rome
⊙	provincial capital
▮	legion headquarters
⚓	major naval base
⊣⊢	fortified frontier (*limes*)
—	major road
	region temporarily held by Rome, with dates
	14 CE Death of Augustus
	14–98 CE expansion, Augustus to Trajan
	98–117 CE expansion during the reign of Trajan

The Roman Empire

51 BCE: Julius Caesar completes conquest of Gallia (Gaul)

30 BCE: Egypt annexed following Octavian's defeat of Mark Antony

9 CE: New province of Pannonia secures Danube frontier

43 CE: Roman invasion of Britain

66–73 CE: First Jewish revolt against Roman rule

106 CE: Trajan conquers Dacia

132–35 CE: Second Jewish Revolt; Jerusalem refounded as Roman city, Aelia Capitolina

50 BCE ——— 1 CE ——— 50 CE ——— 100 CE ——— 150 CE

27 BCE: Assuming the title Augustus, Octavian becomes first Roman emperor

9 CE: After defeat by Germans, Romans retreat to Rhine frontier

14 CE: Death of Augustus

44 CE: Client kingdom of Mauretania absorbed into empire

70 CE: Destruction of Jerusalem by Titus

115–17 CE: In war against Parthia, Trajan extends Roman rule to Persian Gulf

138 CE: Death of Hadrian

Burgundians

Marcomanni · Quadi

Sarmatians

augusta Vindelicorum
Vindobona
Carnuntum
Brigetio · Savaria · Aquincum
NORICUM
15 BCE
Virunum
PANNONIA
SUPERIOR
Siscia
Mursa
Sirmium · Singidunum
33 BCE
DALMATIA · ILLYRICUM
Salonae
DACIA
107 CE
Apulum
Sarmizegethusa
Viminacium
MOESIA
SUPERIOR
29 BCE
Novae
Oescus
Serdica
THRACIA
Philippopolis
45 CE
Nicopolis
Troesmis
Tomi
Durostorum
MOESIA INFERIOR
Roxolani

PANNONIA
INFERIOR
9 CE

Puteoli
Neapolis
Misenum
Dyrrhachium
Stobi
Heraclea
Brundisium
MACEDONIA
148 BCE
Tarantum
Thessalonica
EPIRUS
140 BCE
Nicopolis

Messana
Rhegium
SICILIA
Syracuse

ACHAIA
146 BCE
Corinth
Athens
Delphi
Sparta

Pergamum
ASIA
133 BCE
Ephesus
Miletus
Laodicea
Cnidus
Rhodus
74 CE
Myra

Byzantium
Hadrianopolis
Nicomedia
Cyzicus
Prusa
BITHYNIA ET PONTUS
74 BCE
Ancyra
GALATIA
25 BCE
Dorylaeum
Antiochia
Iconium
LYCIA
74 CE
Attalia
101 BCE
CILICIA

Heraclea
Pontica
Sinope
Pompeiopolis
Gangra
Zela
18 CE
CAPPADOCIA
Caesarea

Trapezus
Satala
Nicopolis
Melitene
Samosata
Zeugma
Cyrrhus
Tarsus
Seleucia
Antioch
Euphrates
Laodicea
Raphanaea
SYRIA
64 BCE
115 CE

LAZICA

ARMENIA
114–117 CE

Caucasus

Caspian Sea

PARTHIAN
EMPIRE

ASSYRIA
116–117 CE
MESOPOTAMIA
115–117 CE
Tigris
Dura
Europos
Ctesiphon

Black Sea

BOSPORAN
KINGDOM
vassal of Rome
from 63 BCE

CYPRUS
58 BCE
Salamis
Paphus
Tripolis
Heliopolis
Damascus
Tyrus
Caparcotna
Caesarea Maritima
JUDAEA
6 CE
Jerusalem
(Aelia Capitolina)
Bostra
Syrian
Desert

Arabian
Peninsula

67 BCE
Gortyn

Ptolemais
Cyrene
74 BCE
CYRENE
ET CRETA

Alexandria
Nicopolis

Memphis
20 BCE
AEGYPTUS
30 BCE

ARABIA
106 CE
Petra

Red Sea

Nile

Mediterranean Sea

HAN CHINA

THE UNIFICATION OF CHINA by the Qin in 221 BCE paved the way for the Han, who assumed control in 206 BCE. The Han established a domain by far the greatest the world had ever seen, and provided a template for Chinese territorial aspirations for the next two millennia.

What factors limited Han expansion?

The Han dynasty

141 BCE: Han emperor Wudi expands into Central Asia **138–126 BCE:** Embassy Zhang Qian to Xiongnu and Central Asia

250 BCE   150 BCE

221 BCE: The First Emperor (Shi Huangdi) unites China under Qin dynasty (to 207) **206 BCE:** Foundation of Han dynasty; capital at Chang'an

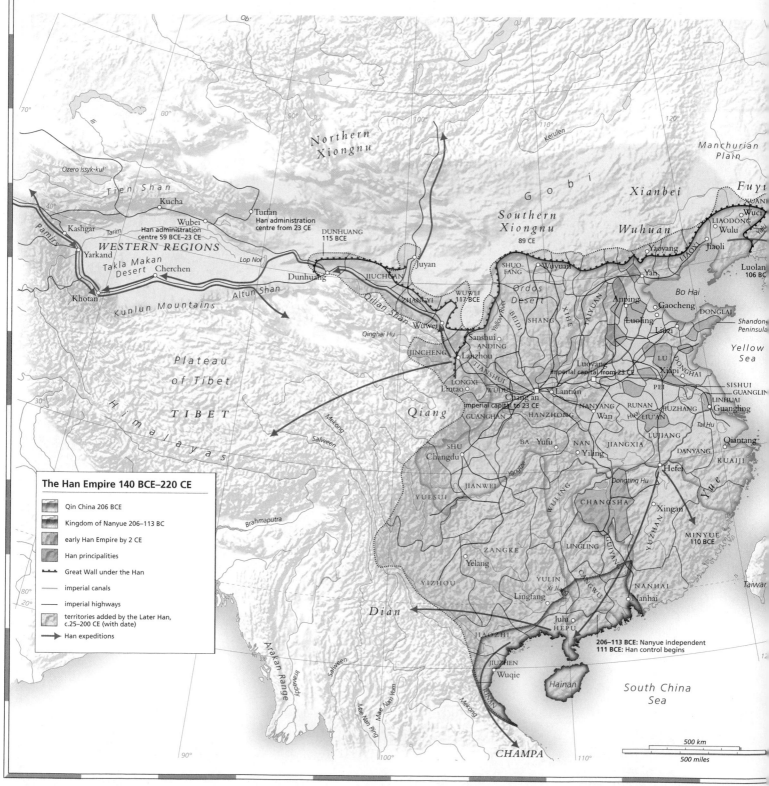

The Han Empire 140 BCE–220 CE

- Qin China 206 BCE
- Kingdom of Nanyue 206–113 BC
- early Han Empire by 2 CE
- Han principalities
- Great Wall under the Han
- imperial canals
- imperial highways
- territories added by the Later Han, c.25–200 CE (with date)
- Han expeditions

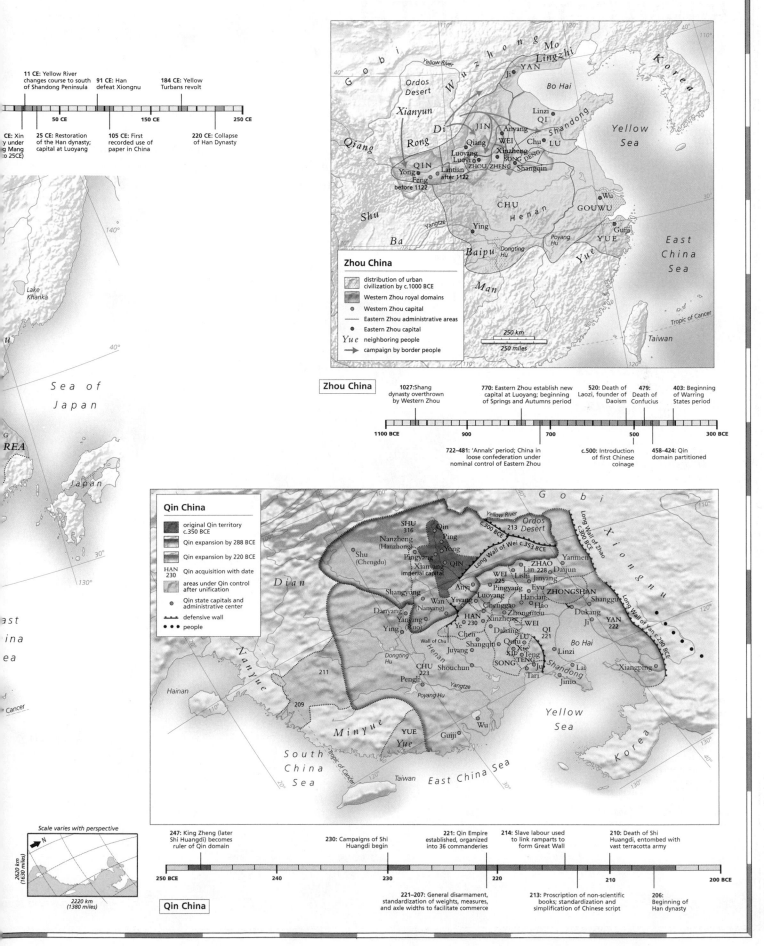

Timeline (top left)

11 CE: Yellow River changes course to south of Shandong Peninsula

91 CE: Han defeat Xiongnu

184 CE: Yellow Turbans revolt

50 CE — 150 CE — 250 CE

CE: Xin ... under ... Mang ... to 25CE)

25 CE: Restoration of the Han dynasty; capital at Luoyang

105 CE: First recorded use of paper in China

220 CE: Collapse of Han Dynasty

Zhou China (legend)

Zhou China

- distribution of urban civilization by c.1000 BCE
- Western Zhou royal domains
- Western Zhou capital
- Eastern Zhou administrative areas
- Eastern Zhou capital
- *Yue* neighboring people
- → campaign by border people

250 km
250 miles

Zhou China timeline

Zhou China

1027: Shang dynasty overthrown by Western Zhou

770: Eastern Zhou establish new capital at Luoyang; beginning of Springs and Autumns period

520: Death of Laozi, founder of Daoism

479: Death of Confucius

403: Beginning of Warring States period

1100 BCE — 900 — 700 — 500 — 300 BCE

722–481: 'Annals' period; China in loose confederation under nominal control of Eastern Zhou

c.500: Introduction of first Chinese coinage

458–424: Qin domain partitioned

Qin China (legend)

Qin China

- original Qin territory c.350 BCE
- Qin expansion by 288 BCE
- Qin expansion by 220 BCE
- HAN 230 Qin acquisition with date
- areas under Qin control after unification
- Qin state capitals and administrative center
- defensive wall
- people

Qin China timeline

247: King Zheng (later Shi Huangdi) becomes ruler of Qin domain

230: Campaigns of Shi Huangdi begin

221: Qin Empire established, organized into 36 commanderies

214: Slave labour used to link ramparts to form Great Wall

210: Death of Shi Huangdi, entombed with vast terracotta army

250 BCE — 240 — 230 — 220 — 210 — 200 BCE

221–207: General disarmament, standardization of weights, measures, and axle widths to facilitate commerce

213: Proscription of non-scientific books; standardization and simplification of Chinese script

206: Beginning of Han dynasty

Qin China

Scale varies with perspective

2620 km (1630 miles)

2220 km (1380 miles)

RELIGIONS OF THE WORLD AFTER 400 CE

BETWEEN 400 CE and the advent of Islam in the mid-7th century, the disintegration of the Old World political order was balanced by the spread and diversification of world religions. Christianity became firmly established throughout the Roman Empire and its successor states. In South Asia, Hinduism became deeply rooted. Meanwhile, Buddhism spread overland to Central Asia and China. Between 400 and 650 CE, the political order disintegrated, but Buddhism spread into maritime Southeast Asia. In the west, Christianity spawned many sects, including Africa's Coptic church.

The growth of early Christianity

46–57: Journeys of St. Paul

132: Suppression of Jewish revolt in Palestine; beginning of diaspora

304: Persecution of Christians by Diocletian (284–305)

325: Council of Nicaea assembled by Constantine

404: Vulgate (Latin version of Bible) completed

| 0 | 100 | 200 | 300 | 400 | 500 |

c.32CE: Crucifixion of Christ

64: Probable martyrdom of St. Paul by Nero (37–68)

274: Mithras admitted into pantheon of Roman Empire

313: Edict of Milan under Constantine (306–337) confirms Christianity as official imperial creed

Compare this map with the map on pages 40–41. What are the connections between the movement of goods and the movement of ideas?

Religions of the Old World after 400 CE

- area largely embracing Christianity by 600
- spread of Gnosticism 200–400
- spread of Arianism 300–500
- spread of Manichaeism 300–500
- Coptic missions by 350
- Nestorian/Jacobite missions 600–1000
- area largely embracing Zoroastrianism by 500
- extent of Hinduism by 400
- spread of Hinduism 400–600
- extent of Jainism by 700
- extent of Buddhism by 400
- spread of Mahayana Buddhism 400–1000
- spread of Buddhism 400–1000
- heartland of Tibetan (Tantric) Buddhism by 800
- spread of Tibetan (Tantric) Buddhism 800–1100
- Shinto

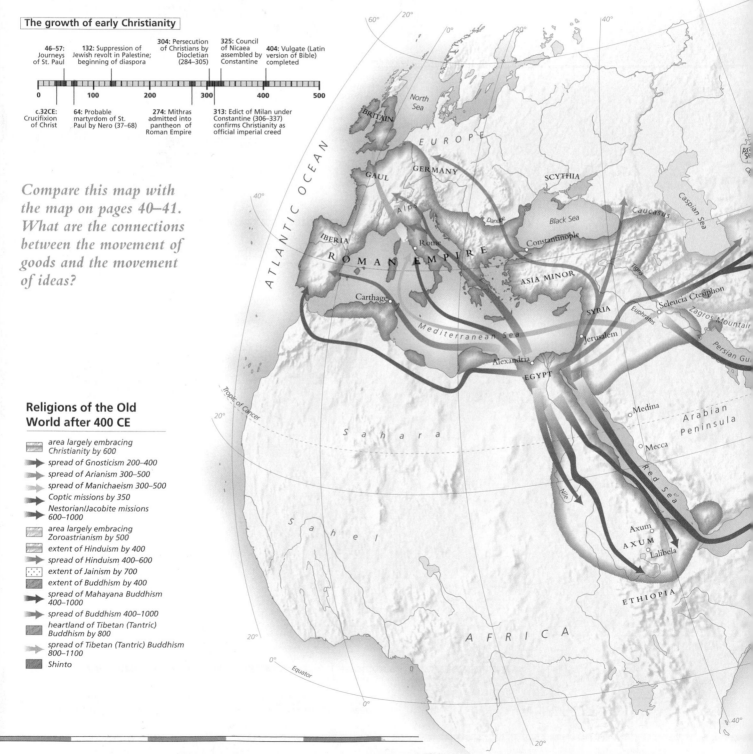

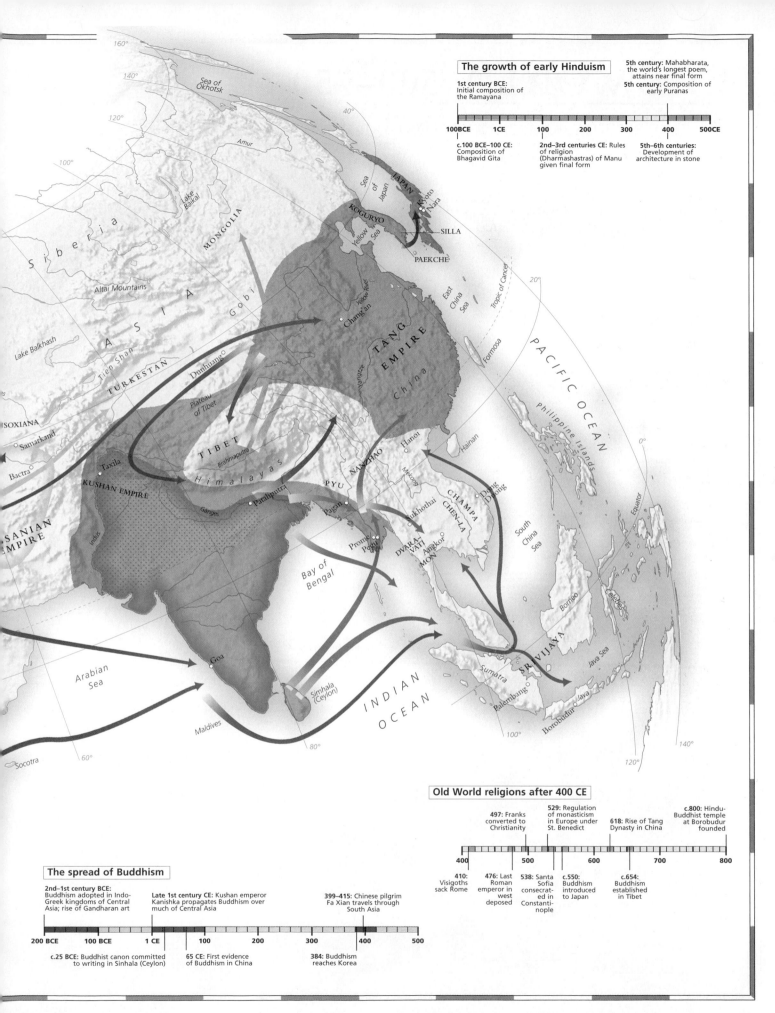

The growth of early Hinduism

1st century BCE: Initial composition of the Ramayana

5th century: Mahabharata, the world's longest poem, attains near final form

5th century: Composition of early Puranas

100BCE	1CE	100	200	300	400	500CE

c.100 BCE–100 CE: Composition of Bhagavid Gita

2nd–3rd centuries CE: Rules of religion (Dharmashastras) of Manu given final form

5th–6th centuries: Development of architecture in stone

Map labels

Sea of Okhotsk
Siberia
Lake Baikal
Amur
MONGOLIA
Altai Mountains
Lake Balkhash
A S I A
Gobi
Tien Shan
TURKESTAN
SOXIANA
Samarkand
Bactra
Taxila
KUSHAN EMPIRE
Indus
Ganges
Pataliputra
TIBET
Plateau of Tibet
Dunhuang
Brahmaputra
H i m a l a y a s
PYU
Pagan
Prome
Pegu
NANZHAO
DVARA-VATI
MON
Goa
Simhala (Ceylon)
Maldives
Arabian Sea
INDIAN OCEAN
Bay of Bengal
Socotra
SASANIAN EMPIRE
Yellow River
Chang'an
TANG EMPIRE
China
Yangtze
Yellow Sea
KOGURYO
PAEKCHE
SILLA
JAPAN
Kyoto
Nara
Sea of Japan
East China Sea
Tropic of Cancer
Formosa
PACIFIC OCEAN
Philippine Islands
Hainan
Hanoi
Mekong
Sukhothai
CHAMPA
CHEN-LA
Dong Duong
Angkor
South China Sea
Borneo
Celebes
Sumatra
SRIVIJAYA
Palembang
Java Sea
Borobudur
Java
Equator

Old World religions after 400 CE

497: Franks converted to Christianity

529: Regulation of monasticism in Europe under St. Benedict

618: Rise of Tang Dynasty in China

c.800: Hindu-Buddhist temple at Borobudur founded

400	500	600	700	800

410: Visigoths sack Rome

476: Last Roman emperor in west deposed

538: Santa Sofia consecrated in Constantinople

c.550: Buddhism introduced to Japan

c.654: Buddhism established in Tibet

The spread of Buddhism

2nd–1st century BCE: Buddhism adopted in Indo-Greek kingdoms of Central Asia; rise of Gandharan art

Late 1st century CE: Kushan emperor Kanishka propagates Buddhism over much of Central Asia

399–415: Chinese pilgrim Fa Xian travels through South Asia

200 BCE	100 BCE	1 CE	100	200	300	500

c.25 BCE: Buddhist canon committed to writing in Sinhala (Ceylon)

65 CE: First evidence of Buddhism in China

384: Buddhism reaches Korea

THE WORLD: 500–750 CE

THE RAPID RECOVERY of the ancient world from the onslaught of invading nomads is evident in the rise of two great empires in Eurasia: the Umayyads in the Middle East and the Tang in China. In the Americas, the Maya remained the most advanced civilization. In Southeast Asia, the maritime empire of Srivijaya dominated an international trade network.

How did the cultural landscape change in the post-classical world?

The World in 750

	Tang Empire
	Byzantine Empire
	Umayyad Caliphate
	Kök Türk Empire 551–572
	East Roman Empire 554–565
	Horsha's Empire c.640
	Avar Empire c.595
	Mayan cultural zone
	Srivijaya

The Americas

c.500: Teotihuacán thriving as a major trading center

c.600: Maya civilization in Central America reaches its height

c.600: Rise of closely-related Tiahuanaco and Huari civilizations in South America

c.700: Beginnings of Puebloan culture

750: Devastation of city of Teotihuacán

| 500 | 550 | 600 | 650 | 700 | 750 |

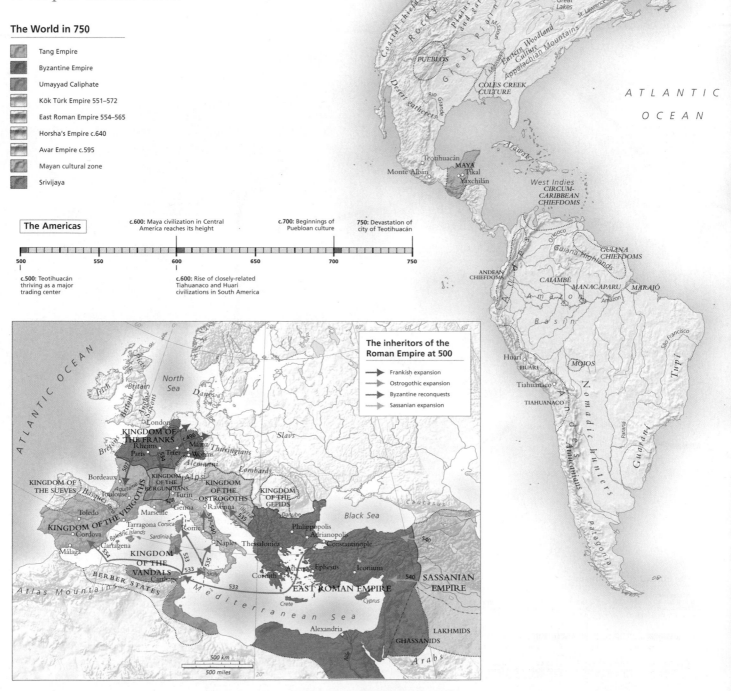

The inheritors of the Roman Empire at 500

→ Frankish expansion
→ Ostrogothic expansion
→ Byzantine reconquests
→ Sassanian expansion

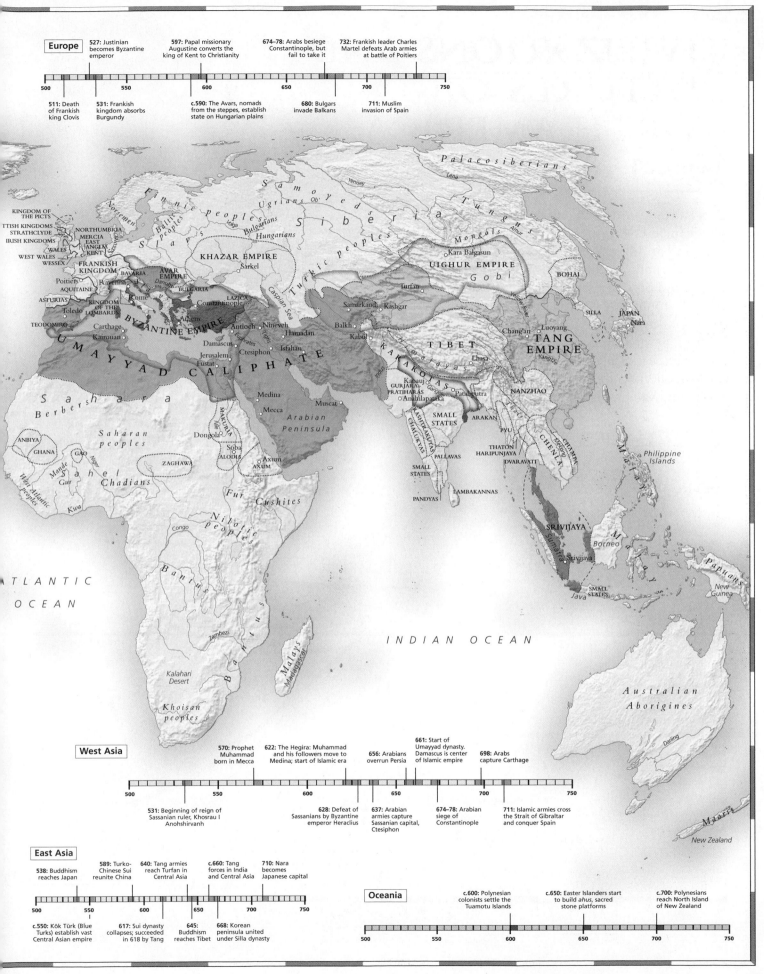

Europe

527: Justinian becomes Byzantine emperor

597: Papal missionary Augustine converts the king of Kent to Christianity

674–78: Arabs besiege Constantinople, but fail to take it

732: Frankish leader Charles Martel defeats Arab armies at battle of Poitiers

500   550   600   650   700   750

511: Death of Frankish king Clovis

531: Frankish kingdom absorbs Burgundy

c.590: The Avars, nomads from the steppes, establish state on Hungarian plains

680: Bulgars invade Balkans

711: Muslim invasion of Spain

Palaeosiberians

Lena

Yenisey

Ob

Norsemen

Finnic peoples

Samoyeds

S i b e r i a

Tungus

KINGDOM OF THE PICTS

TTISH KINGDOMS
STRATHCLYDE
IRISH KINGDOMS

NORTHUMBRIA
MERCIA
EAST
ANGL
KENT

WALES
WEST WALES
WESSEX

Baltic peoples

Ugrians

Mongols

Amur

Volga

Slavs

Bulgarians

Hungarians

Turkic peoples

Kara Balgasun

UIGHUR EMPIRE

Gobi

BOHAI

FRANKISH KINGDOM

BAVARIA

AVAR EMPIRE

KHAZAR EMPIRE

Sarkel

Danube

Poitiers
AQUITAINE

Ravenna
Rome

BULGARIA

Caspian Sea

Samarkand

Kashgar

SILLA

JAPAN
Nara

ASTURIAS

LAZICA
Constantinople

Athens

Turfan

Chang'an

Luoyang

TANG EMPIRE

TEODOMIRO

KINGDOM OF THE LOMBARDS

Toledo

BYZANTINE EMPIRE

Antioch
Nineveh

Hamadan

Balkh

Kabul

Yellow River

TIBET

Yangtze

Carthage

Kairouan

UMAYYAD CALIPHATE

Damascus
Ctesiphon

Euphrates

Tigris

Isfahan

KARAKORAS

Lhasa

NANZHAO

Jerusalem
Fustat

Himalayas

Indus

Ganges

Kanauj
GURJARA-
PRATIHARAS

Anahilapataka

Pataliputra

S a h a r a

Berbers

Medina

Mecca

Nile

MAKURIA

Dongola

Arabian Peninsula

Muscat

RASHTRAKUTAS

SMALL STATES

ARAKAN

PYU

CHAMPA

Mekong

Malays

Philippine Islands

Saharan peoples

ANBIYA
GHANA
GAO

SOBA
ALODIA

ZAGHAWA

AXUM
AXUM

CHALUKYAS

PALLAVAS

THATON
HARIPUNJAYA
DVARAVATI

CHENLA

Sahel

Chadians

Mande
Gur
Kwa

West Atlantic peoples

Fur

Cushites

SMALL STATES

PANDYAS

LAMBAKANNAS

ATLANTIC OCEAN

Nilotic peoples

Congo

Bantus

Kalahari Desert

Zambezi

Malays
Madagascar

SRIVIJAYA

Sumatra

Srivijaya

Borneo

Malay

Java

SMALL STATES

Papuans

New Guinea

INDIAN OCEAN

Khoisan peoples

Australian Aborigines

Darling

Maori

New Zealand

West Asia

570: Prophet Muhammad born in Mecca

622: The Hegira: Muhammad and his followers move to Medina; start of Islamic era

656: Arabians overrun Persia

661: Start of Umayyad dynasty. Damascus is center of Islamic empire

698: Arabs capture Carthage

500   550   600   650   700   750

531: Beginning of reign of Sassanian ruler, Khosrau I Anohshirvanh

628: Defeat of Sassanians by Byzantine emperor Heraclius

637: Arabian armies capture Sassanian capital, Ctesiphon

674–78: Arabian siege of Constantinople

711: Islamic armies cross the Strait of Gibraltar and conquer Spain

East Asia

538: Buddhism reaches Japan

589: Turko-Chinese Sui reunite China

640: Tang armies reach Turfan in Central Asia

c.660: Tang forces in India and Central Asia

710: Nara becomes Japanese capital

500   550   600   650   700   750

c.550: Kök Türk (Blue Turks) establish vast Central Asian empire

617: Sui dynasty collapses; succeeded in 618 by Tang

645: Buddhism reaches Tibet

668: Korean peninsula united under Silla dynasty

Oceania

c.600: Polynesian colonists settle the Tuamotu Islands

c.650: Easter Islanders start to build *ahus*, sacred stone platforms

c.700: Polynesians reach North Island of New Zealand

500   550   600   650   700   750

CIVILIZATIONS AND CULTURES OF NORTH AMERICA: 100–1500 CE

CENTRAL AMERICA in antiquity was split into Mexican and Maya areas, between which there were some major differences, including languages, writing systems, art and architectural styles. City-states dominated both areas: in the Maya area these tended to be small, multi-city regional polities or autonomous cities, while Mexico was dominated by a series of empires. Several overlapping cultures settled the desert southwest, including the Hohokam, Anasazi, and Mogollon. In the southeast, larger settlements in the Mississippi Valley replaced the Hopewell by 800 CE.

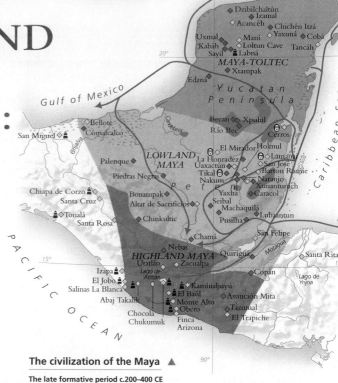

The civilization of the Maya ▲

The late formative period c.200–400 CE

◇ Maya site

⊖ giant stucco mask site

▲ monumental architecture

The Classic period c.290–790 CE

◆ important Classic center

→ trade route

▮ area of intensive agriculture

▨ wetland

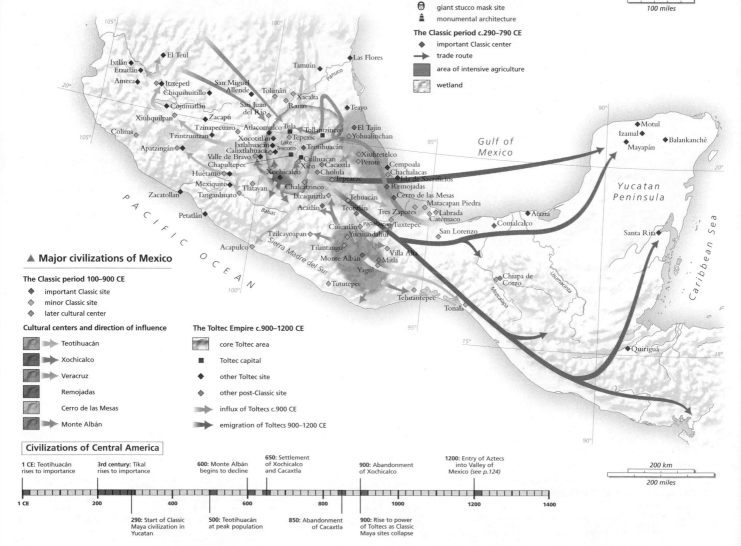

▲ Major civilizations of Mexico

The Classic period 100–900 CE

◆ important Classic site

◇ minor Classic site

◇ later cultural center

Cultural centers and direction of influence

➤ Teotihuacán

➤ Xochicalco

➤ Veracruz

➤ Remojadas

➤ Cerro de las Mesas

➤ Monte Albán

The Toltec Empire c.900–1200 CE

▨ core Toltec area

■ Toltec capital

◆ other Toltec site

◆ other post-Classic site

➤ influx of Toltecs c.900 CE

➤ emigration of Toltecs 900–1200 CE

Civilizations of Central America

1 CE: Teotihuacán rises to importance	**3rd century:** Tikal rises to importance	**600:** Monte Albán begins to decline	**650:** Settlement of Xochicalco and Cacaxtla	**900:** Abandonment of Xochicalco	**1200:** Entry of Aztecs into Valley of Mexico (see p.124)

1 CE	200	400	600	800	1000	1200	1400

290: Start of Classic Maya civilization in Yucatan

500: Teotihuacán at peak population

850: Abandonment of Cacaxtla

900: Rise to power of Toltecs as Classic Maya sites collapse

50

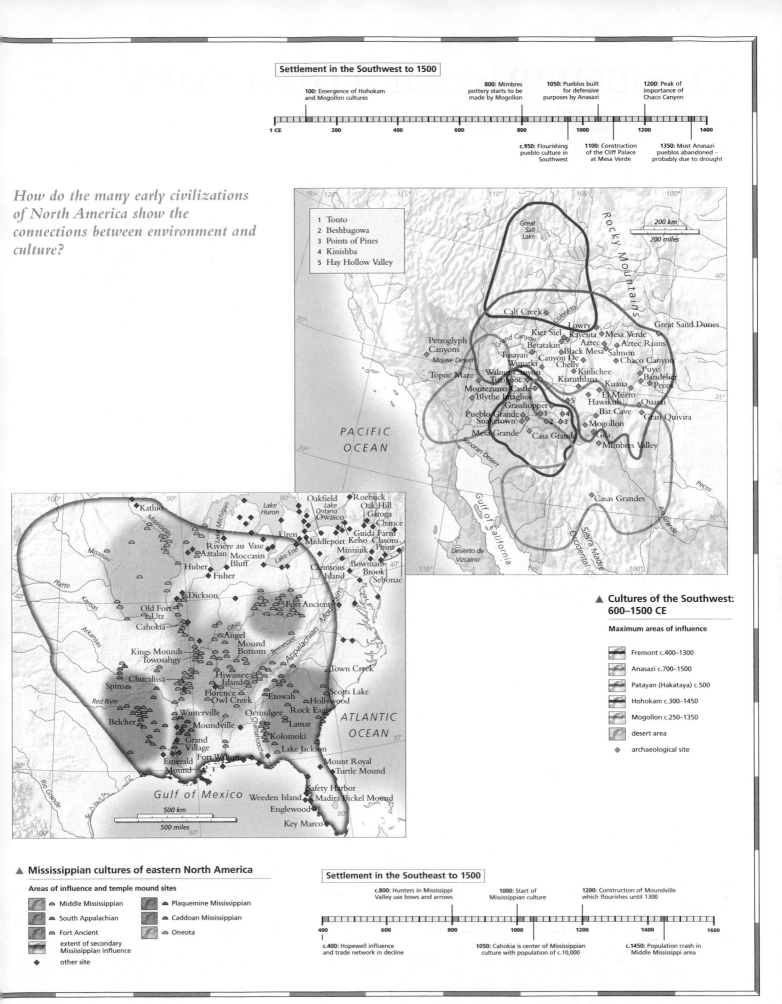

Settlement in the Southwest to 1500

100: Emergence of Hohokam and Mogollon cultures

800: Mimbres pottery starts to be made by Mogollon

1050: Pueblos built for defensive purposes by Anasazi

1200: Peak of importance of Chaco Canyon

1 CE — 200 — 400 — 600 — 800 — 1000 — 1200 — 1400

c.950: Flourishing pueblo culture in Southwest

1100: Construction of the Cliff Palace at Mesa Verde

1350: Most Anasazi pueblos abandoned – probably due to drought

How do the many early civilizations of North America show the connections between environment and culture?

1 Tonto
2 Beshbagowa
3 Points of Pines
4 Kinishba
5 Hay Hollow Valley

▲ Cultures of the Southwest: 600–1500 CE

Maximum areas of influence

- Fremont c.400–1300
- Anasazi c.700–1500
- Patayan (Hakataya) c.500
- Hohokam c.300–1450
- Mogollon c.250–1350
- desert area
- ◆ archaeological site

▲ Mississippian cultures of eastern North America

Areas of influence and temple mound sites

- ⏚ Middle Mississippian
- ⏚ South Appalachian
- ⏚ Fort Ancient
- extent of secondary Mississippian influence
- ◆ other site
- ⏚ Plaquemine Mississippian
- ⏚ Caddoan Mississippian
- ⏚ Oneota

Settlement in the Southeast to 1500

c.800: Hunters in Mississippi Valley use bows and arrows

1000: Start of Mississippian culture

1200: Construction of Moundville which flourishes until 1300

400 — 600 — 800 — 1000 — 1200 — 1400 — 1600

c.400: Hopewell influence and trade network in decline

1050: Cahokia is center of Mississippian culture with population of c.10,000

c.1450: Population crash in Middle Mississippi area

THE EMPIRES OF THE ANDES: 350 BCE–1475 CE

THE CULTURES AND EMPIRES that flourished in the Andes region at intervals from the fourth millennium BCE to about 1475 CE–the Nazca, the Moche, Tiahuanaco, Huari, and the Chimú–were important precursors of the Inca, laying down the religious and social foundations, and the authoritarian government, that were to serve the Inca so well.

What challenges did the Andes pose to the formation of states and empires? How did the cultures of this region overcome these obstacles?

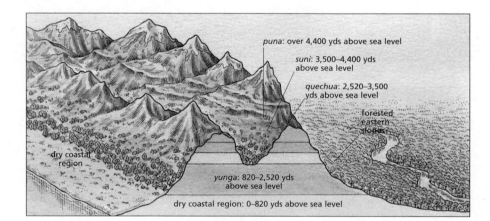

puna: over 4,400 yds above sea level

suni: 3,500–4,400 yds above sea level

quechua: 2,520–3,500 yds above sea level

forested eastern slopes

dry coastal region

yunga: 820–2,520 yds above sea level

dry coastal region: 0–820 yds above sea level

THE VERTICAL ECONOMY OF THE ANDES

The rugged terrain of the Andes provided a series of contiguous, but contrasting environments, fully exploited by the Incas and their predecessors. High, treeless, grassy plains (the *puna*) were used for grazing llamas. Below this, at heights up to 4,400 yds above sea level, lay the *suni*, where potatoes and tubers could be cultivated. Corn, squash, fruits, and cocoa grew in lower, frost-free valleys (the *quechua*), while the lower slopes of the mountains (the *yunga*) were planted with peppers, coca plants, and other fruits. Sources of shellfish and fish from the ocean were periodically disrupted by El Niño, an irregular climatic disturbance which warmed the ocean, leading to torrential rains and disastrous flooding.

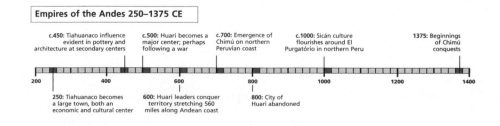

Empires of the Andes 250–1375 CE

c.450: Tiahuanaco influence evident in pottery and architecture at secondary centers

c.500: Huari becomes a major center; perhaps following a war

c.700: Emergence of Chimú on northern Peruvian coast

c.1000: Sicán culture flourishes around El Purgatório in northern Peru

1375: Beginnings of Chimú conquests

250: Tiahuanaco becomes a large town, both an economic and cultural center

600: Huari leaders conquer territory stretching 560 miles along Andean coast

800: City of Huari abandoned

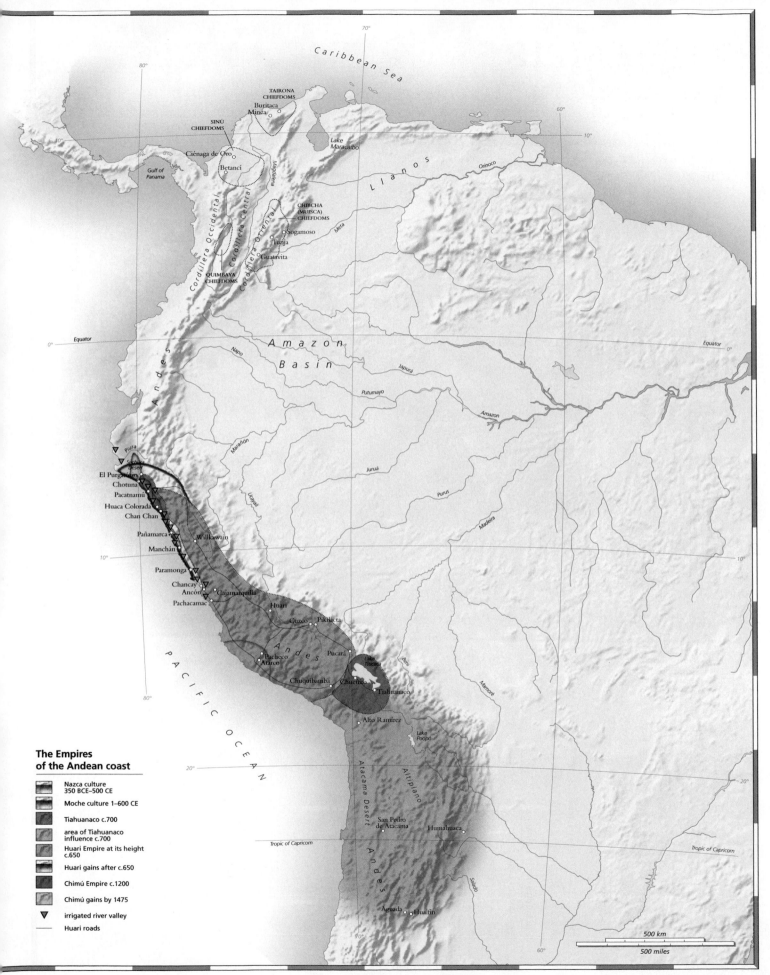

Caribbean Sea

TAIRONA
CHIEFDOMS
Buritaca
Minca

SINÚ
CHIEFDOMS

Ciénaga de Oro
Betancí

Gulf of
Panama

Lake
Maracaibo

Llanos

Orinoco

CHIBCHA
(MUISCA)
CHIEFDOMS

Sogamoso

Tunja

Guatavita

Meta

QUIMBAYA
CHIEFDOMS

Cordillera Occidental
Cordillera Central
Cordillera Oriental

Equator   Equator

Andes

Amazon
Basin

Napo

Japurá

Putumayo

Marañón

Amazon

Juruá

Purus

Ucayali

Piura

Sechura
Desert

El Purgatorio
Chotuna
Pacatnamú
Huaca Colorada
Chan Chan

Madera

Pañamarca
Willkawain

Manchán

10°   10°

Paramonga

Chancay
Ancón
Pachacamac

Cajamarquilla

Huari

Cuzco   Pikillacta

Andes

Pucará

Pacheco
Atarco

Beni

Chuquibamba
Chucuito
Tiahuanaco

Lake
Titicaca

Alto Ramírez

Lake
Poopó

**The Empires
of the Andean coast**

Nazca culture
350 BCE–500 CE

Moche culture 1–600 CE

Tiahuanaco c.700

area of Tiahuanaco
influence c.700

Huari Empire at its height
c.650

Huari gains after c.650

Chimú Empire c.1200

Chimú gains by 1475

▽   irrigated river valley

—   Huari roads

PACIFIC OCEAN

Atacama Desert

Altiplano

Andes

San Pedro
de Atacama

Humahuaca

Tropic of Capricorn   Tropic of Capricorn

Salado

Aguada
Hualfín

500 km

500 miles

53

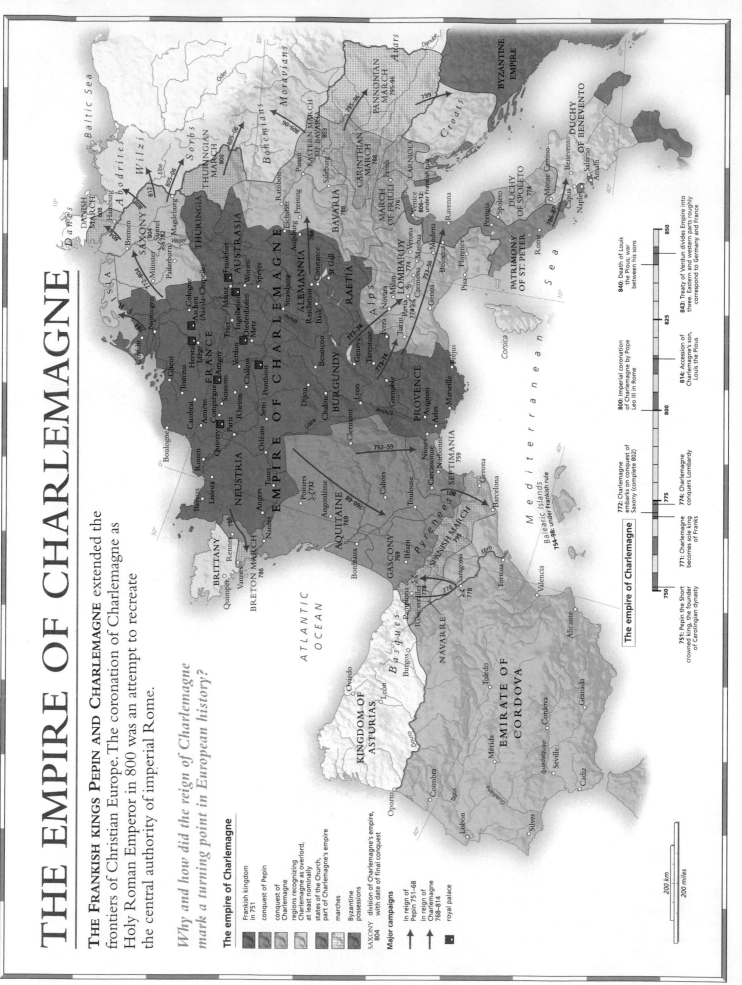

THE EMPIRE OF CHARLEMAGNE

THE FRANKISH KINGS PEPIN AND CHARLEMAGNE extended the frontiers of Christian Europe. The coronation of Charlemagne as Holy Roman Emperor in 800 was an attempt to recreate the central authority of imperial Rome.

Why and how did the reign of Charlemagne mark a turning point in European history?

The empire of Charlemagne

- Frankish kingdom in 751
- conquest of Pepin
- conquest of Charlemagne
- regions recognizing Charlemagne as overlord, at least nominally
- states of the Church, part of Charlemagne's empire
- marches
- Byzantine possessions

SAXONY division of Charlemagne's empire, with date of final conquest
804

Major campaigns

- in reign of Pepin 751–68
- in reign of Charlemagne 768–814
- royal palace

The empire of Charlemagne

751: Pepin the Short crowned king, the founder of Carolingian dynasty

771: Charlemagne becomes sole king of Franks

772: Charlemagne embarks on conquest of Saxony (complete 802)

774: Charlemagne conquers Lombardy

800: Imperial coronation of Charlemagne by Pope Leo III in Rome

814: Accession of Charlemagne's son, Louis the Pious

840: Death of Louis the Pious; war between his sons

843: Treaty of Verdun divides Empire into three. Eastern and western parts roughly correspond to Germany and France

750 775 800 825 850

200 km
200 miles

THE ABBASID CALIPHATE

By 750 CE, Arab armies had carried Islam west to the Iberian peninsula and east to Central Asia. The Abbasid Caliphate, with its capital at Baghdad, was founded in 750. It was an era of great prosperity, especially in the reign of Harun al-Rashid.

How would you compare the empire ruled by Harun al-Rashid with that of his contemporary Charlemagne on the preceding page?

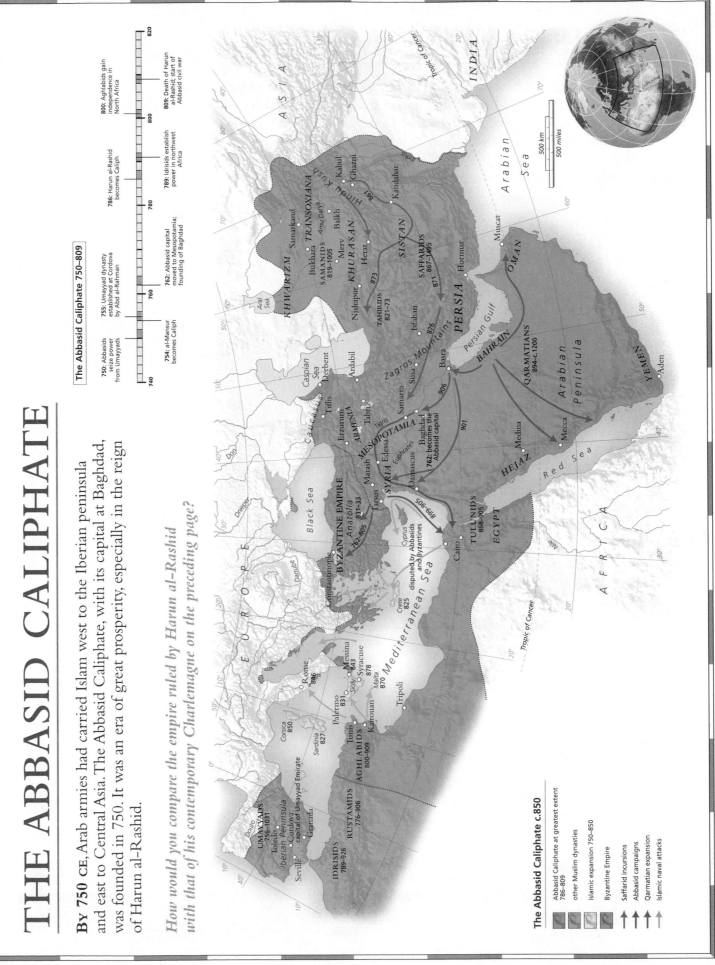

The Abbasid Caliphate 750–809

740	760	780	800	820

750: Abbasids seize power from Umayyads

754: al-Mansur becomes Caliph

755: Umayyad dynasty established at Cordova by Abd al-Rahman

762: Abbasid capital moved to Mesopotamia; founding of Baghdad

786: Harun al-Rashid becomes Caliph

789: Idrisids establish power in northwest Africa

800: Aghlabids gain independence in North Africa

809: Death of Harun al-Rashid; start of Abbasid civil war

The Abbasid Caliphate c.850

- ▬ Abbasid Caliphate at greatest extent 786–809
- ▬ other Muslim dynasties
- ▬ Islamic expansion 750–850
- ▬ Byzantine Empire
- ↑ Saffarid incursions
- ↑ Abbasid campaigns
- ↑ Qarmatian expansion
- ↑ Islamic naval attacks

55

THE ISLAMIC IMPRINT

THE RAPID SPREAD OF ISLAM was one of the most decisive developments of the medieval period. Muslims controlled Eurasian trade on land and by sea – trade which would spread the faith further afield, deep into Africa, across the Indian Ocean, and north into Central Asia, over the subsequent centuries.

What was the relationship between trade and the spread of Islam?

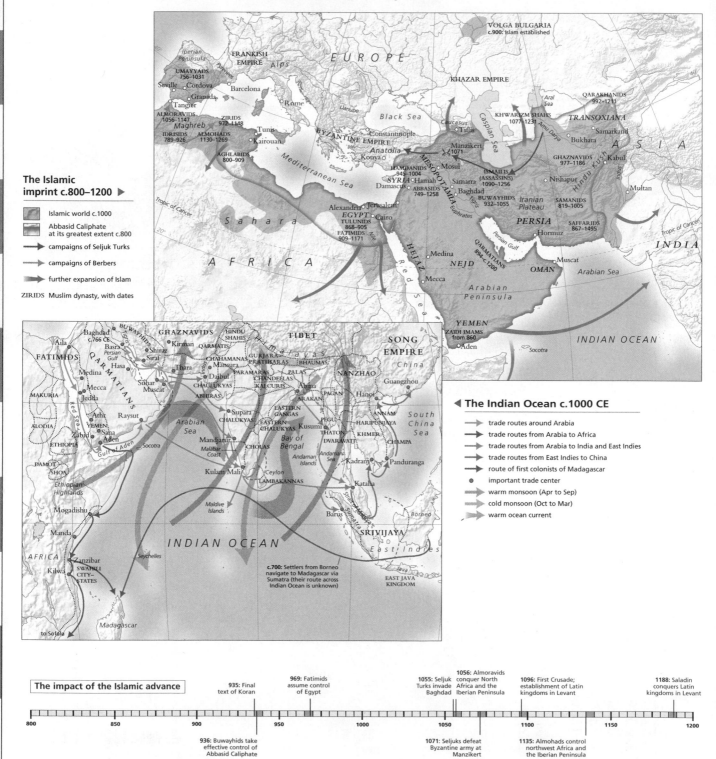

The Islamic imprint c.800–1200 ▶

- Islamic world c.1000
- Abbasid Caliphate at its greatest extent c.800
- → campaigns of Seljuk Turks
- → campaigns of Berbers
- → further expansion of Islam

ZIRIDS Muslim dynasty, with dates

◀ The Indian Ocean c.1000 CE

- → trade routes around Arabia
- → trade routes from Arabia to Africa
- → trade routes from Arabia to India and East Indies
- → trade routes from East Indies to China
- → route of first colonists of Madagascar
- ● important trade center
- → warm monsoon (Apr to Sep)
- → cold monsoon (Oct to Mar)
- → warm ocean current

The impact of the Islamic advance

- **935:** Final text of Koran
- **969:** Fatimids assume control of Egypt
- **1055:** Seljuk Turks invade Baghdad
- **1056:** Almoravids conquer North Africa and the Iberian Peninsula
- **1096:** First Crusade; establishment of Latin kingdoms in Levant
- **1188:** Saladin conquers Latin kingdoms in Levant
- **936:** Buwayhids take effective control of Abbasid Caliphate
- **1071:** Seljuks defeat Byzantine army at Manzikert
- **1135:** Almohads control northwest Africa and the Iberian Peninsula

800 850 900 950 1000 1050 1100 1150 1200

AFRICAN EMPIRES AND CITY-STATES

THE PERIOD BETWEEN 800 AND 1500 witnessed the growth of several
powerful African states, some of which – for example, Mali and Songhay –
were centered on trans-Saharan trade routes.

What factors contributed to state development in Africa during this period?

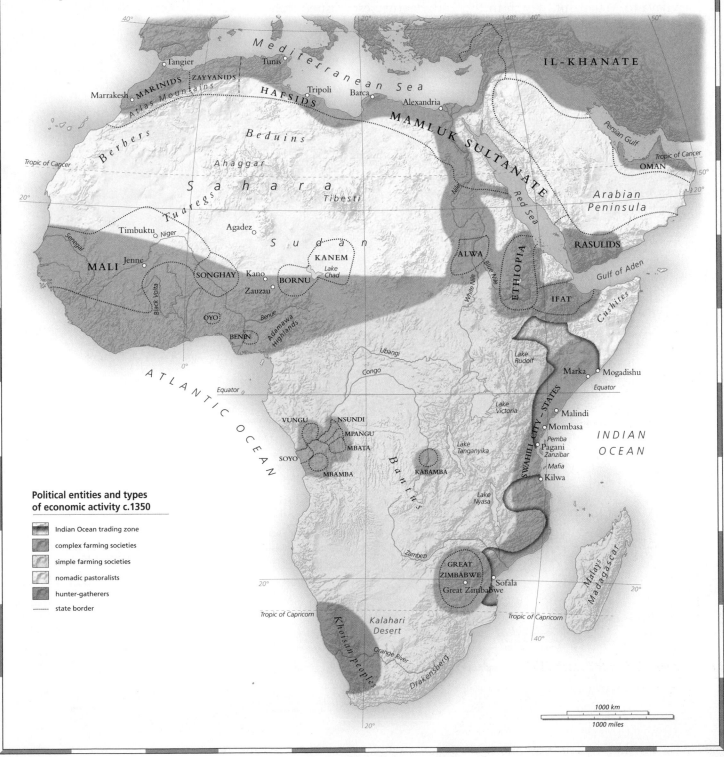

**Political entities and types
of economic activity c.1350**

- Indian Ocean trading zone
- complex farming societies
- simple farming societies
- nomadic pastoralists
- hunter-gatherers
- ·········· state border

1000 km

1000 miles

STATES AND EMPIRES IN SOUTH ASIA: 300–1550

SOUTH ASIA WAS RULED by a great diversity of regional powers for much of this period. In the 4th century CE, the Gupta dynasty succeeded in uniting much of the Indian subcontinent. In the 13th century, much of India again came under the control of a single state, the Delhi Sultanate. In the East Indies, dominance passed from Srivijaya to Majapahit, which in the 14th century established the most extensive commercial empire that the area was to see in precolonial times.

What were the challenges to state-building in South and Southeast Asia at this time?

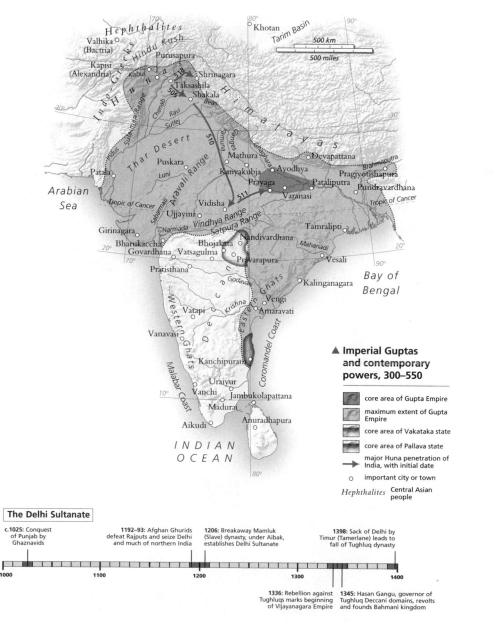

▲ Imperial Guptas and contemporary powers, 300–550

- core area of Gupta Empire
- maximum extent of Gupta Empire
- core area of Vakataka state
- core area of Pallava state
- → major Huna penetration of India, with initial date
- ○ important city or town
- *Hephthalites* Central Asian people

▲ The Delhi Sultanate, 1206–1526

- area of Sultanate at accession of Jalal ud-din Khalji, 1290
- additional territory at some time under direct Khalji administration
- limit of nominal Khalji vassals
- → possible route of Khalji raids against Mongols
- extent of Sultanate at accession of Ghiyas ud-din Tughluq, 1320
- maximum extent of Sultanate under direct Tughluq administration
- limit of nominal Tughluq vassals
- *Ahoms* peoples and dynasties
- *SIND* cultural region

The Delhi Sultanate

c.1025: Conquest of Punjab by Ghaznavids

1192–93: Afghan Ghurids defeat Rajputs and seize Delhi and much of northern India

1206: Breakaway Mamluk (Slave) dynasty, under Aibak, establishes Delhi Sultanate

1398: Sack of Delhi by Timur (Tamerlane) leads to fall of Tughluq dynasty

| 1000 | 1100 | 1200 | 1300 | 1400 |

1336: Rebellion against Tughluqs marks beginning of Vijayanagara Empire

1345: Hasan Gangu, governor of Tughluq Deccani domains, revolts and founds Bahmani kingdom

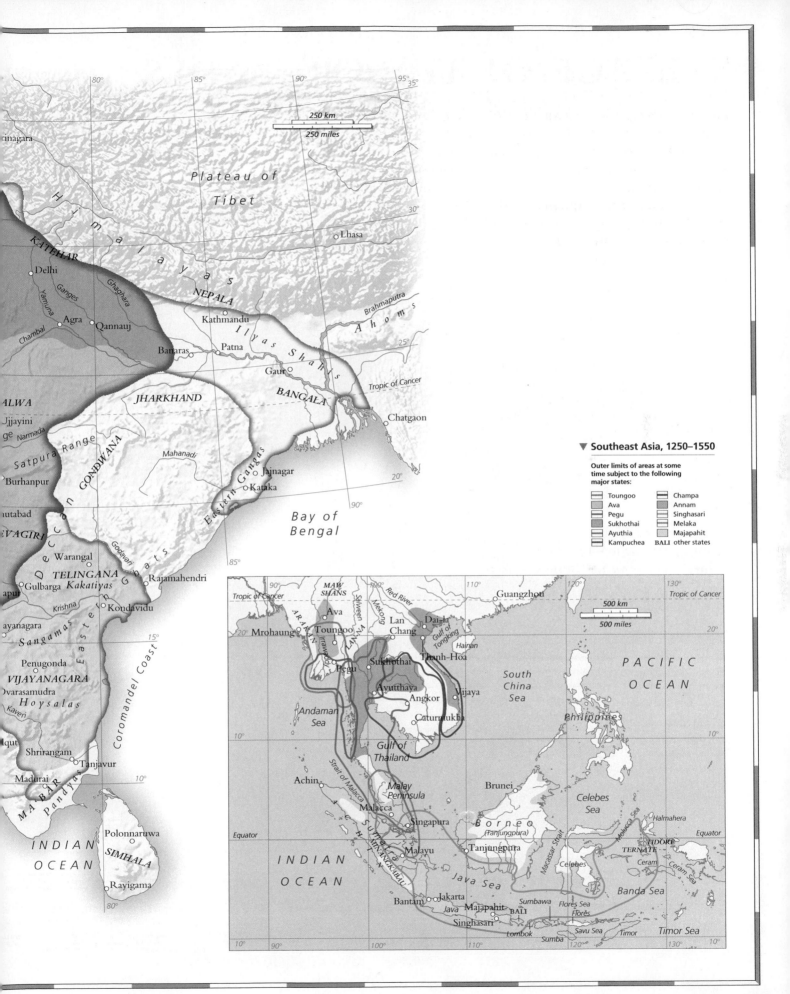

▼ Southeast Asia, 1250–1550

Outer limits of areas at some time subject to the following major states:

Toungoo	Champa
Ava	Annam
Pegu	Singhasari
Sukhothai	Melaka
Ayuthia	Majapahit
Kampuchea	**BALI** other states

THE AGE OF THE CRUSADES

HOLY WAR WAS NEVER PART of the doctrine of the early Church. This changed in 1095 when Pope Urban II urged French barons and knights to liberate the Holy Land from Muslim 'infidels.' In 1099, the Crusaders captured Jerusalem. The crusading ideal became firmly established in European consciousness, and there were many subsequent expeditions to defend or recapture Jerusalem, but none was as successful as the first.

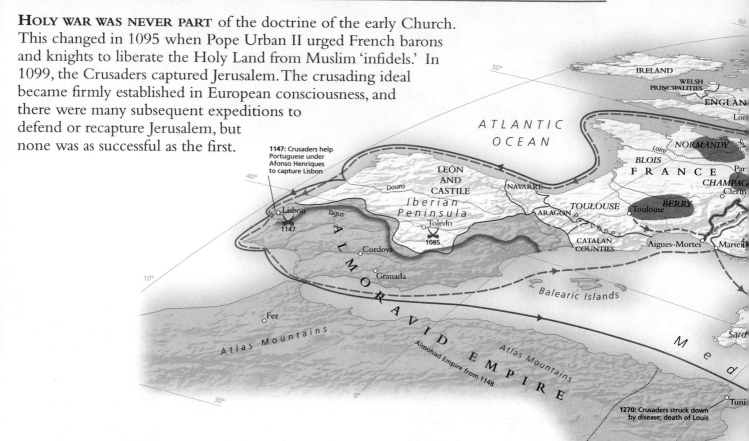

1147: Crusaders help Portuguese under Afonso Henriques to capture Lisbon

1270: Crusaders struck down by disease; death of Louis

What effect did the Crusades have on western Europe, the Byzantine Empire, and Islam?

The Crusades 1096–1270

Muslim territory 1096	**First Crusade routes 1096–99**	**Third Crusade routes 1189–92**
Byzantine Empire 1096	→ Godfrey of Bouillon	→ Richard I
major areas of recruiting for First Crusade	→ Raymond of Toulouse	→ Richard I's fleet
Muslim/Christian frontier c.1150	→ Robert of Normandy	→ Frederick Barbarossa
✂ Christian victory	→ Baldwin of Boulogne	→ Philip Augustus of France
✂ Muslim victory	**Second Crusade routes 1147–49**	**Fourth Crusade route 1202–1204**
Holy Roman Empire	→ English and Flemish Crusaders	→
···· frontiers c.1096	→ Conrad III	
	→ Louis VII of France	

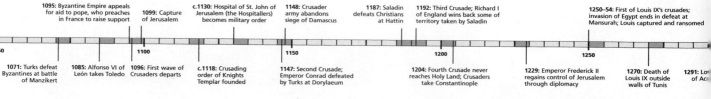

The Crusades 1050–1350

1095: Byzantine Empire appeals for aid to pope, who preaches in France to raise support

1099: Capture of Jerusalem

c.1130: Hospital of St. John of Jerusalem (the Hospitallers) becomes military order

1148: Crusader army abandons siege of Damascus

1187: Saladin defeats Christians at Hattin

1192: Third Crusade; Richard I of England wins back some of territory taken by Saladin

1250–54: First of Louis IX's crusades; invasion of Egypt ends in defeat at Mansurah; Louis captured and ransomed

1050 — 1100 — 1150 — 1200 — 1250 —

1071: Turks defeat Byzantines at battle of Manzikert

1085: Alfonso VI of León takes Toledo

1096: First wave of Crusaders departs

c.1118: Crusading order of Knights Templar founded

1147: Second Crusade; Emperor Conrad defeated by Turks at Dorylaeum

1204: Fourth Crusade never reaches Holy Land; Crusaders take Constantinople

1229: Emperor Frederick II regains control of Jerusalem through diplomacy

1270: Death of Louis IX outside walls of Tunis

1291: Lo... of Ac...

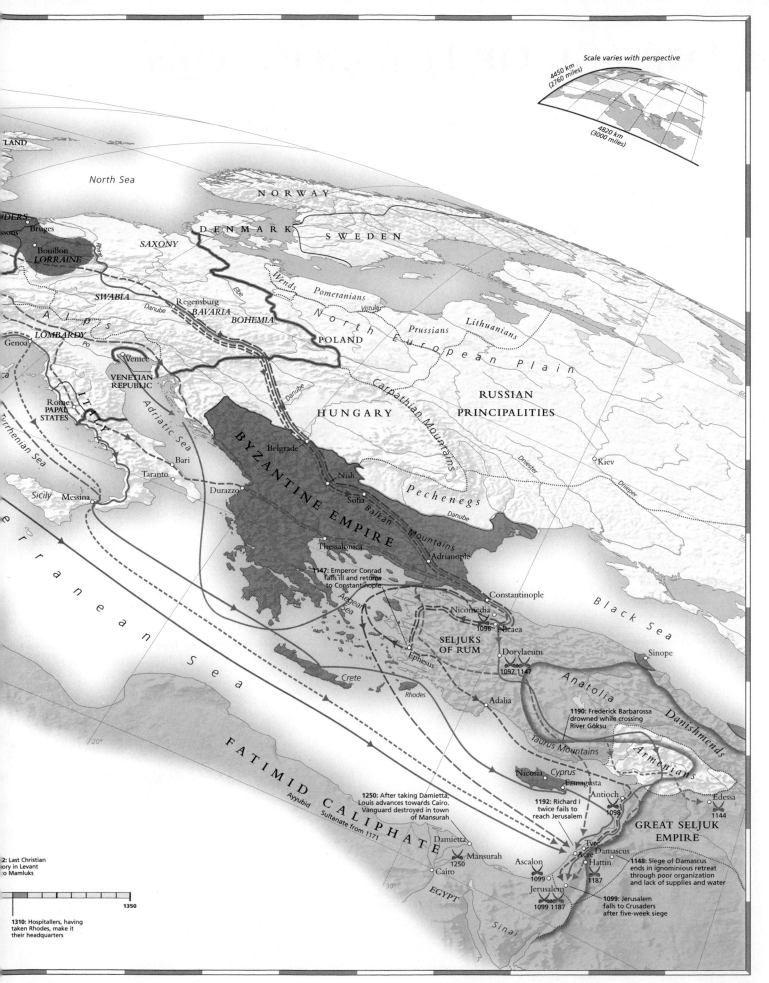

North Sea

LAND

DERS
Bruges

Bouillon
LORRAINE

NORWAY

DENMARK   SWEDEN

SAXONY

SWABIA

Rhine

Regensburg
BAVARIA
Danube
BOHEMIA

Elbe

Wends

Pomeranians

Vistula

Prussians

Lithuanians

North European Plain

POLAND

Carpathian Mountains

RUSSIAN
PRINCIPALITIES

LOMBARDY
Genoa
Po

A l p s

Venice

VENETIAN
REPUBLIC

Rome
PAPAL
STATES

ITALY

Tyrrhenian
Sea

Sicily

Messina

Bari

Taranto

Adriatic Sea

Durazzo

Danube

HUNGARY

Belgrade

BYZANTINE
EMPIRE

Nish

Sofia

Balkan Mountains

Pechenegs

Danube

Dniester

Kiev

Dnieper

Black Sea

Thessalonica

Adrianople

1147: Emperor Conrad
falls ill and returns
to Constantinople

Aegean
Sea

Ephesus

Crete

Rhodes

Constantinople

Nicomedia

1096   Nicaea

SELJUKS
OF RUM

Dorylaeum

1097 1147

Adalia

Anatolia

Danishmends

Sinope

1190: Frederick Barbarossa
drowned while crossing
River Göksu

Taurus Mountains

Armenians

Mediterranean Sea

FATIMID CALIPHATE

Ayyubid Sultanate from 1171

20°

30°

1250: After taking Damietta,
Louis advances towards Cairo.
Vanguard destroyed in town
of Mansurah

Nicosia   Cyprus

Famagusta

1192: Richard I
twice fails to
reach Jerusalem

Antioch

1098

Edessa

1144

GREAT SELJUK
EMPIRE

2: Last Christian
ory in Levant
o Mamluks

Damietta

Mansurah

1250

Cairo

EGYPT

Tyre

Acre   Damascus

Ascalon   Hattin

1099   1187

Jerusalem

1099 1187

Sinai

1148: Siege of Damascus
ends in ignominious retreat
through poor organization
and lack of supplies and water

1099: Jerusalem
falls to Crusaders
after five-week siege

1350

1310: Hospitallers, having
taken Rhodes, make it
their headquarters

Scale varies with perspective

4450 km
(2760 miles)

4820 km
(3000 miles)

THE AGE OF THE MONGOLS

By the 13th century, the Chinese empire had become weak and fragmented. Into this power vacuum burst the Mongols, a fierce race of skilled horsemen united under the inspired leadership of Genghis Khan. Genghis's successors extended his conquests across Asia and deep into Europe, but the empire then split into four khanates (see p. 68).

What were the consequences for world history of Mongol expansion?

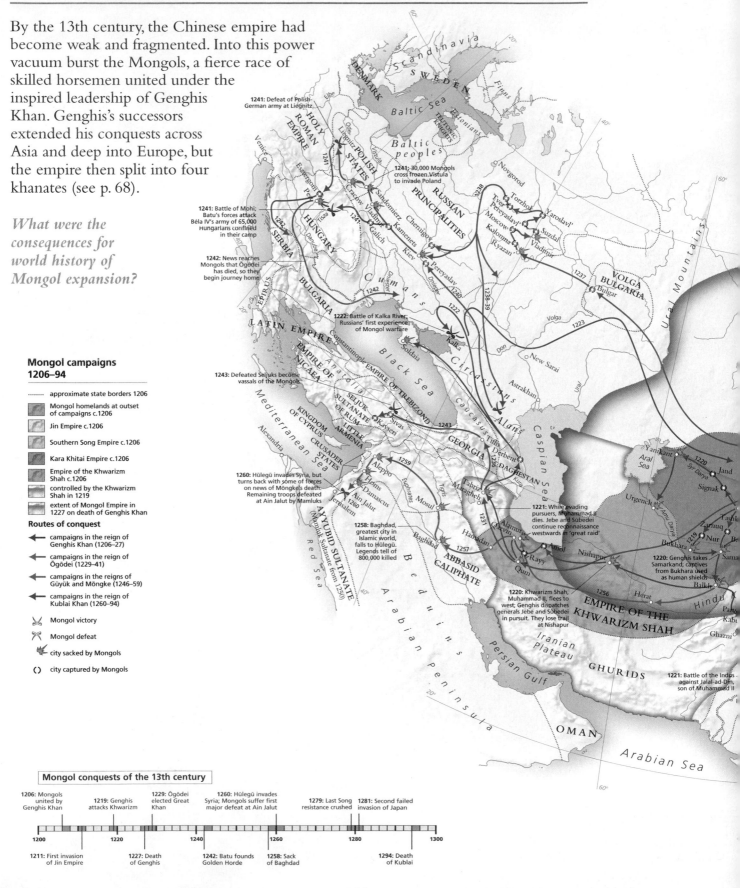

Mongol campaigns 1206–94

.... approximate state borders 1206

▨ Mongol homelands at outset of campaigns c.1206

▨ Jin Empire c.1206

▨ Southern Song Empire c.1206

▨ Kara Khitai Empire c.1206

▨ Empire of the Khwarizm Shah c.1206

▨ controlled by the Khwarizm Shah in 1219

▨ extent of Mongol Empire in 1227 on death of Genghis Khan

Routes of conquest

← campaigns in the reign of Genghis Khan (1206–27)

← campaigns in the reign of Ögödei (1229–41)

← campaigns in the reigns of Güyük and Möngke (1246–59)

← campaigns in the reign of Kublai Khan (1260–94)

⚔ Mongol victory

⚔ Mongol defeat

🔥 city sacked by Mongols

() city captured by Mongols

1241: Defeat of Polish-German army at Liegnitz

1241: 30,000 Mongols cross frozen Vistula to invade Poland

1241: Battle of Mohi; Batu's forces attack Béla IV's army of 65,000 Hungarians confined in their camp

1242: News reaches Mongols that Ögödei has died, so they begin journey home

1222: Battle of Kalka River; Russians' first experience of Mongol warfare

1243: Defeated Seljuks become vassals of the Mongols

1260: Hülegü invades Syria, but turns back with some of forces on news of Möngkel's death; Remaining troops defeated at Ain Jalut by Mamluks

1258: Baghdad, greatest city in Islamic world, falls to Hülegü. Legends tell of 800,000 killed

1221: While evading pursuers, Muhammad II dies. Jebe and Sübedei continue reconnaissance westwards in 'great raid'

1220: Genghis takes Samarkand; captives from Bukhara used as human shields

1220: Khwarizm Shah, Muhammad II, flees to west; Genghis dispatches generals Jebe and Sübedei in pursuit. They lose trail at Nishapur

1221: Battle of the Indus against Jalal-ad-Din, son of Muhammad II

Mongol conquests of the 13th century

1206: Mongols united by Genghis Khan

1219: Genghis attacks Khwarizm

1229: Ögödei elected Great Khan

1260: Hülegü invades Syria; Mongols suffer first major defeat at Ain Jalut

1279: Last Song resistance crushed

1281: Second failed invasion of Japan

| 1200 | 1220 | 1240 | 1260 | 1280 | 1300 |

1211: First invasion of Jin Empire

1227: Death of Genghis

1242: Batu founds Golden Horde

1258: Sack of Baghdad

1294: Death of Kublai

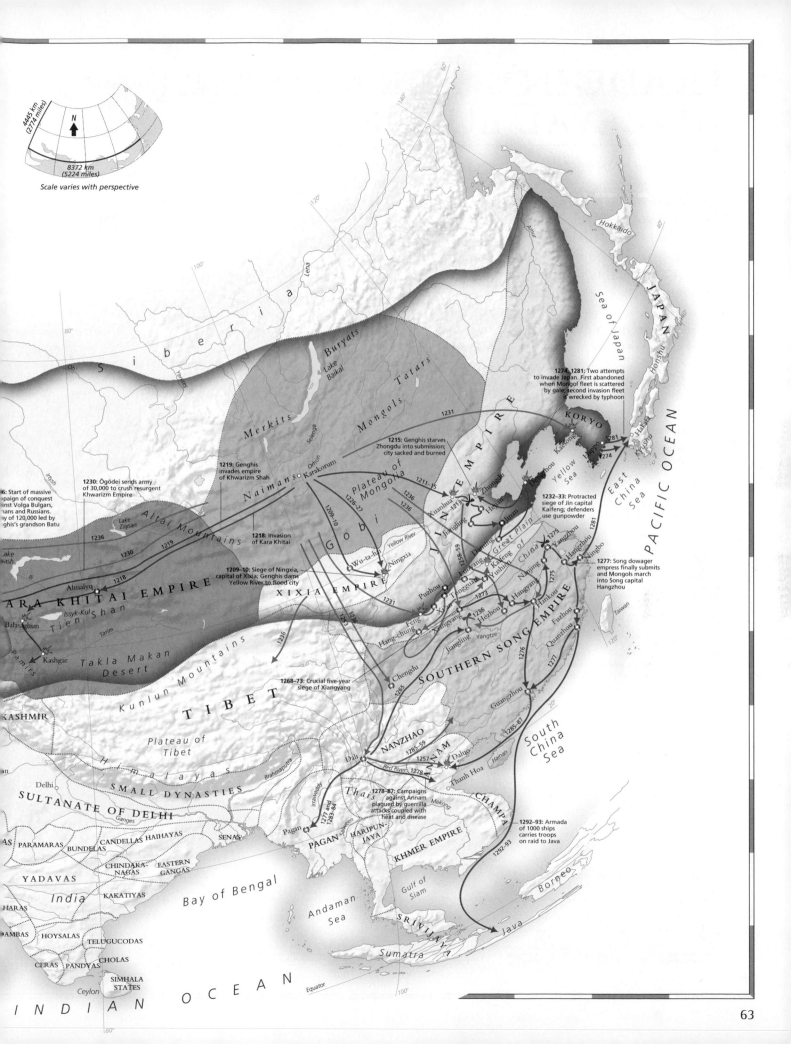

Scale varies with perspective

4445 km
(2774 miles)

N

8372 km
(5224 miles)

S i b e r i a

Lena

Ob

Yenisey

Buryats

Lake
Baikal

Merkits

Mongols

Tatars

1231

Naimans

Karakorum

Plateau
of Mongolia

1274, 1281: Two attempts
to invade Japan. First abandoned
when Mongol fleet is scattered
by gale; second invasion fleet
is wrecked by typhoon

JAPAN

Hokkaido

Sea
of Japan

Honshu

PACIFIC
OCEAN

KORYO

Kaifeng

Hakata

Kyushu

1281

1274

1215: Genghis starves
Zhongdu into submission;
city sacked and burned

1219: Genghis
invades empire
of Khwarizm Shah

1230: Ögödei sends army
of 30,000 to crush resurgent
Khwarizm Empire

J I N   E M P I R E

1211–15

1236

1236

Kuanhua

1213

Henan

Zhongdu

Dengzhou

Yellow
Sea

East
China
Sea

1232–33: Protracted
siege of Jin capital
Kaifeng; defenders
use gunpowder

Jiangling

Jinan

6: Start of massive
paign of conquest
inst Volga Bulgars,
ans and Russians.
y of 120,000 led by
ghis's grandson Batu

Lake
Zaysan

Altai Mountains

1236

1230

1219

1218

1218: Invasion
of Kara Khitai

1209–10

G o b i

1236

Yellow River

Wu-ta-hu

Ningxia

XIXIA EMPIRE

Daming

Great Plain

Luoyang

Kaifeng

1268–59

Gulf
of
China

Nanjing

1275

Yangzhou

Hangzhou

1275

Ningbo

1281

1277: Song dowager
empress finally submits
and Mongols march
into Song capital
Hangzhou

Almalyq

1218

1209–10: Siege of Ningxia,
capital of Xixia; Genghis dams
Yellow River to flood city

1231

Puzhou

Xi'an

Tongguan

1273

1236

Hezhou

Xiangyang

Yushan

Hangyang

Hankou

Fuzhou

Quanzhou

1277

ARA KHITAI EMPIRE

Issyk-Kul

Tien Shan

Balasaghun

Kashgar

Tarim

Pamirs

Takla Makan
Desert

Kunlun Mountains

1236

1253

1236

1231

Feng

Hang-chung

Jiangling

Yangtze

Taiwan

1276

SOUTHERN SONG EMPIRE

South
China
Sea

1285–87

KASHMIR

T I B E T

Plateau
of
Tibet

Himalayas

1268–73: Crucial five-year
siege of Xiangyang

Chengdu

1265

NANZHAO

1285–59

1257

Daluo

Hainan

Thanh Hoa

A N N A M

Guangzhou

1292–93

1277

Delhi

SULTANATE OF DELHI

SMALL DYNASTIES

Ganges

Brahmapura

Dali

Red River

1278

1277 and
1283–84

Thais

Irrawaddy

Salween

Pagan

PAGAN

HARIPUN
JAYA

Mekong

KHMER EMPIRE

CHAMPA

1278–87: Campaigns
against Annam
plagued by guerrilla
attacks coupled with
heat and disease

1292–93: Armada
of 1000 ships
carries troops
on raid to Java

AS   PARAMARAS

BUNDELAS

CANDELLAS   HAIHAYAS

CHINDAKA-
NAGAS

EASTERN
GANGAS

SENAS

YADAVAS

KAKATIYAS

India

Bay of Bengal

Andaman
Sea

Gulf
of Siam

Borneo

HARAS

AMBAS   HOYSALAS   TELUGUCODAS

CERAS   PANDYAS   CHOLAS

SIMHALA
STATES

Ceylon

Java

Sumatra

SRIVIJAYA

I N D I A N   O C E A N

Equator

TRADE IN MEDIEVAL EUROPE

THE EXPLOSION IN EUROPE'S POPULATION, which nearly doubled between the 10th and 14th centuries, was caused by greatly increased agricultural productivity and large land–clearance projects which brought marginal land, such as marshes and forests, under cultivation. This demographic surge led to increased trading activity; trade and commerce went hand in hand with urban development. As cities prospered, a new class, the bourgeoisie, emerged.

How did trade and commerce affect the growth of European states and cities in the Middle Ages?

Trade in Europe c.1300

Principal trade routes

— Venetian
— Genoese
— Catalan
— Hanseatic
— main overland route

- region of commercially produced cereals
- region of commercially produced wine
- ● town with population over 50,000
- ○ other trading center
- major textile town
- important fair
- ℗ branch or agency of Florentine Peruzzi company
- silver mine
- wax
- timber
- salt
- fish
- furs

frontier of Islamic world 1300

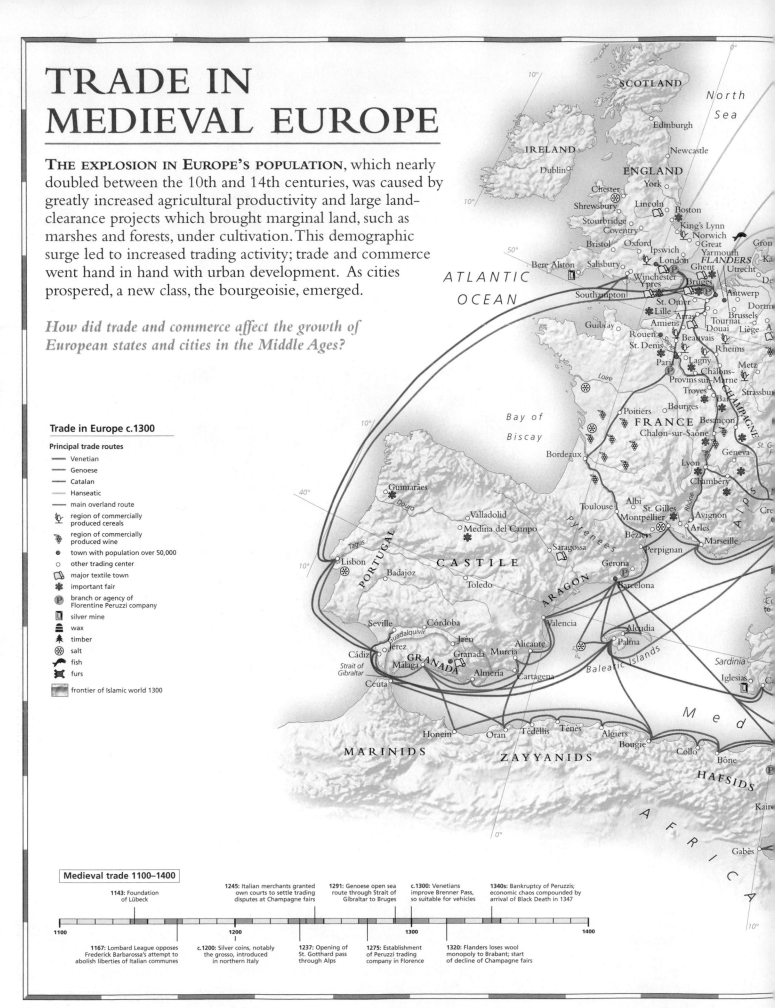

Medieval trade 1100–1400

1143: Foundation of Lübeck

1167: Lombard League opposes Frederick Barbarossa's attempt to abolish liberties of Italian communes

c.1200: Silver coins, notably the grosso, introduced in northern Italy

1237: Opening of St. Gotthard pass through Alps

1245: Italian merchants granted own courts to settle trading disputes at Champagne fairs

1275: Establishment of Peruzzi trading company in Florence

1291: Genoese open sea route through Strait of Gibraltar to Bruges

c.1300: Venetians improve Brenner Pass, so suitable for vehicles

1320: Flanders loses wool monopoly to Brabant; start of decline of Champagne fairs

1340s: Bankruptcy of Peruzzis; economic chaos compounded by arrival of Black Death in 1347

1100   1200   1300   1400

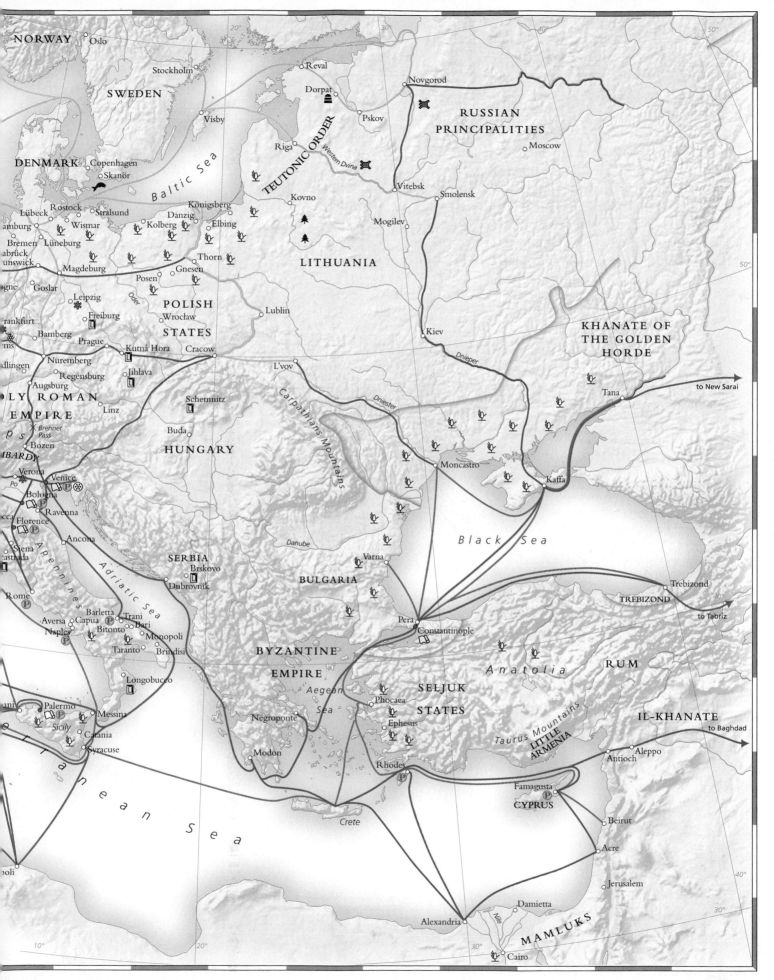

NORWAY
Oslo
Stockholm
SWEDEN
Reval
Dorpat
Novgorod
RUSSIAN
PRINCIPALITIES
Visby
Pskov
Moscow
Baltic Sea
Riga
Western Dvina
DENMARK
Copenhagen
Skanör
TEUTONIC ORDER
Vitebsk
Smolensk
Lübeck
Rostock
Stralsund
Königsberg
Kovno
Hamburg
Wismar
Danzig
Kolberg
Elbing
Mogilev
Bremen
Lüneburg
Osnabrück
Brunswick
Magdeburg
Oder
Posen
Thorn
Gnesen
LITHUANIA
Cologne
Goslar
Leipzig
POLISH
Lublin
Kiev
Dnieper
KHANATE OF
THE GOLDEN
HORDE
Frankfurt
Freiburg
Bamberg
Wrocław
STATES
Worms
Prague
Kutná Hora
Cracow
L'vov
Nördlingen
Nuremberg
Jihlava
Dniester
Tana
to New Sarai
Augsburg
Regensburg
Schemnitz
HOLY ROMAN
Linz
Carpathians Mountains
EMPIRE
Brenner
Pass
Buda
Moncastro
Kaffa
Bozen
HUNGARY
LOMBARDY
Verona
Venice
Po
Bologna
Ravenna
Black   Sea
Lucca
Florence
Ancona
Danube
Siena
Castradia
Apennines
SERBIA
Brskovo
Varna
Trebizond
Rome
Adriatic Sea
Dubrovnik
BULGARIA
TREBIZOND
Barletta
Trani
Aversa
Capua
Bitonto
Bari
to Tabriz
Naples
Monopoli
Pera
Taranto
Brindisi
Constantinople
BYZANTINE
Anatolia
RUM
Longobucco
EMPIRE
IL-KHANATE
Palermo
Messina
Aegean
Sea
SELJUK
Taurus Mountains
to Baghdad
Sicily
Catania
Negroponte
Phocaea
STATES
LITTLE
ARMENIA
Syracuse
Modon
Ephesus
Antioch
Aleppo
Mediterranean Sea
Rhodes
Famagusta
Crete
CYPRUS
Beirut
Acre
Tripoli
Jerusalem
Damietta
Alexandria
Nile
Cairo
MAMLUKS

20°
30°
40°
50°
50°
40°
30°
10°
20°
30°

65

THE BLACK DEATH

FROM 500 TO 1500 CE, imperial expansion, mass migration, cross-cultural trade, and long-distance travel all facilitated the spread of crops, domesticated animals, and diseases throughout much of the Old World. In the early 14th century, Mongol armies helped infected fleas spread from Yunnan to the rest of China. From China, bubonic plague spread rapidly west along the Silk Road. By 1346 it had reached the Black Sea. Muslim merchants carried it south and west, while Italian merchants carried it to western Europe, where it became known as the Black Death. Up to one third of Europe's population is thought to have died from the plague.

How did the Black Death affect the societies of the Old World?

The spread of the Black Death

───	Arab trade route
───	Chinese trade route
───	Genoese trade route
───	main Hanseatic trade routes
───	Silk Road } routes opened during the 'Mongol Peace' c.1250–1350
- - -	other route
───	Venetian trade route
───	other trade route
·····	principal route of Hajj pilgrimage to Mecca
➤	progress of bubonic plague
▓	area of earliest outbreak of bubonic plague
░	area of outbreak of bubonic plague
☣	recorded outbreak of bubonic plague

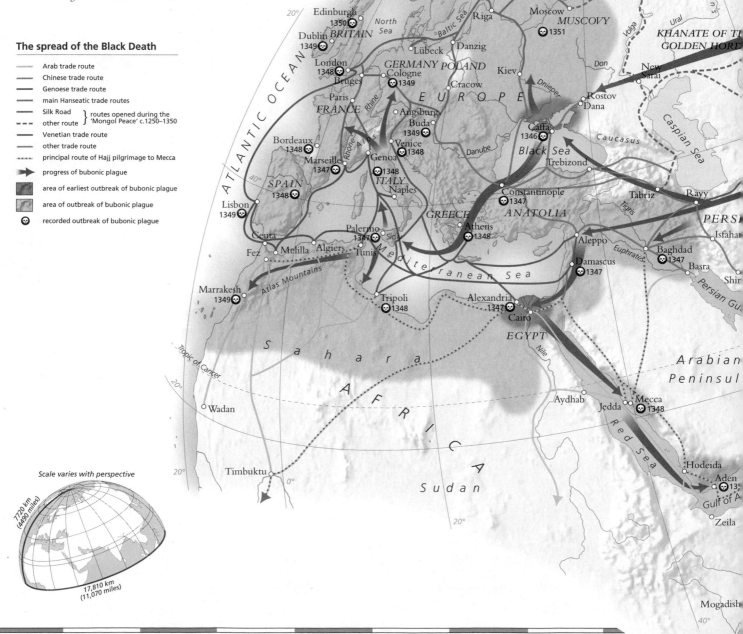

Scale varies with perspective

7720 km (4490 miles)

17,810 km (11,070 miles)

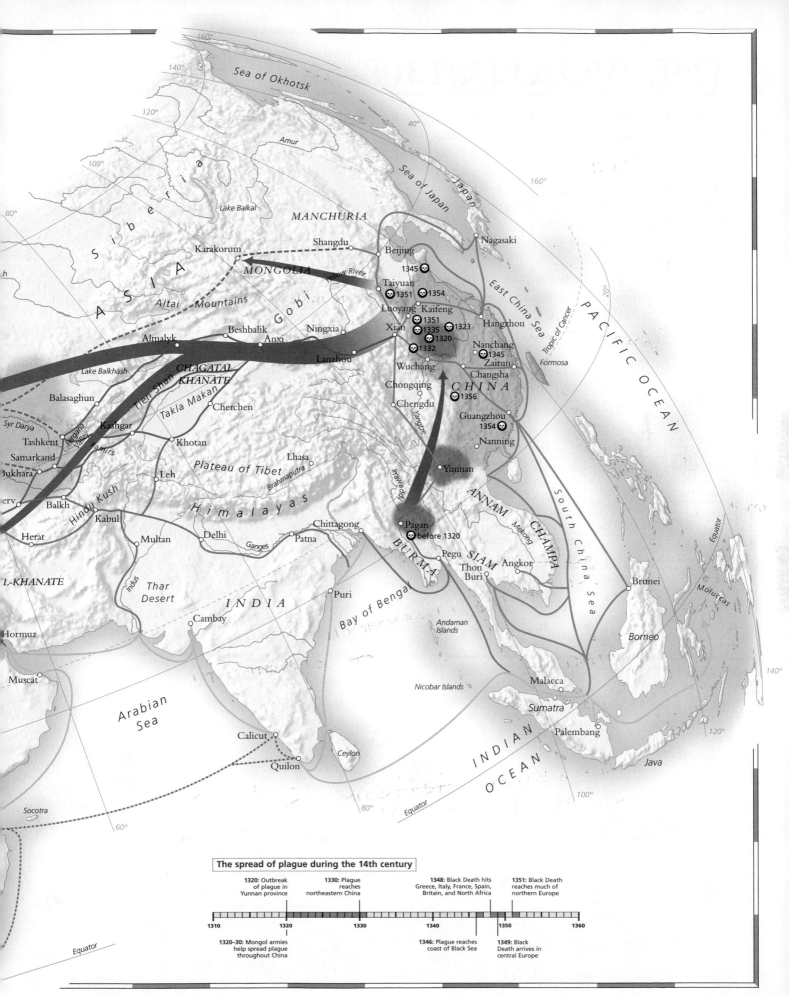

The spread of plague during the 14th century

1320: Outbreak of plague in Yunnan province

1330: Plague reaches northeastern China

1348: Black Death hits Greece, Italy, France, Spain, Britain, and North Africa

1351: Black Death reaches much of northern Europe

1310 — 1320 — 1330 — 1340 — 1350 — 1360

1320–30: Mongol armies help spread plague throughout China

1346: Plague reaches coast of Black Sea

1349: Black Death arrives in central Europe

THE WORLD: 1300–1400

DURING THE 14TH CENTURY, dramatic demographic decline led to economic and social disruption that weakened states throughout Eurasia and North Africa. The Mongol Empire, which had dominated Eurasia for over a century, began to disintegrate. In China, a new dynasty, the Ming, emerged, while in west Asia, the Ottoman Turks seized Anatolia and encroached on Byzantine holdings in southeastern Europe. The Islamic Mali Empire controlled the trans-Saharan caravan trade, using the profits to maintain a powerful army and dominate West Africa, but by 1400 it was in decline.

What factors contributed to political change in Europe and new empires in Asia?

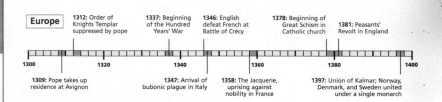

Europe

1312: Order of Knights Templar suppressed by pope	**1337:** Beginning of the Hundred Years' War	**1346:** English defeat French at Battle of Crécy	**1378:** Beginning of Great Schism in Catholic church	**1381:** Peasants' Revolt in England		

1300   **1320**   **1340**   **1360**   **1380**   **1400**

1309: Pope takes up residence at Avignon

1347: Arrival of bubonic plague in Italy

1358: The Jacquerie, uprising against nobility in France

1397: Union of Kalmar; Norway, Denmark, and Sweden united under a single monarch

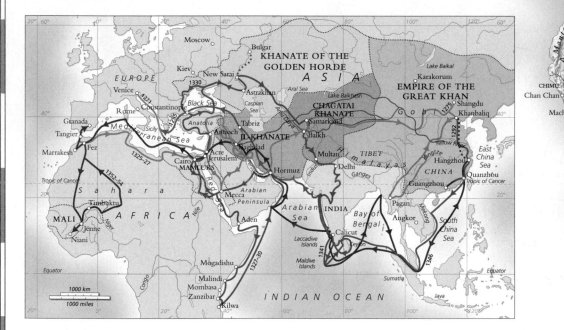

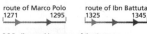

▲ **Eurasia and Africa c.1300**

route of Marco Polo
1271   1295

route of Ibn Battuta
1325   1345

⋮⋮⋮► disputed journeys of Ibn Battuta

— Silk Road

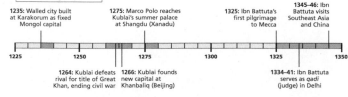

The Mongol peace

1235: Walled city built at Karakorum as fixed Mongol capital

1275: Marco Polo reaches Kublai's summer palace at Shangdu (Xanadu)

1325: Ibn Battuta's first pilgrimage to Mecca

1345–46: Ibn Battuta visits Southeast Asia and China

1225   **1250**   **1275**   **1300**   **1325**   **1350**

1264: Kublai defeats rival for title of Great Khan, ending civil war

1266: Kublai founds new capital at Khanbaliq (Beijing)

1334–41: Ibn Battuta serves as *qadi* (judge) in Delhi

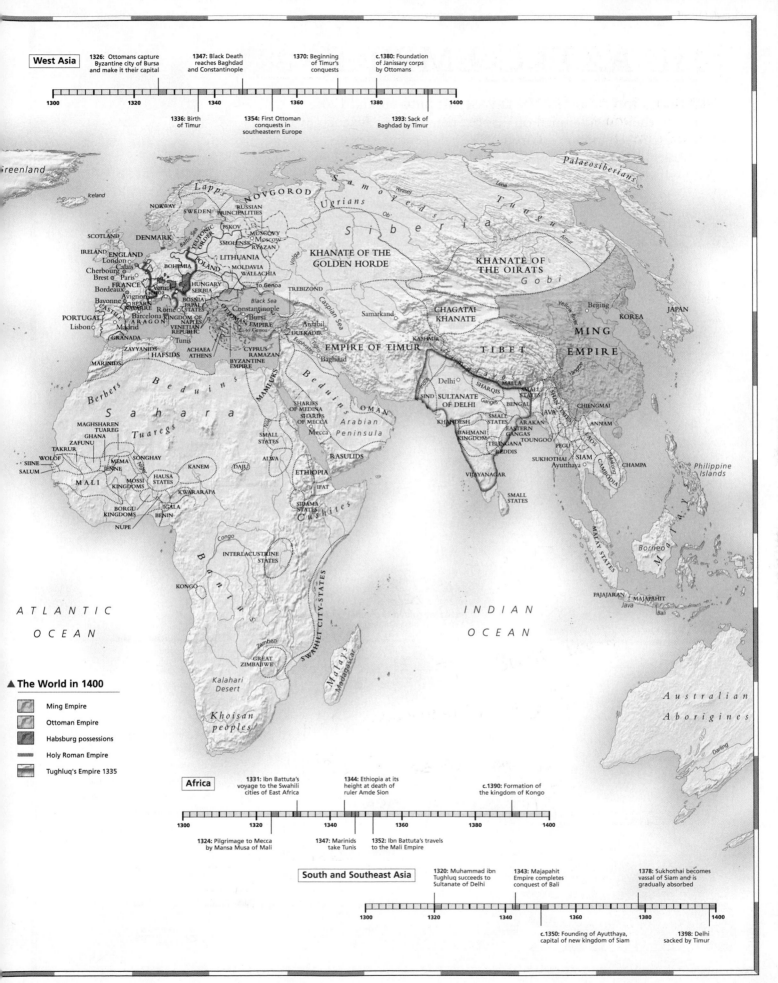

West Asia timeline:

- **1326:** Ottomans capture Byzantine city of Bursa and make it their capital
- **1347:** Black Death reaches Baghdad and Constantinople
- **1370:** Beginning of Timur's conquests
- **c.1380:** Foundation of Janissary corps by Ottomans
- **1336:** Birth of Timur
- **1354:** First Ottoman conquests in southeastern Europe
- **1393:** Sack of Baghdad by Timur

Timeline: 1300 — 1320 — 1340 — 1360 — 1380 — 1400

▲ The World in 1400

Legend:
- Ming Empire
- Ottoman Empire
- Habsburg possessions
- Holy Roman Empire
- Tughluq's Empire 1335

Africa timeline:

- **1331:** Ibn Battuta's voyage to the Swahili cities of East Africa
- **1344:** Ethiopia at its height at death of ruler Amde Sion
- **c.1390:** Formation of the kingdom of Kongo
- **1324:** Pilgrimage to Mecca by Mansa Musa of Mali
- **1347:** Marinids take Tunis
- **1352:** Ibn Battuta's travels to the Mali Empire

Timeline: 1300 — 1320 — 1340 — 1360 — 1380 — 1400

South and Southeast Asia timeline:

- **1320:** Muhammad ibn Tughluq succeeds to Sultanate of Delhi
- **1343:** Majapahit Empire completes conquest of Bali
- **1378:** Sukhothai becomes vassal of Siam and is gradually absorbed
- **c.1350:** Founding of Ayutthaya, capital of new kingdom of Siam
- **1398:** Delhi sacked by Timur

Timeline: 1300 — 1320 — 1340 — 1360 — 1380 — 1400

Map labels include:

Greenland, Iceland, Lapps, NOVGOROD, NORWAY, SWEDEN, RUSSIAN PRINCIPALITIES, Ugrians, Samoyeds, Siberia, Tungus, Palaeosiberians, SCOTLAND, DENMARK, PSKOV, MUSCOVY, Moscow, SMOLENSK, RYAZAN, KHANATE OF THE GOLDEN HORDE, KHANATE OF THE OIRATS, Gobi, IRELAND, ENGLAND, London, Calais, Cherbourg, Brest, Paris, TEUTONIC ORDER, Baltic Sea, LITHUANIA, POLAND, MOLDAVIA, WALLACHIA, to Genoa, Volga, Yenisey, Ob, Lena, Amur, FRANCE, BOHEMIA, HUNGARY, Venice, BOSNIA, SERBIA, TREBIZOND, CHAGATAI KHANATE, Samarkand, Beijing, JAPAN, KOREA, Bayonne, Bordeaux, Avignon, BEARN, NAVARRE, ARAGON, Rome, PAPAL STATES, VENETIAN REPUBLIC, Black Sea, OTTOMAN EMPIRE, Constantinople, Bursa, to Genoa, Caspian Sea, Ardabil, EMPIRE OF TIMUR, MING EMPIRE, TIBET, Yellow River, PORTUGAL, Lisbon, CASTILE, Madrid, Barcelona, KINGDOM OF NAPLES, Tunis, ACHAEA, ATHENS, CYPRUS, RAMAZAN, DULKADIR, KASHMIR, Indus, Delhi, SHARQIS, MALLA, SMALL STATES, SHAN STATES, Yangtze, GRANADA, ZAYYANIDS, HAFSIDS, MARINIDS, Berbers, Beduins, Sahara, MAMLUKS, Beduins, Baghdad, Euphrates, Tigris, SULTANATE OF DELHI, SIND, Ganges, BENGAL, AVA, CHIENGMAI, ANNAM, MAGHSHAREN, TUAREG, GHANA, ZAFUNU, Tuaregs, SHARIFS OF MEDINA, SHARIFS OF MECCA, Mecca, OMAN, Arabian Peninsula, KHANDESH, SMALL STATES, ARAKAN, EASTERN GANGAS, TOUNGOO, LAOS, Mekong, TAKRUR, WOLOF, SIINE, SALUM, MEMA, SONGHAY, JENNE, KANEM, DAJU, ALWA, RASULIDS, BAHMANI KINGDOM, TELINGANA, REDDIS, PEGU, SUKHOTHAI, Ayutthaya, SIAM, CAMBODIA, CHAMPA, Philippine Islands, MALI, MOSSI KINGDOMS, HAUSA STATES, KWARARAFA, ETHIOPIA, IFAT, VIJAYANAGAR, SMALL STATES, MALAY STATES, BORGU KINGDOMS, IGALA, BENIN, NUPE, SIDAMA STATES, Cushites, Congo, INTERLACUSTRINE STATES, Bantus, KONGO, SWAHILI CITY-STATES, INDIAN OCEAN, Borneo, PAJAJARAN, MAJAPAHIT, Java, Bali, Malays, ATLANTIC OCEAN, Zambezi, GREAT ZIMBABWE, Madagascar, Kalahari Desert, Khoisan peoples, Australian Aborigines, Darling

THE AZTEC EMPIRE

The Aztecs entered the Valley of Mexico around 1200, establishing their island capital of Tenochtitlan on Lake Texcoco in 1325. By 1519 the Aztec Empire controlled most of central Mexico as well as Maya areas further east. The Aztecs maintained a state of constant military activity which served to provide a flow of tribute from neighboring states.

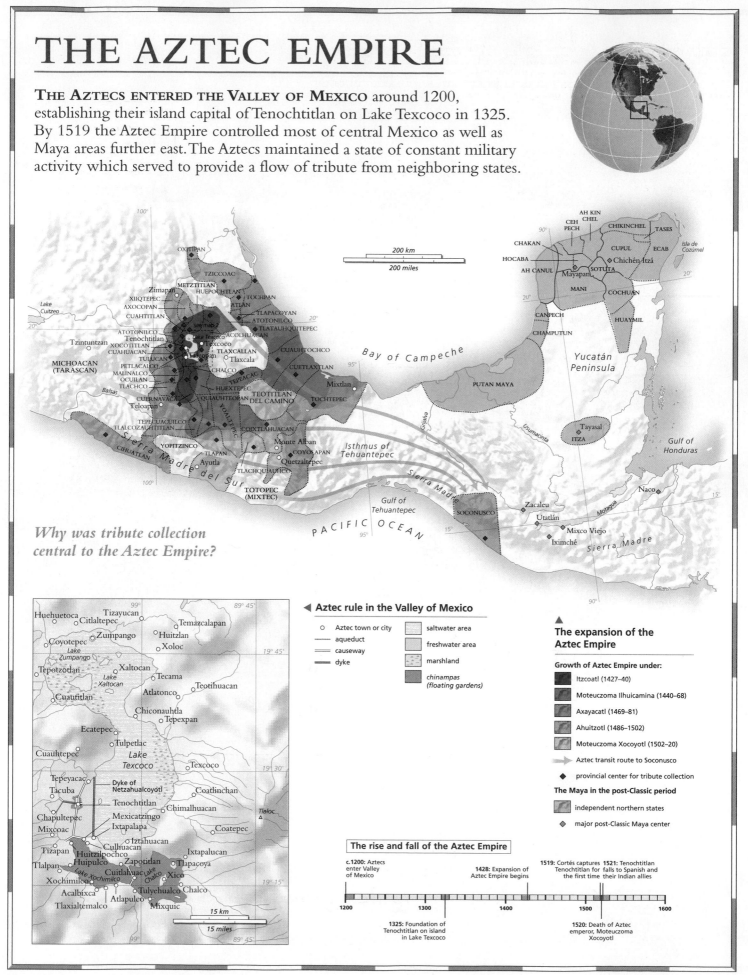

Why was tribute collection central to the Aztec Empire?

Aztec rule in the Valley of Mexico

- ○ Aztec town or city
- ---- aqueduct
- ===== causeway
- ▬▬ dyke

- saltwater area
- freshwater area
- marshland
- *chinampas (floating gardens)*

The expansion of the Aztec Empire

Growth of Aztec Empire under:

- Itzcoatl (1427–40)
- Moteuczoma Ilhuicamina (1440–68)
- Axayacatl (1469–81)
- Ahuitzotl (1486–1502)
- Moteuczoma Xocoyotl (1502–20)
- → Aztec transit route to Soconusco
- ◆ provincial center for tribute collection

The Maya in the post-Classic period

- independent northern states
- ◆ major post-Classic Maya center

The rise and fall of the Aztec Empire

- c.1200: Aztecs enter Valley of Mexico
- 1325: Foundation of Tenochtitlan on island in Lake Texcoco
- 1428: Expansion of Aztec Empire begins
- 1519: Cortés captures Tenochtitlan for the first time
- 1520: Death of Aztec emperor, Moteuczoma Xocoyotl
- 1521: Tenochtitlan falls to Spanish and their Indian allies

Timeline: 1200 — 1300 — 1400 — 1500 — 1600

THE INCA EMPIRE

THE INCA EMERGED, in less than a century, as the preeminent state in South America; from 1470 they ruled vast territories from their capital, Cuzco. An extensive road network bound the empire together.

How did control of varied ecological zones contribute to the development of Inca civilization?

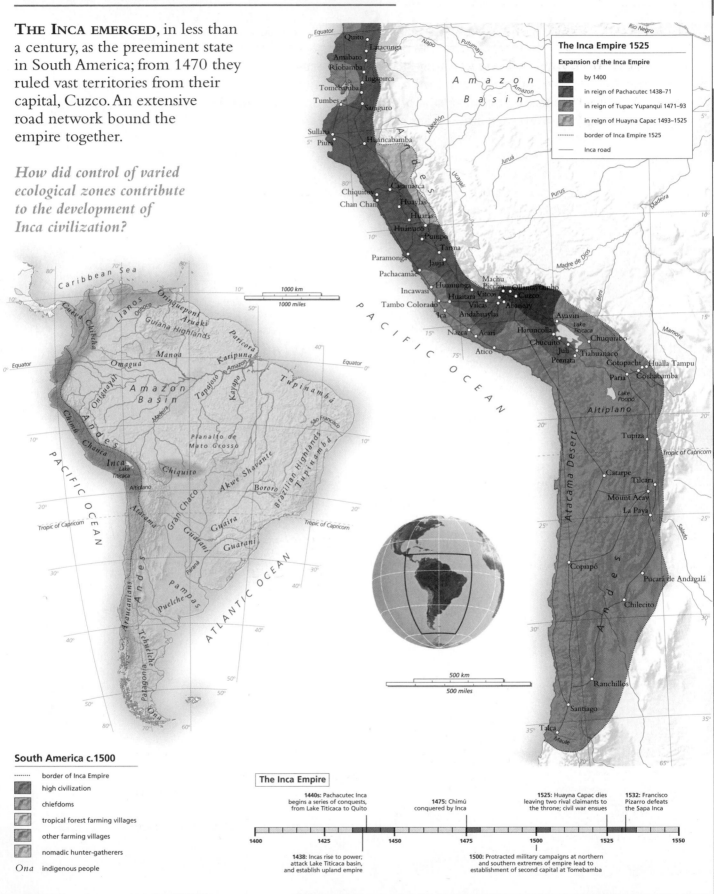

The Inca Empire 1525

Expansion of the Inca Empire

- by 1400
- in reign of Pachacutec 1438–71
- in reign of Tupac Yupanqui 1471–93
- in reign of Huayna Capac 1493–1525
- border of Inca Empire 1525
- Inca road

South America c.1500

- border of Inca Empire
- high civilization
- chiefdoms
- tropical forest farming villages
- other farming villages
- nomadic hunter-gatherers

Ona indigenous people

The Inca Empire

1440s: Pachacutec Inca begins a series of conquests, from Lake Titicaca to Quito

1475: Chimú conquered by Inca

1525: Huayna Capac dies leaving two rival claimants to the throne; civil war ensues

1532: Francisco Pizarro defeats the Sapa Inca

1400 1425 1450 1475 1500 1525 1550

1438: Incas rise to power; attack Lake Titicaca basin, and establish upland empire

1500: Protracted military campaigns at northern and southern extremes of empire lead to establishment of second capital at Tomebamba

GLOBAL ECONOMIES AND TECHNOLOGIES CA. 1500

A GLOBAL WORLDVIEW IS A RELATIVELY MODERN CONCEPT. The Americas were unknown to Old World Eurasia until 500 years ago, and each of the major cultural regions had discrete world views of varying extents, their own means of subsistence, and their own technologies which were in direct responses to their immediate environment.

By 1500, which regions had most intensively modified their environments?

Does this map affirm or contradict the way most people view the history of the world since 1500?

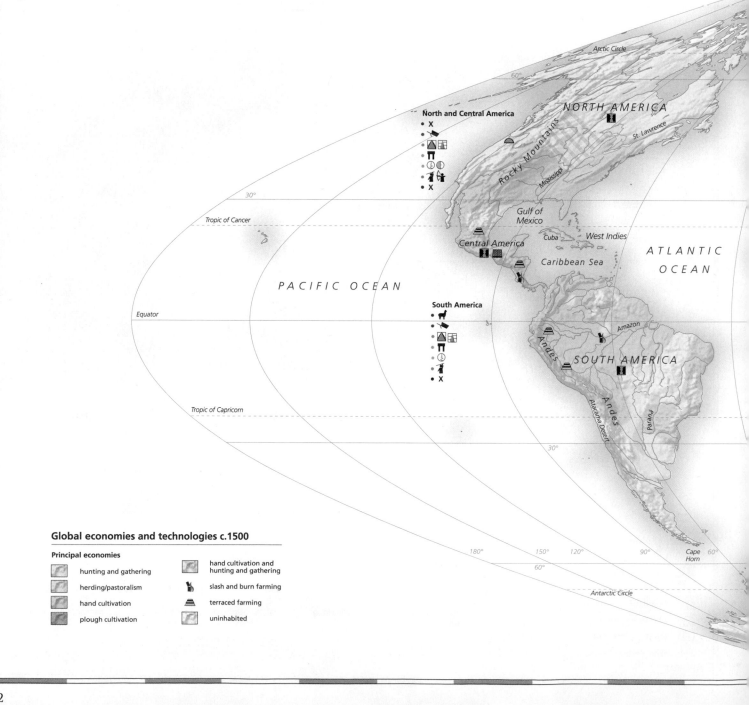

Global economies and technologies c.1500

Principal economies

	hunting and gathering		hand cultivation and hunting and gathering
	herding/pastoralism		slash and burn farming
	hand cultivation		terraced farming
	plough cultivation		uninhabited

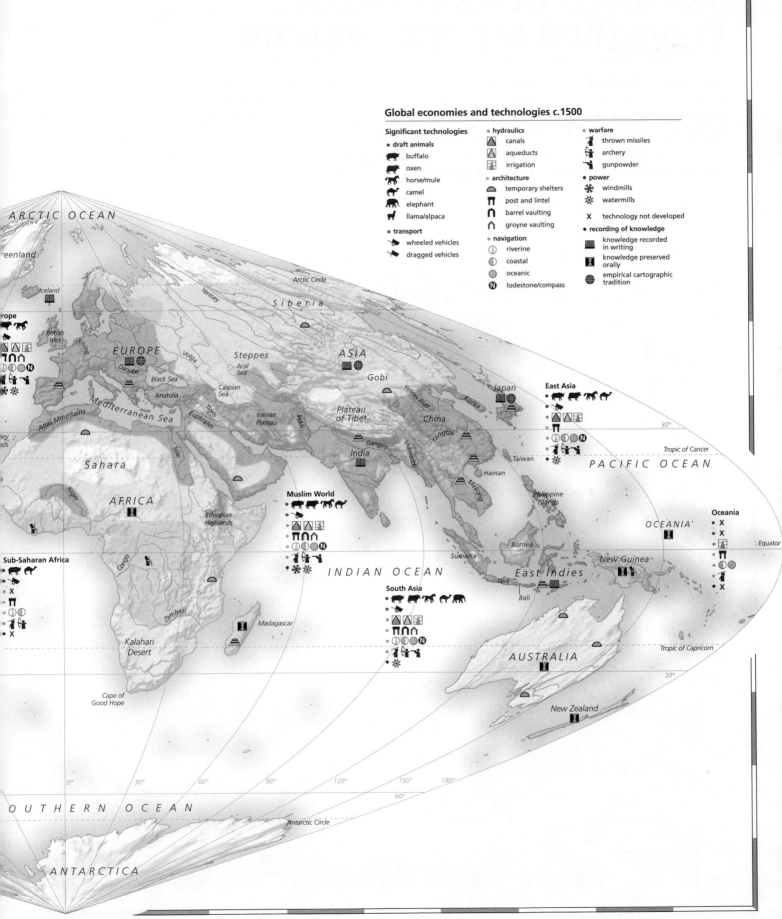

Global economies and technologies c.1500

Significant technologies

● draft animals
- buffalo
- oxen
- horse/mule
- camel
- elephant
- llama/alpaca

● transport
- wheeled vehicles
- dragged vehicles

● hydraulics
- canals
- aqueducts
- irrigation

● architecture
- temporary shelters
- post and lintel
- barrel vaulting
- groyne vaulting

● navigation
- riverine
- coastal
- oceanic
- lodestone/compass

● warfare
- thrown missiles
- archery
- gunpowder

● power
- windmills
- watermills

X technology not developed

● recording of knowledge
- knowledge recorded in writing
- knowledge preserved orally
- empirical cartographic tradition

VOYAGES OF EUROPEAN EXPANSION

THE 16TH CENTURY SAW THE EXPANSION of several European nations far beyond their continental limits. The Spanish and the Portuguese led the way, followed by the French and English. Travelers transported numerous species of fruits, vegetables, and animals from the Americas to Europe. At the same time, settlers introduced European species to the Americas and Oceania. European expansion also led to a spread of European diseases. Vast numbers of indigenous American peoples died from measles and smallpox, which broke out in massive epidemics.

Voyages of expansion 1492–1590

1492: Columbus, in search of Asia, reaches Cuba and the Bahamas

1509–16: Portuguese voyages to Moluccas, Malacca, and Macao

1532: Cartier explores Strait of Belle Isle and St Lawrence

1576: Frobisher reaches Baffin Island

1490 — 1510 — 1530 — 1550 — 1570 — 1590

1498: Vasco da Gama rounds Cape of Good Hope and reaches India

1500: Cabral sights Brazilian coast on voyage to India

1519–22: Magellan and del Cano complete first global circumnavigation reaching Moluccas via the Philippine Islands

1553: Willoughby reaches Archangel on Northeast Passage

1577–80: Drake circumnavigates globe

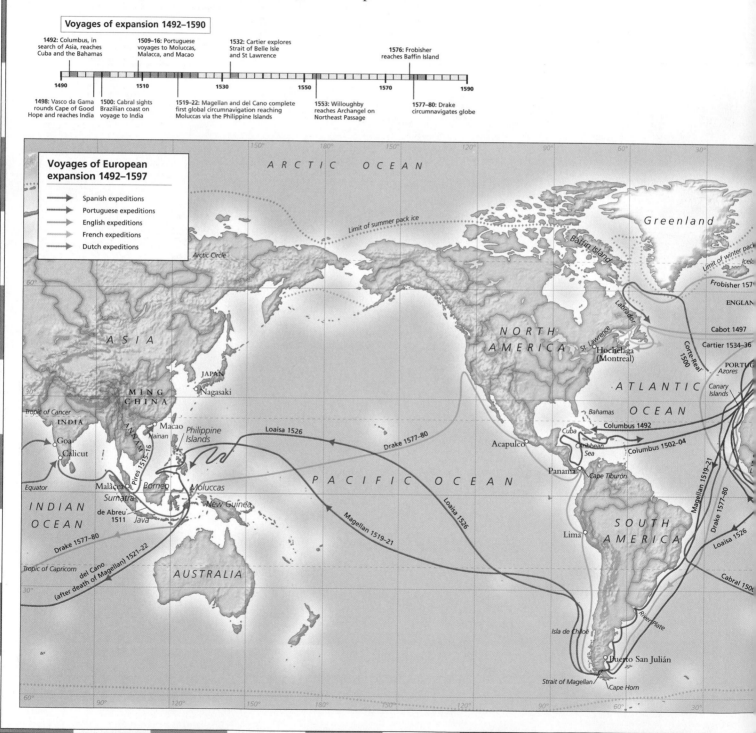

Voyages of European expansion 1492–1597

→ Spanish expeditions
→ Portuguese expeditions
→ English expeditions
→ French expeditions
→ Dutch expeditions

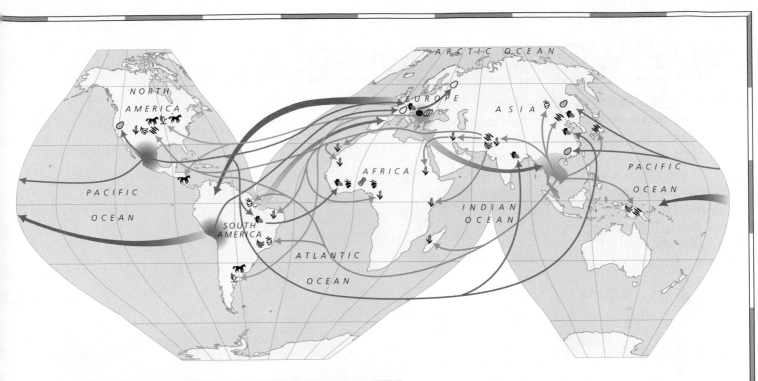

Biological exchanges ▲

Origin and movement of plants and animals

→ from Europe

→ from America

→ from Asia

Plants and animals

🍌 bananas
🌶 chili peppers
🐎 horses
🌽 maize
🌿 manioc
🥜 peanuts
🥔 potatoes
🌾 rice
↓ sugar cane
🥔 sweet potatoes
🌱 tomatoes
🌱 wheat
🌿 yams

Diseases

→ diphtheria, influenza, measles, smallpox, and whooping cough

→ syphilis

How did European expansion transform societies, economies, and environments around the world?

THE WORLD: 1500–1600

IN THE 16TH CENTURY Spain seized a vast land empire that encompassed much of the Americas and the Philippines. Meanwhile, Portugal acquired a large maritime empire stretching from Brazil to Macao. Ferdinand Magellan demonstrated that all of the world's oceans were linked and sea lanes were established through the Indian, Atlantic, and Pacific oceans, creating for the first time a genuine global trading network.

Why is this period often considered the beginning of the modern world?

Europe

1500	1520	1540	1560	1580	1600

1519: Charles V elected Holy Roman Emperor

1545: Council of Trent called to counter threat of Protestantism

1580: Philip II of Spain seizes Portuguese crown

1598: Edict of Nantes ends over 30 years of religious wars in France

1517: Martin Luther's *95 Theses* attack abuses of Catholic church

1534: Act of Supremacy; Henry VIII of England breaks with Rome

1565: Dutch Revolt starts long series of wars to gain independence from Spain

1588: English defeat Spanish Armada

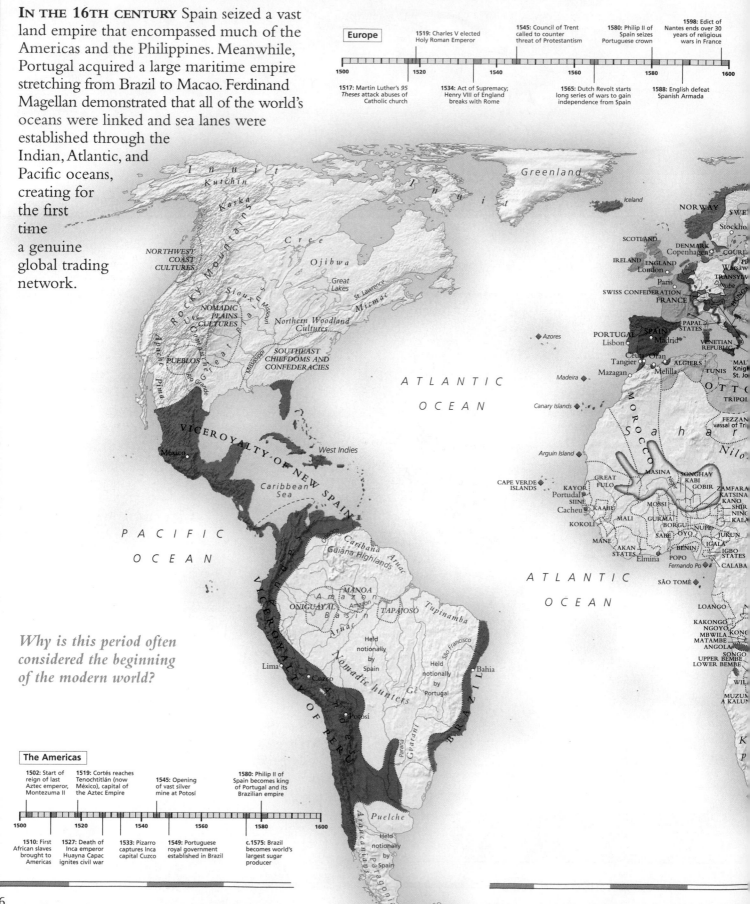

The Americas

1500	1520	1540	1560	1580	1600

1502: Start of reign of last Aztec emperor, Montezuma II

1519: Cortés reaches Tenochtitlán (now México), capital of the Aztec Empire

1545: Opening of vast silver mine at Potosí

1580: Philip II of Spain becomes king of Portugal and its Brazilian empire

1510: First African slaves brought to Americas

1527: Death of Inca emperor Huayna Capac ignites civil war

1533: Pizarro captures Inca capital Cuzco

1549: Portuguese royal government established in Brazil

c.1575: Brazil becomes world's largest sugar producer

West Asia

1500 — 1520 — 1540 — 1560 — 1580 — 1600

1507: Portuguese victory over Ottoman and Arab fleet at Diu
1520: Suleiman the Magnificent becomes Ottoman sultan
1566: Suleiman succeeded by Selim II
1588: Abbas I the Great becomes Safavid shah

1514: Ottomans victory over Safavids at Chaldiran
1526: Battle of Mohács: Ottomans crush Hungarian army
1571: Battle of Lepanto; Ottoman navy defeated by united Christian fleet off Greek coast
1587: Isfahan becomes capital of Safavid Empire

South and Southeast Asia

1500 — 1520 — 1540 — 1560 — 1580 — 1600

1510: Portuguese conquest of Goa
1526: Babur conquers Sultanate of Delhi
1563: Burmese King Bayinnaung invades Siam
1600: English East India Company founded

1511: Portuguese take Malacca
1556: Akbar becomes Mughal emperor
1565: Spanish fleet claims Philippines in name of King Philip II

The World in 1600

- Ming Empire
- Ottoman Empire
- Spain and possessions
- Portugal and possessions (ruled by Kings of Spain 1580–1640)
- England and possessions
- Austrian Habsburg territories
- France
- Denmark and possessions
- United Provinces (fighting for independence from Spain)
- Dutch (United Provinces) possessions
- Mughal Empire at Akbar's accession, 1556
- under Burmese control, 1575
- Songhay to 1590
- Holy Roman Empire

Africa

1500 — 1520 — 1540 — 1560 — 1580 — 1600

c.1500: Establishment of forest states of Oyo and Benin
1517: Ottomans conquer Mamluks in Egypt
1578: Moroccans crush invading Portuguese

1505: First Portuguese trading posts in East Africa
1546: Songhay destroys Mali Empire
1570: Establishment of Portuguese colony in Angola
1591: Songhay Empire falls to Morocco

THE MING AND THE OUTSIDE WORLD

WITH THE ESTABLISHMENT of the Ming Empire in 1368, China returned to control by a native dynasty after a century of foreign rule. Despite its isolationism, in the 16th century Ming China's sheer wealth and productivity made it a great magnet for global trade.

How did Ming China drive the global economy of the early–modern world?

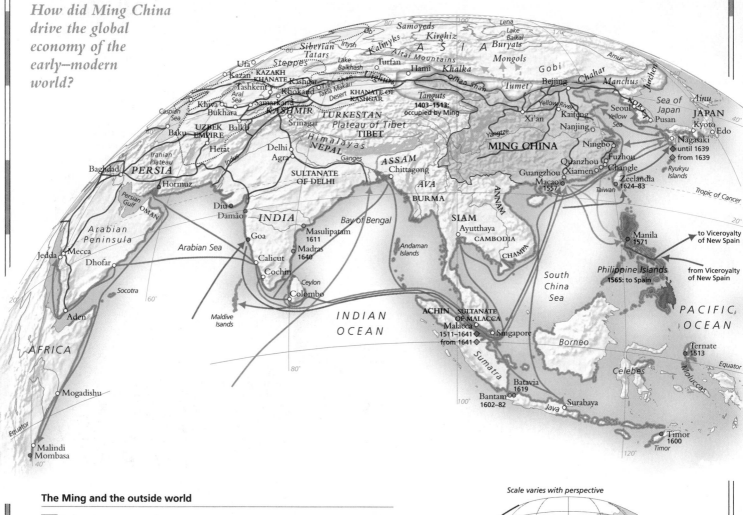

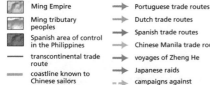

The Ming and the outside world

- Ming Empire
- Ming tributary peoples
- Spanish area of control in the Philippines
- transcontinental trade route
- coastline known to Chinese sailors

- Portuguese trade routes
- Dutch trade routes
- Spanish trade routes
- Chinese Manila trade routes
- voyages of Zheng He
- Japanese raids
- campaigns against the Mongols

- ◆◇ Dutch territory/trading station with date
- ◆◇ Portuguese territory/trading station with date
- ○ English territory/trading station with date
- ● Spanish trading station with date
- ○ major Chinese port

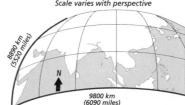

Scale varies with perspective

8890 km (5520 miles)

N

9800 km (6090 miles)

Trade and the first European contacts

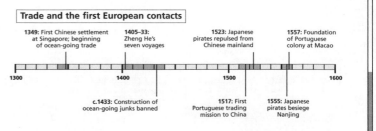

1349: First Chinese settlement at Singapore; beginning of ocean-going trade

1405–33: Zheng He's seven voyages

1523: Japanese pirates repulsed from Chinese mainland

1557: Foundation of Portuguese colony at Macao

| 1300 | 1400 | 1500 | 1600 |

c.1433: Construction of ocean-going junks banned

1517: First Portuguese trading mission to China

1555: Japanese pirates besiege Nanjing

THE REUNIFICATION OF JAPAN

THE STRUGGLE FOR SUPREMACY between *bushido* warlords in 16th-century Japan led to the emergence of two shoguns: Oda Nobunaga, who enforced national unfication under a virtual dictatorship, and his succesor Toyotmi Hideyoshi, whose imperial ambitions led to repeated campaigns in Korea. This period was accompanied by the first contacts with European trade and Christian missions.

What were the challenges to unity in Japan?

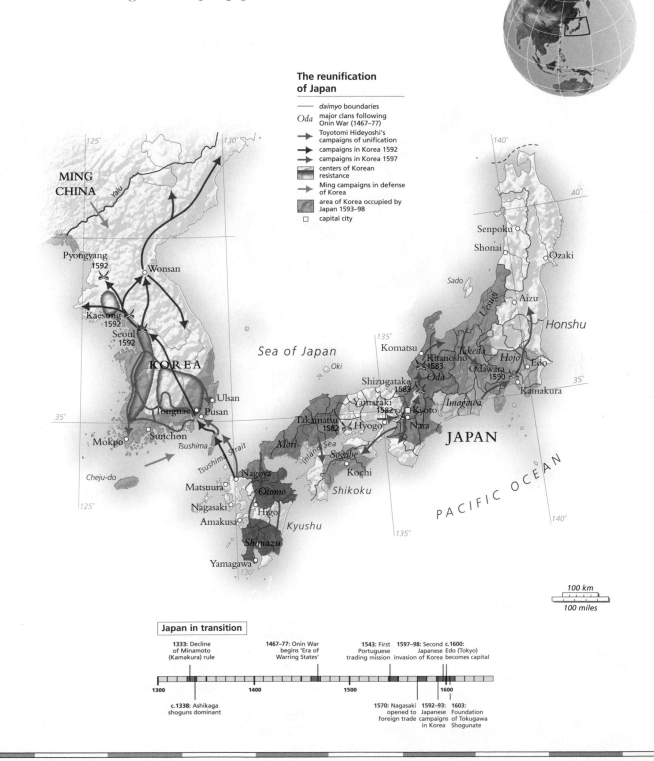

The reunification of Japan

— *daimyo* boundaries
Oda major clans following Onin War (1467–77)
→ Toyotomi Hideyoshi's campaigns of unification
→ campaigns in Korea 1592
→ campaigns in Korea 1597
▨ centers of Korean resistance
→ Ming campaigns in defense of Korea
▨ area of Korea occupied by Japan 1593–98
□ capital city

MING CHINA

Pyongyang 1592
Wonsan
Kaesong 1592
Seoul 1592
KOREA
Ulsan
Tongnae Pusan
Mokpo Sunchon
Tsushima
Tsushima Strait
Cheju-do

Sea of Japan
Oki

Senpoku
Shonai
Ozaki
Sado
Aizu
Uesugi
Honshu

Komatsu
Kitanosho 1583
Takeda
Hojo
Edo
Oda
Odawara 1590
Shizugatake 1583
Kamakura
Yamazaki 1582
Imagawa
Takamatsu 1582
Hyogo
Kyoto
Nara
Mori
Sogabe
JAPAN
Inland Sea
Kochi
Shikoku
Nagoya
Matsuura
Otomo
Nagasaki
Higo
Amakusa
Kyushu
Shimazu
Yamagawa

PACIFIC OCEAN

100 km
100 miles

Japan in transition

1333: Decline of Minamoto (Kamakura) rule
1467–77: Onin War begins 'Era of Warring States'
1543: First Portuguese trading mission
1597–98: Second Japanese invasion of Korea
c.1600: Edo (Tokyo) becomes capital

1300 | 1400 | 1500 | 1600

c.1338: Ashikaga shoguns dominant
1570: Nagasaki opened to foreign trade
1592–93: Japanese campaigns in Korea
1603: Foundation of Tokugawa Shogunate

THE RELIGIOUS MAP OF EUROPE IN 1590

A SERIES OF PROFOUND CHANGES in theological doctrine and practice caused violent political upheavals in 16th century Europe. The Reformation, spearheaded by Martin Luther, divided much of the continent along religious lines.

Why did Protestantism spread throughout northern Europe?

The religious map of Europe 1590

- ▓ mostly Catholic
- ▓ mostly Protestant
- ▓ Catholic majority, but with very strong Protestant minority
- ▓ mainly Catholic, with strong Greek Orthodox presence
- ▓ Greek Orthodox, with significant Muslim presence in some areas of the Balkans
- ▓ Muslim majority
- ---- frontiers 1590
- ━━━ frontier of Holy Roman Empire 1590
- *Calvinist* locally dominant Protestant denomination

The Reformation in Europe 1517–55

1529: At Diet of Speyer, Charles V attempts to reach compromise with Lutheran princes

1535: John Calvin formulates doctrine of predestination in Geneva

1545: Start of Council of Trent, which defines modern Catholicism

1510   1520   1530   1540   1550   1560

1517: Martin Luther posts 95 Theses condemning abuses of Catholic church at Wittenberg

1532: Henry VIII of England declares himself head of Church of England

1555: At Peace of Augsburg; Lutheran princes win right to choose their religion

THE HEIGHT OF OTTOMAN POWER

THE OTTOMAN EMPIRE was one of the great world powers of the early modern era. At its height, the empire stretched from the Persian Gulf to Algiers, Hungary, and the Crimea.

Was the geographical position of the Ottoman Empire a source of strength or weakness?

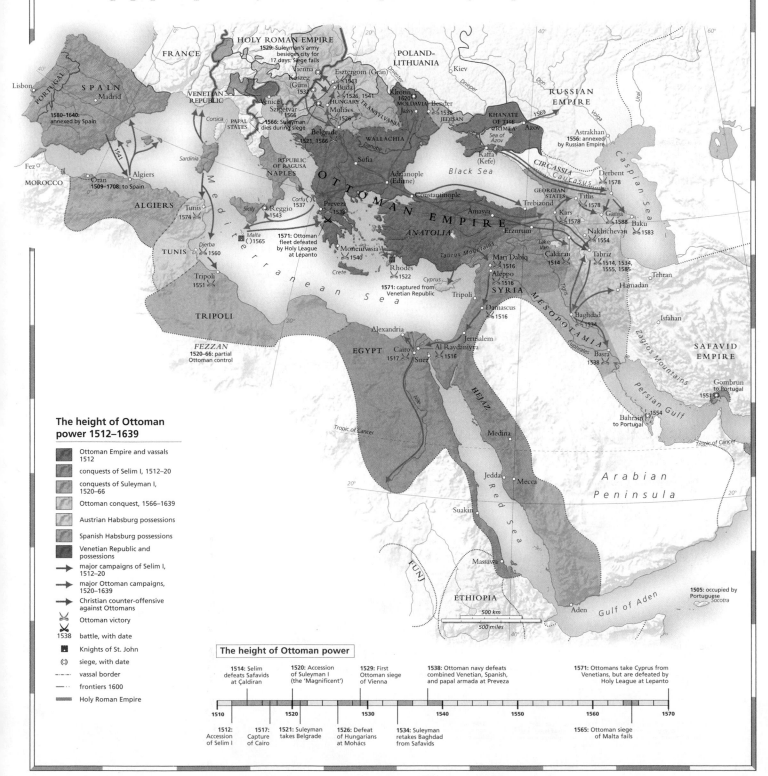

The height of Ottoman power 1512–1639

- Ottoman Empire and vassals 1512
- conquests of Selim I, 1512–20
- conquests of Suleyman I, 1520–66
- Ottoman conquest, 1566–1639
- Austrian Habsburg possessions
- Spanish Habsburg possessions
- Venetian Republic and possessions
- → major campaigns of Selim I, 1512–20
- → major Ottoman campaigns, 1520–1639
- → Christian counter-offensive against Ottomans
- ✕ Ottoman victory
- 1538 battle, with date
- ▣ Knights of St. John
- ⊙ siege, with date
- –·–·– vassal border
- –––– frontiers 1600
- Holy Roman Empire

The height of Ottoman power

1514: Selim defeats Safavids at Çaldiran

1520: Accession of Suleyman I (the 'Magnificent')

1529: First Ottoman siege of Vienna

1538: Ottoman navy defeats combined Venetian, Spanish, and papal armada at Preveza

1571: Ottomans take Cyprus from Venetians, but are defeated by Holy League at Lepanto

1512: Accession of Selim I

1517: Capture of Cairo

1521: Suleyman takes Belgrade

1526: Defeat of Hungarians at Mohács

1534: Suleyman retakes Baghdad from Safavids

1565: Ottoman siege of Malta fails

1510 — 1520 — 1530 — 1540 — 1550 — 1560 — 1570

THE MUGHAL EMPIRE

THE CONQUEST OF NORTHERN INDIA in 1526 by the Muslim Mughal chief, Babur, ushered in a new era, marked by orderly government, economic prosperity, and great achievements in the arts. Vasco da Gama's voyage to India in 1498 opened up new trade routes, enabling European powers to establish commercial toeholds.

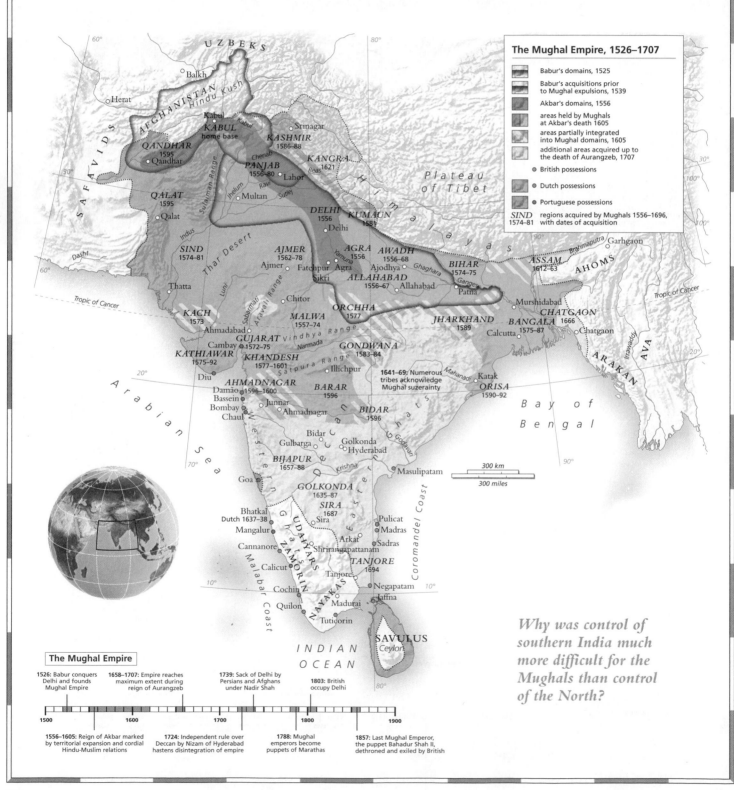

The Mughal Empire, 1526–1707

- Babur's domains, 1525
- Babur's acquisitions prior to Mughal expulsions, 1539
- Akbar's domains, 1556
- areas held by Mughals at Akbar's death 1605
- areas partially integrated into Mughal domains, 1605
- additional areas acquired up to the death of Aurangzeb, 1707
- British possessions
- Dutch possessions
- Portuguese possessions

SIND 1574–81 regions acquired by Mughals 1556–1696, with dates of acquisition

Why was control of southern India much more difficult for the Mughals than control of the North?

The Mughal Empire

1526: Babur conquers Delhi and founds Mughal Empire

1658–1707: Empire reaches maximum extent during reign of Aurangzeb

1739: Sack of Delhi by Persians and Afghans under Nadir Shah

1803: British occupy Delhi

1500 — 1600 — 1700 — 1800 — 1900

1556–1605: Reign of Akbar marked by territorial expansion and cordial Hindu-Muslim relations

1724: Independent rule over Deccan by Nizam of Hyderabad hastens disintegration of empire

1788: Mughal emperors become puppets of Marathas

1857: Last Mughal Emperor, the puppet Bahadur Shah II, dethroned and exiled by British

SAFAVID PERSIA

OTTOMAN EXPANSION TO THE EAST (see p. 75) was checked by the sudden rise to power in 1500 of a new Persian dynasty, the Safavids. The first Safavid ruler, Shah Ismail I, rapidly united Persia, converting it from Sunni to Shiite Islam.

What have been the long-term implications of conflict between the Shiite Safavids and Sunni Ottomans?

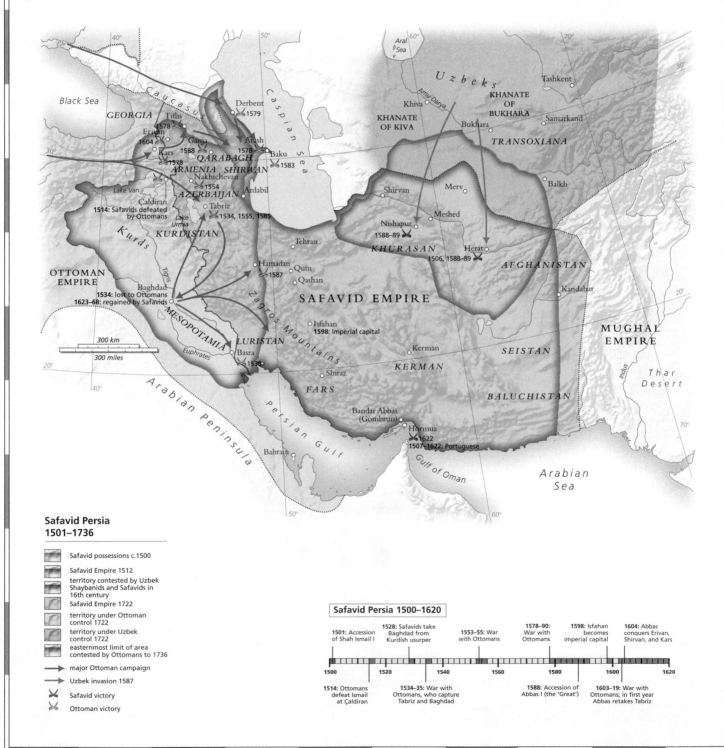

Safavid Persia
1501–1736

- Safavid possessions c.1500
- Safavid Empire 1512
- territory contested by Uzbek Shaybanids and Safavids in 16th century
- Safavid Empire 1722
- territory under Ottoman control 1722
- territory under Uzbek control 1722
- easternmost limit of area contested by Ottomans to 1736
- → major Ottoman campaign
- → Uzbek invasion 1587
- ✗ Safavid victory
- ✗ Ottoman victory

Safavid Persia 1500–1620

1501: Accession of Shah Ismail I

1528: Safavids take Baghdad from Kurdish usurper

1553–55: War with Ottomans

1578–90: War with Ottomans

1598: Isfahan becomes imperial capital

1604: Abbas conquers Erivan, Shirvan, and Kars

1514: Ottomans defeat Ismail at Çaldiran

1534–35: War with Ottomans, who capture Tabriz and Baghdad

1588: Accession of Abbas I (the 'Great')

1603–19: War with Ottomans; in first year Abbas retakes Tabriz

THE WORLD: 1600–1700

DURING THE 17TH CENTURY, Dutch, British, and French mariners followed the Iberians into the world's seas, establishing colonies in North America. Trade between Europe, Africa, and the Americas knitted the Atlantic Ocean basin, while trade in the Indian Ocean linked European and Asian markets.

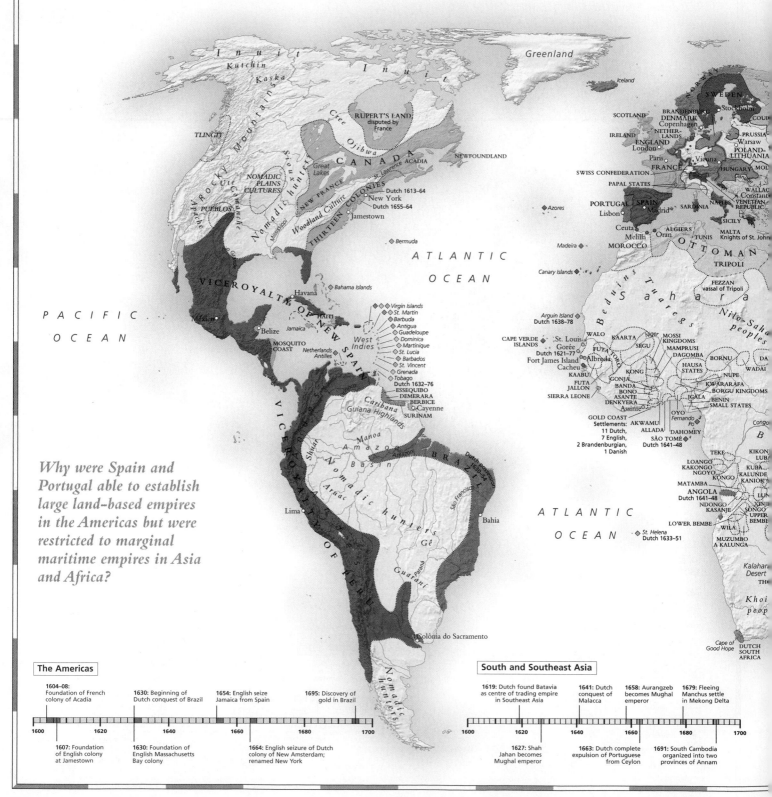

Why were Spain and Portugal able to establish large land-based empires in the Americas but were restricted to marginal maritime empires in Asia and Africa?

The Americas

1604–08: Foundation of French colony of Acadia

1630: Beginning of Dutch conquest of Brazil

1654: English seize Jamaica from Spain

1695: Discovery of gold in Brazil

1607: Foundation of English colony at Jamestown

1630: Foundation of English Massachusetts Bay colony

1664: English seizure of Dutch colony of New Amsterdam; renamed New York

| 1600 | 1620 | 1640 | 1660 | 1680 | 1700 |

South and Southeast Asia

1619: Dutch found Batavia as centre of trading empire in Southeast Asia

1641: Dutch conquest of Malacca

1658: Aurangzeb becomes Mughal emperor

1679: Fleeing Manchus settle in Mekong Delta

1627: Shah Jahan becomes Mughal emperor

1663: Dutch complete expulsion of Portuguese from Ceylon

1691: South Cambodia organized into two provinces of Annam

| 1600 | 1620 | 1640 | 1660 | 1680 | 1700 |

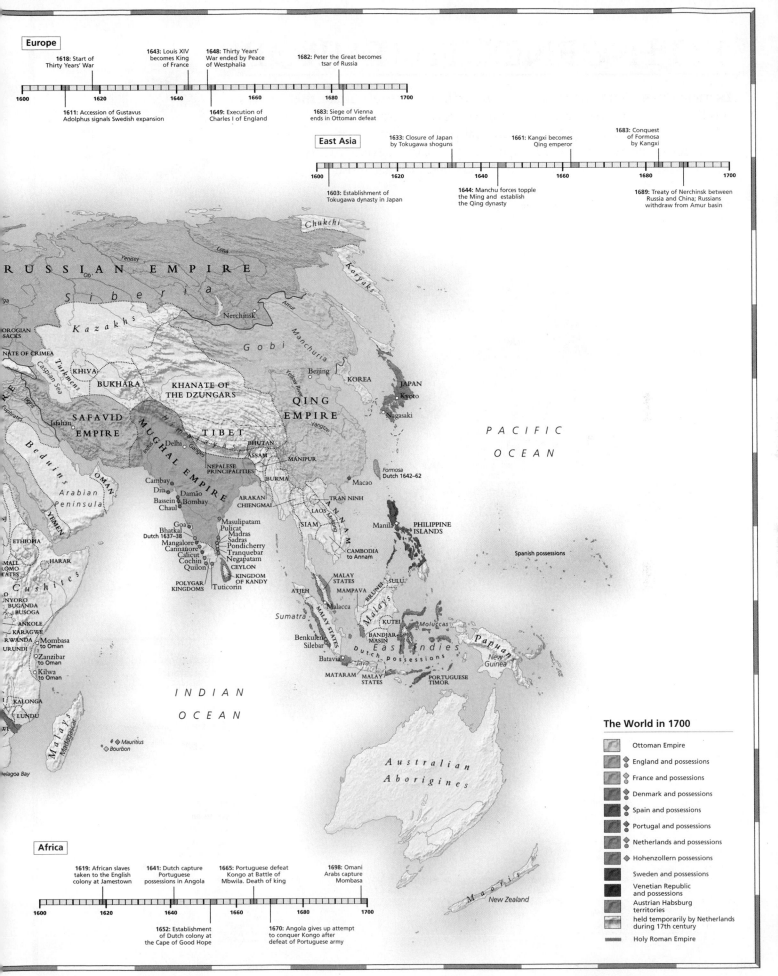

1618: Start of Thirty Years' War

1643: Louis XIV becomes King of France

1648: Thirty Years' War ended by Peace of Westphalia

1682: Peter the Great becomes tsar of Russia

1600 1620 1640 1660 1680 1700

1611: Accession of Gustavus Adolphus signals Swedish expansion

1649: Execution of Charles I of England

1683: Siege of Vienna ends in Ottoman defeat

East Asia

1633: Closure of Japan by Tokugawa shoguns

1661: Kangxi becomes Qing emperor

1683: Conquest of Formosa by Kangxi

1600 1620 1640 1660 1680 1700

1603: Establishment of Tokugawa dynasty in Japan

1644: Manchu forces topple the Ming and establish the Qing dynasty

1689: Treaty of Nerchinsk between Russia and China; Russians withdraw from Amur basin

Chukchi

Yenisey

Lena

RUSSIAN EMPIRE

Koryaks

Ob'

Siberia

ga

OROGIAN SACKS

Nerchinsk

Amur

Manchuria

NATE OF CRIMEA

Kazakhs

Gobi

KHIVA

Turkmens

Caspian Sea

BUKHARA

KHANATE OF THE DZUNGARS

Yellow River

Beijing

KOREA

JAPAN

Kyoto

Isfahan

SAFAVID EMPIRE

TIBET

QING EMPIRE

Yangtze

Nagasaki

PACIFIC OCEAN

Beduins

Euphrates

OMAN

MUGHAL EMPIRE

Delhi

Ganges

BHUTAN

ASSAM

Macao

Arabian Peninsula

YEMEN

Indus

Himalayas

NEPALESE PRINCIPALITIES

MANIPUR

Formosa Dutch 1642–62

Cambay

Diu

Damão

BURMA

ARAKAN

CHIENGMAI

TRAN NINH

Macao

Bassein

Bombay

Chaul

LAOS

ETHIOPIA

HARAR

Goa

Bhatkal Dutch 1637–38

Mangalore

Cannanore

Calicut

Cochin

Quilon

Masulipatam

Pulicat

Madras

Sadras

Pondicherry

Tranquebar

Negapatam

CEYLON

SIAM

Mekong

ANNAM

Manila

PHILIPPINE ISLANDS

MALL LOMO TES

Cushites

POLYGAR KINGDOMS

Tuticorin

KINGDOM OF KANDY

CAMBODIA to Annam

Spanish possessions

JNYORO BUGANDA BUSOGA

ATJEH

MALAY STATES

MAMPAVA

SULU

BRUNEI

ANKOLE

KARAGWE

RWANDA

URUNDI

Mombasa to Oman

Malays

Mulacca

Sumatra

Malays

MALAY STATES

KUTEI

Moluccas

Zanzibar to Oman

Kilwa to Oman

Benkulen

Silebar

BANDJAR MASIN

East Indies Dutch possessions

Papuans

New Guinea

KALONGA

LUNDU

Malays

Madagascar

Batavia

Java

MATARAM

MALAY STATES

PORTUGUESE TIMOR

INDIAN OCEAN

Mauritius

Bourbon

Australian Aborigines

lagoa Bay

The World in 1700

Ottoman Empire

England and possessions

France and possessions

Denmark and possessions

Spain and possessions

Portugal and possessions

Netherlands and possessions

Hohenzollern possessions

Sweden and possessions

Venetian Republic and possessions

Austrian Habsburg territories

held temporarily by Netherlands during 17th century

Holy Roman Empire

Maoris

New Zealand

Africa

1619: African slaves taken to the English colony at Jamestown

1641: Dutch capture Portuguese possessions in Angola

1665: Portuguese defeat Kongo at Battle of Mbwila. Death of king

1698: Omani Arabs capture Mombasa

1600 1620 1640 1660 1680 1700

1652: Establishment of Dutch colony at the Cape of Good Hope

1670: Angola gives up attempt to conquer Kongo after defeat of Portuguese army

17TH-CENTURY EUROPE

IN THE 17TH CENTURY, following years of destructive warfare, the modern European state system began to evolve. European states were transformed in a process of internal political centralization and external consolidation. The legitimacy of these developments was often questioned, leading to civil wars and popular resistance.

What were the roots of civil unrest in early-modern Europe?

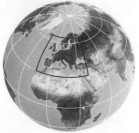

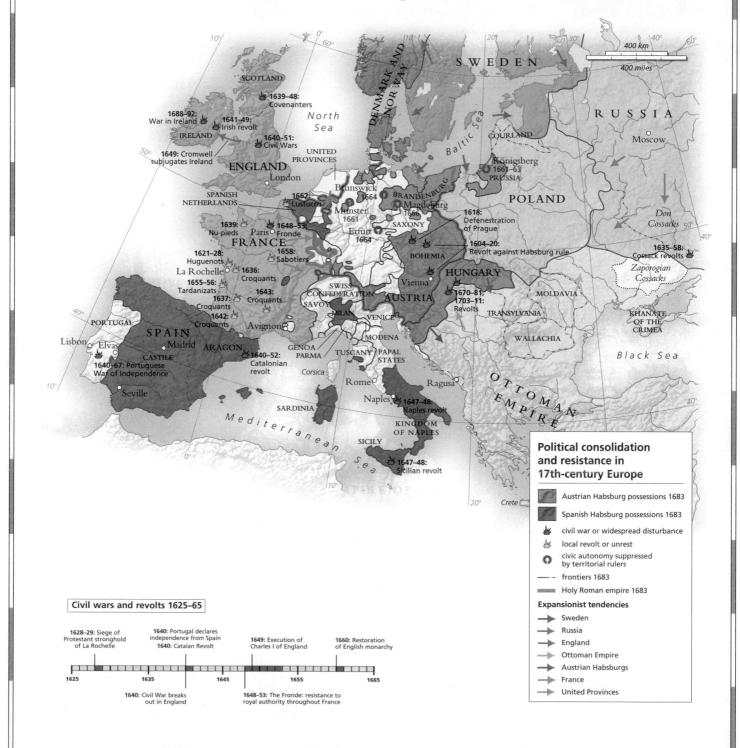

1639–48: Covenanters

1688–92: War in Ireland
1641–49: Irish revolt
1640–51: Civil Wars
1649: Cromwell subjugates Ireland

North Sea

SCOTLAND

IRELAND

ENGLAND
London

SPANISH NETHERLANDS

UNITED PROVINCES

Brunswick
1662: Lustucru
Münster 1661
Erfurt 1664

Magdeburg 1666

BRANDENBURG

SAXONY

1639: Nu-pieds
Paris **1648–53:** Fronde
FRANCE
1621–28: Huguenots
La Rochelle
1636: Croquants
1655–56: Tardanizats
1637: Croquants
1643: Croquants
1642: Croquants
Avignon

1658: Sabotiers

SWISS CONFEDERATION
SAVOY
MILAN
VENICE

1618: Defenestration of Prague

1604–20: Revolt against Habsburg rule

BOHEMIA
Vienna
AUSTRIA

HUNGARY

1670–81:
1703–11: Revolts

SWEDEN

COURLAND

Königsberg
1661–63: PRUSSIA

POLAND

MOLDAVIA
TRANSYLVANIA
WALLACHIA

RUSSIA
Moscow

Don Cossacks

1635–58: Cossack revolts

Zaporogian Cossacks

KHANATE OF THE CRIMEA

Black Sea

PORTUGAL
Lisbon
Elvas
SPAIN
Madrid
CASTILE
ARAGON
Seville
1640–67: Portuguese War of Independence

1640–52: Catalonian revolt

GENOA
PARMA
Corsica
MODENA
TUSCANY
PAPAL STATES
Rome
Ragusa

OTTOMAN EMPIRE

SARDINIA

Naples **1647–48:** Naples revolt
KINGDOM OF NAPLES

SICILY **1647–48:** Sicilian revolt

Mediterranean Sea

Crete

Political consolidation and resistance in 17th-century Europe

	Austrian Habsburg possessions 1683
	Spanish Habsburg possessions 1683
	civil war or widespread disturbance
	local revolt or unrest
	civic autonomy suppressed by territorial rulers
—	frontiers 1683
	Holy Roman empire 1683

Expansionist tendencies

→ Sweden
→ Russia
→ England
→ Ottoman Empire
→ Austrian Habsburgs
→ France
→ United Provinces

Civil wars and revolts 1625–65

1628–29: Siege of Protestant stronghold of La Rochelle

1640: Portugal declares independence from Spain
1640: Catalan Revolt

1649: Execution of Charles I of England

1660: Restoration of English monarchy

1625 1635 1645 1655 1665

1640: Civil War breaks out in England

1648–53: The Fronde: resistance to royal authority throughout France

QING CHINA: 1644–1800

THE MANCHUS had already built a state along Chinese lines in southern Manchuria, based at Mukden, and were poised to take advantage of the Ming collapse in 1644. They swiftly suppressed the rebels and by the end of the 17th century had reduced Ming resistance in the south. The 18th century was a stable period of expansion and prosperity, as the Manchu, or Qing dynasty, adopted Chinese ways. Successive campaigns established an enormous empire and an array of tributary states, while regional uprisings were ruthlessly crushed. But by the 19th century the pressures of European imperial expansion and internal dissent on an unprecedented scale brought regression, isolationism, resistance to reform, and political decay.

Compare this map with a map of modern China?

What are the similarities and differences?

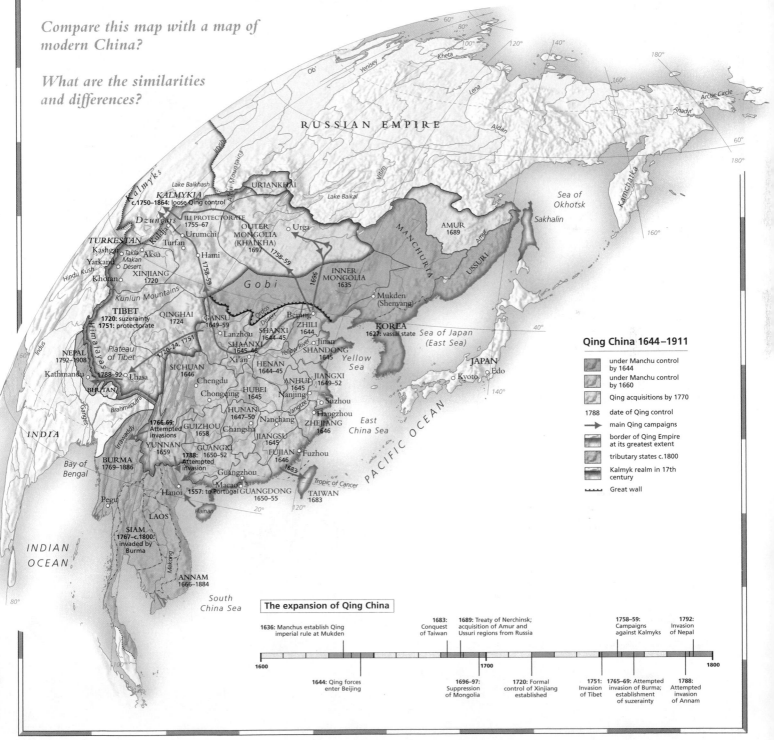

Qing China 1644–1911

- under Manchu control by 1644
- under Manchu control by 1660
- Qing acquisitions by 1770
- 1788 date of Qing control
- → main Qing campaigns
- border of Qing Empire at its greatest extent
- tributary states c.1800
- Kalmyk realm in 17th century
- ···· Great wall

The expansion of Qing China

1636: Manchus establish Qing imperial rule at Mukden

1683: Conquest of Taiwan

1689: Treaty of Nerchinsk; acquisition of Amur and Ussuri regions from Russia

1758–59: Campaigns against Kalmyks

1792: Invasion of Nepal

1600

1700

1800

1644: Qing forces enter Beijing

1696–97: Suppression of Mongolia

1720: Formal control of Xinjiang established

1751: Invasion of Tibet

1765–69: Attempted invasion of Burma; establishment of suzerainty

1788: Attempted invasion of Annam

THE WORLD SLAVE TRADE

THE USE OF SLAVES is endemic in most human societies. Between the 9th and 19th centuries Muslim merchants may have transported as many as 14 million slaves across the Sahara to destinations in the Middle East and the Indian Ocean. The establishment of European colonies between the 16th and 19th centuries saw the creation of a slave trade on an industrial scale. Between 1600 and 1800 over seven and a half million African slaves were shipped across the Atlantic.

What is the relationship between the trade in slaves and the trade in manufactured goods?

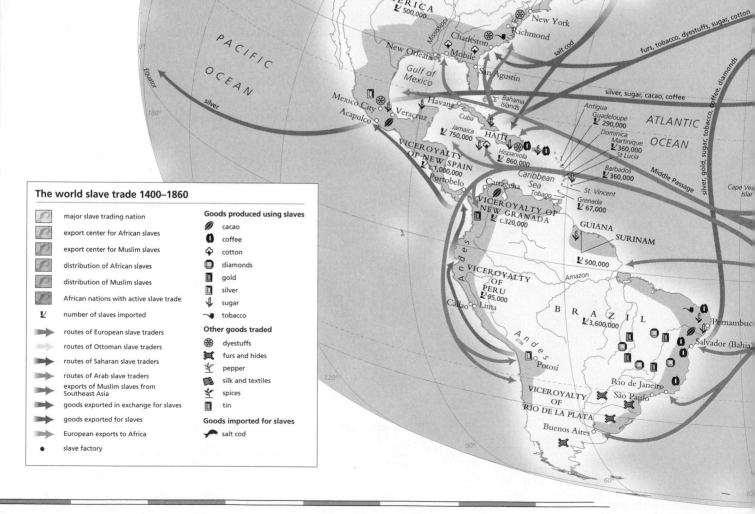

The world slave trade 1400–1860

	major slave trading nation
	export center for African slaves
	export center for Muslim slaves
	distribution of African slaves
	distribution of Muslim slaves
	African nations with active slave trade
⚓	number of slaves imported
➤	routes of European slave traders
➤	routes of Ottoman slave traders
➤	routes of Saharan slave traders
➤	routes of Arab slave traders
➤	exports of Muslim slaves from Southeast Asia
➤	goods exported in exchange for slaves
➤	goods exported for slaves
➤	European exports to Africa
●	slave factory

Goods produced using slaves

	cacao
	coffee
	cotton
	diamonds
	gold
	silver
	sugar
	tobacco

Other goods traded

⊕	dyestuffs
	furs and hides
	pepper
	silk and textiles
	spices
	tin

Goods imported for slaves

	salt cod

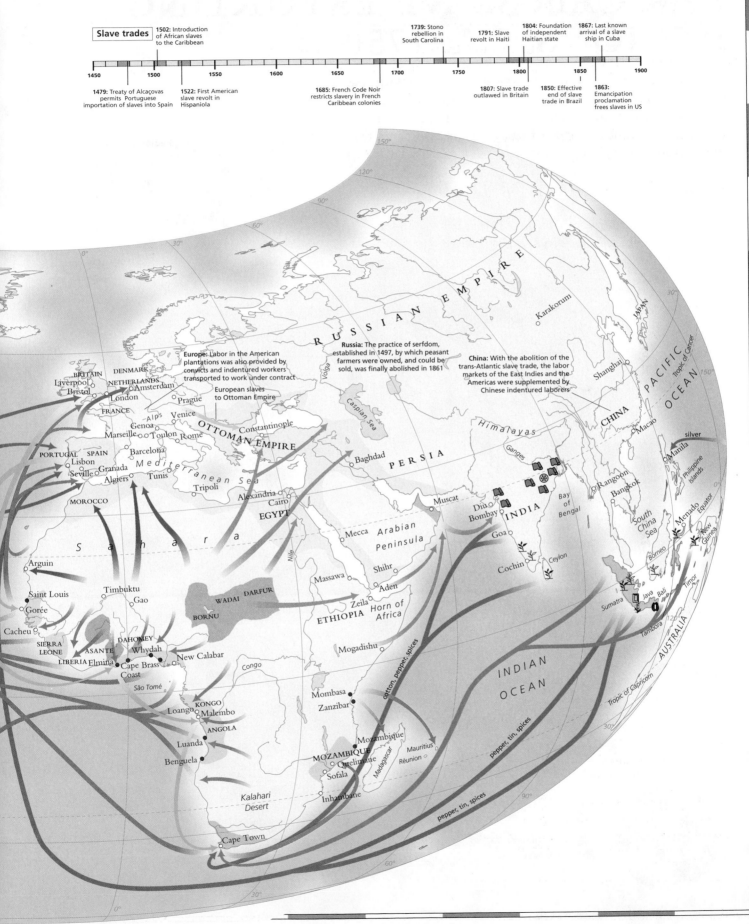

Slave trades

1479: Treaty of Alcaçovas permits Portuguese importation of slaves into Spain

1502: Introduction of African slaves to the Caribbean

1522: First American slave revolt in Hispaniola

1685: French Code Noir restricts slavery in French Caribbean colonies

1739: Stono rebellion in South Carolina

1791: Slave revolt in Haiti

1807: Slave trade outlawed in Britain

1804: Foundation of independent Haitian state

1850: Effective end of slave trade in Brazil

1867: Last known arrival of a slave ship in Cuba

1863: Emancipation proclamation frees slaves in US

1450 · 1500 · 1550 · 1600 · 1650 · 1700 · 1750 · 1800 · 1850 · 1900

Europe: Labor in the American plantations was also provided by convicts and indentured workers transported to work under contract

European slaves to Ottoman Empire

Russia: The practice of serfdom, established in 1497, by which peasant farmers were owned, and could be sold, was finally abolished in 1861

China: With the abolition of the trans-Atlantic slave trade, the labor markets of the East Indies and the Americas were supplemented by Chinese indentured laborers

RUSSIAN EMPIRE

Karakorum

JAPAN

Shanghai

CHINA

PACIFIC OCEAN

Tropic of Cancer

BRITAIN
Liverpool
Bristol
DENMARK
NETHERLANDS
Amsterdam
London
Prague
FRANCE
Alps
Venice
Genoa
Marseille
Toulon
Rome
Constantinople
OTTOMAN EMPIRE
PORTUGAL SPAIN
Lisbon
Granada
Seville
Barcelona
Algiers
Tunis
Tripoli
Mediterranean Sea
MOROCCO
Alexandria
Cairo
EGYPT

Baghdad
PERSIA
Himalayas
Ganges
Macao
Manila
silver
Philippine Islands
Rangoon
Bangkok
Muscat
Diu
Bombay
Goa
INDIA
Bay of Bengal
South China Sea
Menado
New Guinea
Equator

Caspian Sea

Volga

Nile

Sahara

Arguin

Saint Louis
Gorée
Timbuktu
Gao
WADAI DARFUR
BORNU
Mecca
Arabian Peninsula
Massawa
Shihr
Aden
Zeila
ETHIOPIA
Horn of Africa

Cochin
Ceylon

cotton, pepper, spices

Sumatra
Java
Bali
Timor
Borneo
Tambora
AUSTRALIA

Cacheu
SIERRA LEONE
LIBERIA
ASANTE
DAHOMEY
Whydah
Elmina
Cape Brass Coast
New Calabar
São Tomé
Congo
Mogadishu

Mombasa
Zanzibar

INDIAN OCEAN

KONGO
Loango
Malembo
ANGOLA
Luanda
Benguela

Mozambique
MOZAMBIQUE
Quelimane
Sofala
Madagascar
Réunion
Mauritius

pepper, tin, spices

Tropic of Capricorn

Kalahari Desert

Inhambane

pepper, tin, spices

Cape Town

AFRICAN SLAVE EXPORTING REGIONS, CA. 1750

ORIGINS OF AFRICAN SLAVES SENT TO THE AMERICAS.
Captive Africans came from the eight regions. West Central
Africa sent more captives to the Americas than any other
region. Overall, nearly 40% of enslaved Africans came from
this region.

*How does this map show the impact of the slave trade on
African societies?*

*How does it not reveal how enslaved Africans responded,
endured, and resisted captivity?*

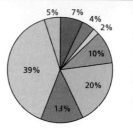

African Slave Exporting Regions, ca. 1750

- 5%
- 7%
- 4%
- 2%
- 10%
- 20%
- 13%
- 39%

- Senegambia
- Sierra Leone
- Windward Coast
- Gold Coast
- Bight of Benin
- Bight of Biafra
- West Central Africa
- Southeast Africa

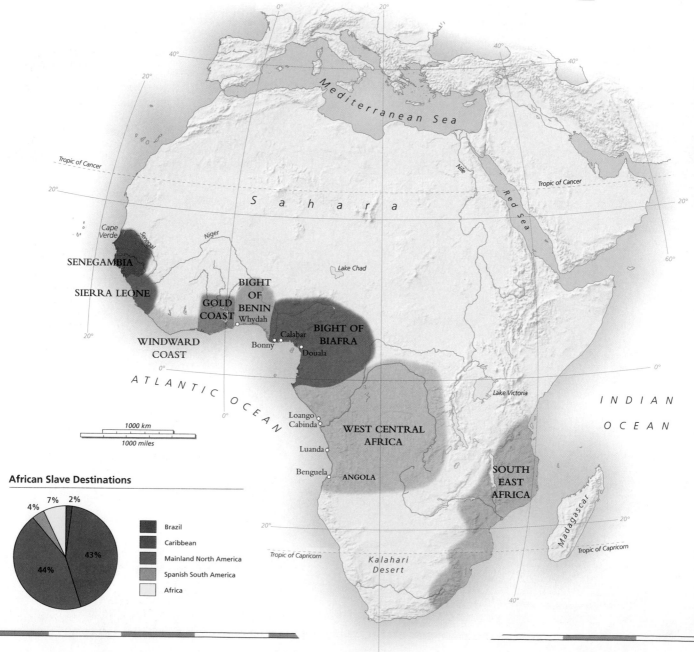

African Slave Destinations

- 4%
- 7%
- 2%
- 43%
- 44%

- Brazil
- Caribbean
- Mainland North America
- Spanish South America
- Africa

THE COLONIZATION OF NORTH AMERICA

FROM THE EARLY 17TH CENTURY, British, French, and Dutch migrants settled along the Atlantic seaboard and in the Gulf of St. Lawrence. As they grew in numbers, they displaced Native American peoples from their lands.

Why do you think that Native Americans had more conflicts with British colonists than with the French or Spanish?

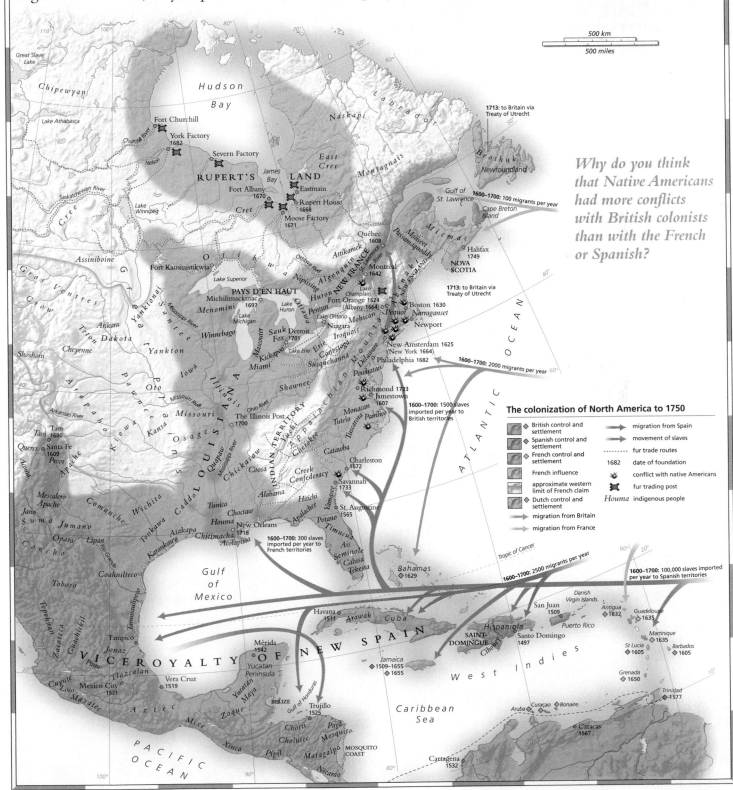

500 km
500 miles

1713: to Britain via Treaty of Utrecht

Great Slave Lake

Chipewyan

Hudson Bay

Lake Athabasca

Fort Churchill
York Factory 1682
Severn Factory

Churchill River
Nelson

Naskapi
Labrador

East Cree
Montagnais

Beothuk
Newfoundland

RUPERT'S LAND
James Bay
Fort Albany 1670
Eastmain
Rupert House 1668
Moose Factory 1671

Gulf of St. Lawrence
Cape Breton Island

1600–1700: 100 migrants per year

Cree
Assiniboine
Lake Winnipeg
Saskatchewan River

Gros Ventres
Crow
Arikara
Yanktonai
Santee
Teton Dakota
Cheyenne
Yankton
Shoshoni

Assiniboine

Fort Kaministikwia
Ojibwa
Lake Superior
Michilimackinac 1697
PAYS D'EN HAUT
Menomini
Winnebago
Lake Michigan

Québec 1608
Maliseet
Passamaquoddy
Attikamek
Micmac
Halifax 1749
NOVA SCOTIA

1713: to Britain via Treaty of Utrecht

Nipissing
Ottawa River
Algonquin
Huron **NEW FRANCE**
Montreal 1642
Lake Champlain
Fort Orange 1624 (Albany 1664)
Abenaki
NEW ENGLAND
Boston 1630
Pequot *Narraganset*
Newport

Sauk Detroit 1701
Fox
Mascoutec
Kickapoo
Miami
Lake Erie
Niagara
Lake Ontario
Mohican
Iroquois
Conestoga
Susquehanna
Delaware
Mountains

New Amsterdam 1625 (New York 1664)
Philadelphia 1682

1600–1700: 2000 migrants per year

Arapaho
Pawnee
Iowa
Oto
Illinois
Missouri
Kansa
Osage
Kiowa

The Illinois Post 1700
Shawnee
Ohio River
INDIAN TERRITORY
Yuchi
Powhatan
Monacan
Tutelo
Tuscarora
Pamlico
Richmond 1733
Jamestown 1607

1600–1700: 1500 slaves imported per year to British territories

Taos 1680
Quères
Santa Fe 1609
Pecos
Acoma
Apache
Mescalero Apache
Jano
Suma *Jumano*
Opata
Lipan
Cancho

Comanche
Wichita
Caddo
Quapaw
Chickasaw
Coosa
Catawba
Cherokee
Creek Confederacy
Charleston 1672
Alabama
Hitichi
Savannah 1733
Yamasee
St. Augustine 1565

1600–1700: 300 slaves imported per year to French territories

Tonkawa
Atakapa
Karankawa
Chitimacha
Acolapissa
Tunica
Choctaw
Houma
New Orleans 1718
Apalachee
Potano
Timucua
Ais
Seminole
Calusa
Tekesta

Bahamas 1629

Coahuilteco
Toboso

Tepehuan
Zacateca
Chichiquil
Jonaz
Cuyute
Loco
Mazatec
Tampico
Mérida 1542
VICEROYALTY OF NEW SPAIN
Vera Cruz
Mexico City 1519
1521
Tlazcalan
Aztec
Yucatán Peninsula
Zoque *Maya*
Mixe
Xinca
Pipil
BELIZE
Chorti
Cholutec
Paya
Mosquito
Matagalpa
MOSQUITO COAST
Nicarao
Gulf of Honduras
Trujillo 1525

Gulf of Mexico

1600–1700: 2500 migrants per year

Tropic of Cancer

1600–1700: 100,000 slaves imported per year to Spanish territories

Havana 1511
Arawak
Cuba
Jamaica 1509–1655
1655

Danish Virgin Islands
San Juan 1509
Ciboney
Santo Domingo 1497
SAINT-DOMINGUE
Hispaniola
Puerto Rico

Antigua 1632
Guadeloupe 1635
Martinique 1635
St Lucia 1605
Barbados 1605
Grenada 1650
Trinidad 1577

West Indies

Caribbean Sea

Aruba Curaçao Bonaire
Caracas 1567

Cartagena 1532

PACIFIC OCEAN

ATLANTIC OCEAN

The colonization of North America to 1750

British control and settlement	migration from Spain
Spanish control and settlement	movement of slaves
French control and settlement	fur trade routes
French influence	1682 date of foundation
approximate western limit of French claim	conflict with native Americans
Dutch control and settlement	fur trading post
migration from Britain	*Houma* indigenous people
migration from France	

ENLIGHTENMENT IN EUROPE: SUBSCRIPTIONS TO THE *ENCYCLOPEDIA*

SUBSCRIPTIONS TO THE ENCYCLOPEDIA. The largest publishing venture of eighteenth-century Europe, the *Encyclopedia: A Classified Dictionary of the Sciences, Arts, and Trades* by Denis Diderot (1713–1784) aimed to encapsulate all of human knowledge. It contained 60,000 illustrated articles. Its thirty-five volumes took more than thirty years to publish. The *Encyclopedia* profoundly affected the way Europeans viewed their world.

Which countries and cities were most affected by the ideas of the Encyclopedia?

Subscriptions to the Encyclopedia

- ■ 1–10
- ■ 11–50
- ■ 51–100
- ■ more than 100

SOUTH AND SOUTHEAST ASIA: 1765

EVEN AFTER THE COLLAPSE of the Mughal Empire in 1761, significant states stood in the path of Western colonial expansion in both India and Southeast Asia. In India, the foremost power was the Maratha Confederacy, while in Southeast Asia, Burma, Siam, and Vietnam expanded in size and strength.

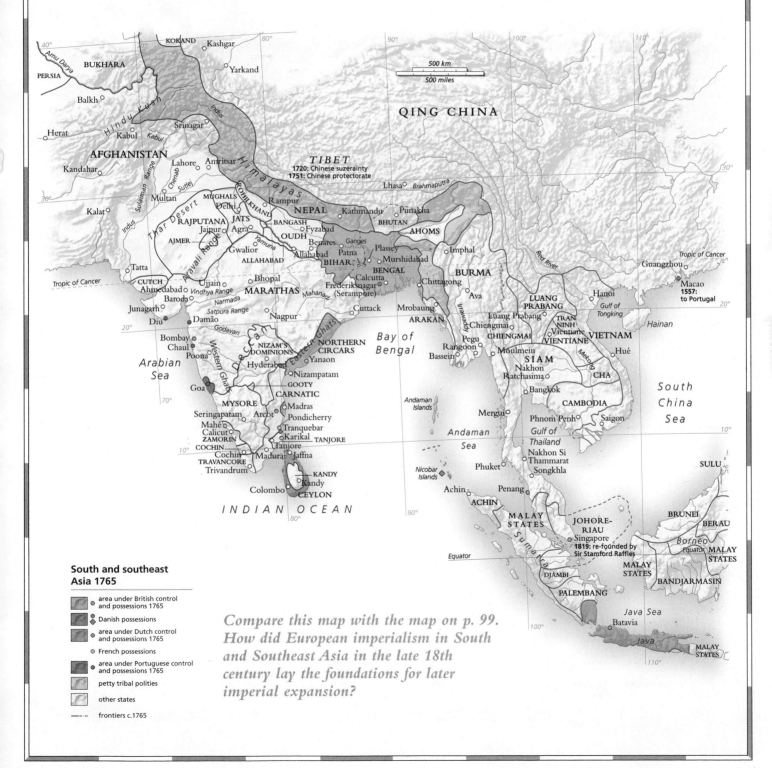

South and southeast Asia 1765

- area under British control and possessions 1765
- Danish possessions
- area under Dutch control and possessions 1765
- French possessions
- area under Portuguese control and possessions 1765
- petty tribal polities
- other states
- --- frontiers c.1765

Compare this map with the map on p. 99. How did European imperialism in South and Southeast Asia in the late 18th century lay the foundations for later imperial expansion?

AN ERA OF REVOLUTION

RAPID POPULATION GROWTH, the creation of the first industrial societies, the maturing of Europe's American colonies, and new ideas about statehood and freedom of the individual, combined to create an overwhelming demand for political change in the 18th century, most notably exemplified by the French Revolution of 1789. Uprisings and revolutions continued into the middle of the 19th century.

Does this map reveal any connections between revolution and empire?

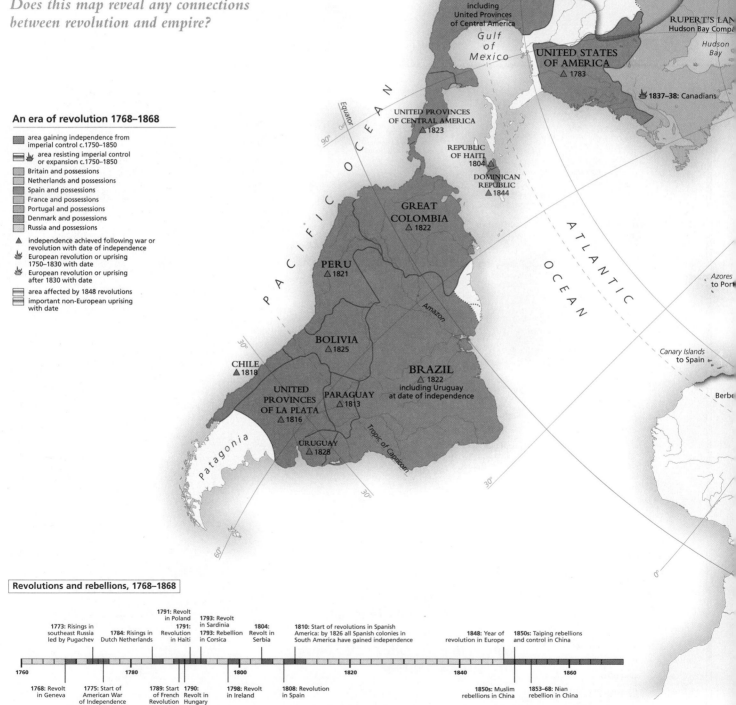

An era of revolution 1768–1868

- area gaining independence from imperial control c.1750–1850
- area resisting imperial control or expansion c.1750–1850
- Britain and possessions
- Netherlands and possessions
- Spain and possessions
- France and possessions
- Portugal and possessions
- Denmark and possessions
- Russia and possessions
- ▲ independence achieved following war or revolution with date of independence
- European revolution or uprising 1750–1830 with date
- European revolution or uprising after 1830 with date
- area affected by 1848 revolutions
- important non-European uprising with date

Map labels:

NORTH AMERICA
Plains Indians
RUPERT'S LAND — Hudson Bay Compa[ny]
Hudson Bay
MEXICO 1821 including United Provinces of Central America
Gulf of Mexico
UNITED STATES OF AMERICA ▲ 1783
1837–38: Canadians
UNITED PROVINCES OF CENTRAL AMERICA ▲ 1823
REPUBLIC OF HAITI 1804 ▲
DOMINICAN REPUBLIC ▲ 1844
GREAT COLOMBIA ▲ 1822
PERU ▲ 1821
Amazon
BOLIVIA ▲ 1825
CHILE ▲ 1818
BRAZIL ▲ 1822 including Uruguay at date of independence
UNITED PROVINCES OF LA PLATA ▲ 1816
PARAGUAY ▲ 1813
URUGUAY ▲ 1828
Patagonia
PACIFIC OCEAN
ATLANTIC OCEAN
Azores to Por[tugal]
Canary Islands to Spain
Berbe[ra]
Tropic of Cancer
Equator
Tropic of Capricorn

Revolutions and rebellions, 1768–1868

- 1768: Revolt in Geneva
- 1773: Risings in southeast Russia led by Pugachev
- 1775: Start of American War of Independence
- 1784: Risings in Dutch Netherlands
- 1789: Start of French Revolution
- 1790: Revolt in Hungary
- 1791: Revolt in Poland
- 1791: Revolution in Haiti
- 1793: Revolt in Sardinia
- 1793: Rebellion in Corsica
- 1798: Revolt in Ireland
- 1804: Revolt in Serbia
- 1808: Revolution in Spain
- 1810: Start of revolutions in Spanish America: by 1826 all Spanish colonies in South America have gained independence
- 1848: Year of revolution in Europe
- 1850s: Muslim rebellions in China
- 1850s: Taiping rebellions and control in China
- 1853–68: Nian rebellion in China

Timeline: 1760 — 1780 — 1800 — 1820 — 1840 — 1860

ALASKA

Arctic Circle

Greenland

ARCTIC OCEAN

Iceland

Siberia

JAPAN

KOREA

Yellow Sea

RUSSIAN EMPIRE

Tropic of Cancer

DUTCH
NETHERLANDS

NORWAY

1853–68:
Nian rebellion

1853–63:
Taiping
rebellion

1863–73: Northwest
Muslim revolts

*Philippine
Islands*

local
tribes

Equator

ELAND
1798

BRITAIN

DENMARK

POLAND
1791,
1830–31

1825: Decembrist
uprising

QING EMPIRE

HONG KONG
1842: to Britain

Macao

UM
7
1

1784

HOLY
ROMAN
EMPIRE

1831: Ostrolenka

1850–53:
Taiping advance

Jiantian
1850: Beginning of
Taiping rebellion

FRANCE
1789,
1830

*South
China
Sea*

UGAL
21

1821

HUNGARY
1790
1848–49

1773–74: Pugachev's
and Cossack revolt

Kazakhs
and
Turkmen

1855–73: Yunnan
Muslim rising

SPAIN
1808,
1820–23

Corsica
1793

1793, 1821

SARDINIA

SERBIA
1804

1840–60:
Circassians

1834–59: Shamil

Shan Tribes

Celebes

PORTUGUESE
TIMOR

ALGERIA
1832–47:
Abd-el Kader

SICILY
1820–21
GREECE
1830

Nepal

Chandernagore

1844–50:
Babism

Pashtun

*Bay
of
Bengal*

*Gulf
of
Siam*

Borneo

Timor

OTTOMAN EMPIRE

PERSIA

Nile

1857–59:
The Mutiny

Dayaks

Flores

DUTCH POSSESSIONS AND DEPENDENCIES

AFRICA

Wahhabis

*Arabian
Peninsula*

INDIA

Diu
Damão

Yanaon

*Arabian
Sea*

Nicobar Islands
to Denmark

Sumba

Goa

Pondicherry
Karikal

Achin

Mahé

Ceylon

Sumatra

INDIAN OCEAN

Equator

1825–30:
Dipo Negoro

Java

THE NAPOLEONIC EMPIRE

THE BRILLIANT revolutionary general Napoleon Bonaparte in 1799 staged a coup d'etat which made him ruler of France. In 1804, just ten years after revolutionaries had executed Louis XVI, Napoleon took the title of emperor and began to create a dynasty. His imperial ambitions were ultimately thwarted by Britain: its navy blockaded France and overran French colonies, while a series of alliances completed an encirclement that contained and eventually defeated Napoleon.

What role did geography play in the downfall of Napoleon's empire?

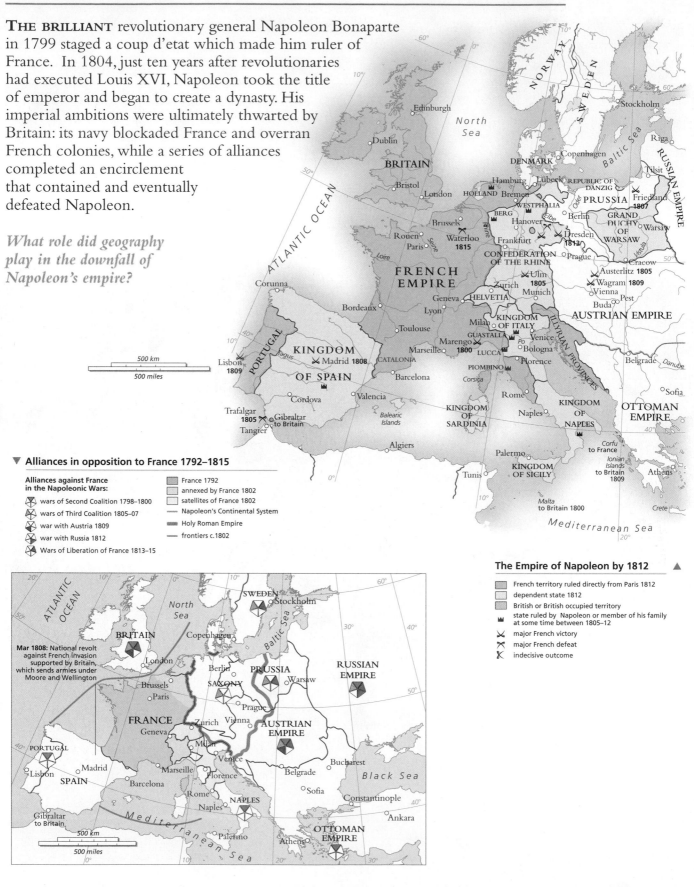

Alliances in opposition to France 1792–1815

Alliances against France in the Napoleonic Wars:

- wars of Second Coalition 1798–1800
- wars of Third Coalition 1805–07
- war with Austria 1809
- war with Russia 1812
- Wars of Liberation of France 1813–15

- France 1792
- annexed by France 1802
- satellites of France 1802
- Napoleon's Continental System
- Holy Roman Empire
- frontiers c.1802

The Empire of Napoleon by 1812

- French territory ruled directly from Paris 1812
- dependent state 1812
- British or British occupied territory
- state ruled by Napoleon or member of his family at some time between 1805–12
- major French victory
- major French defeat
- indecisive outcome

Mar 1808: National revolt against French invasion supported by Britain, which sends armies under Moore and Wellington

EUROPE AFTER THE CONGRESS OF VIENNA: 1815–1852

TO RESTORE STABLITY after the turmoil of the Napoleonic wars, the Congress of Vienna redrew the political map of Europe and restored many former ruling houses. The result was three decades of reactionary rule, during which nationalist and republican movements challenged the status quo.

Europe after the Congress of Vienna 1815–1852

- small German states
- German Confederation
- threat to Vienna System 1817–39
- revolution in 1848–49
- frontiers 1815

NORWAY
1814: Denmark forced to cede Norway to Sweden

SWEDEN
Stockholm

Helsingfors

St. Petersburg

SCOTLAND
Edinburgh

North Sea

Riga

Moscow

IRELAND
1822–29: Catholic Emancipation campaign

BRITAIN
Dublin

ENGLAND
WALES

DENMARK
Copenhagen
Bornholm

RUSSIAN EMPIRE

1830–32: First Reform Act crisis

1840s: Chartist agitation

Amsterdam

SCHLESWIG-HOLSTEIN

Hamburg

HANOVER
Hanover

1817–31: German student protests

EAST PRUSSIA
Danzig

London

1831: Belgium gains independence from United Netherlands

Brussels

PRUSSIA
Cologne

Berlin

Posen

Warsaw

POLAND

Brest-Litovsk

UNITED NETHERLANDS

SAXONY

PRUSSIA

Vistula

1830–31: national revolt

Kiev

ATLANTIC OCEAN

1830: Revolution
Paris

Prague

BAVARIA

Cracow

REP. OF CRACOW
1847: to Austria

1847: Peasant uprising

1831: Vendean uprising

FRANCE

Jan–Mar 1848: Fighting at the barricades

Stuttgart
WÜRTTEMBERG

GALICIA

Bay of Biscay

Bordeaux

PR. OF NEUCHÂTEL

BADEN

BAVARIA
Munich

Vienna

Dniester

Odessa

Lyon

Geneva

SWITZERLAND

1847–48: Swiss Civil War

AUSTRIAN EMPIRE

Buda Pest

HUNGARY

TRANSYLVANIA

MOLDAVIA

1829: to Russia

Sebastopol

Oporto
1820: Revolution in Portugal against British control of country

1833–39: First Carlist War

Marseille

SARDINIA

LOMBARDY-VENETIA
Milan

1821: Piedmontese revolution

PARMA

Venice

ILLYRIAN KINGDOM

DALMATIA

MILITARY FRONTIER

1807–33: Serbian revolts

Belgrade

WALLACHIA

Bucharest

1821: Revolts in Wallachia and Moldavia

ANDORRA

1820: Revolution
Madrid

Barcelona

MONACO

MODENA

MASSA AND CARRARA

SAN MARINO

BOSNIA

SERBIA

Danube

Black Sea

BULGARIA

SPAIN
1846–48: Second Carlist War

LUCCA

TUSCANY

PAPAL STATES

Corsica

Rome

MONTENEGRO

RUMELIA

Balearic Islands

SARDINIA

1820: Revolution
Naples

ALBANIA

OTTOMAN EMPIRE

THRACE

Constantinople

GIBRALTAR to Britain

Palermo

1821: Revolution

KINGDOM OF THE TWO SICILIES

Corfu
1815: to Britain

GREECE

Salonica

1821–33: War of Independence

Smyrna

ANATOLIA

Mediterranean Sea

Ionian Islands
1815: to Britain

Athens

Malta
1800: to Britain

Crete

Cyprus

Compare this map with the map on page 96.

How did the Congress of Vienna alter the borders of European states?

400 km

400 miles

INDUSTRIAL DEVELOPMENT IN EUROPE: 1850–1914

IN THE 18TH AND 19TH CENTURIES, technological, social, and economic changes transformed Europe into an urban, industrial society.

By 1914, which regions of Europe were the most industrialized? Which regions were the least industrialized?

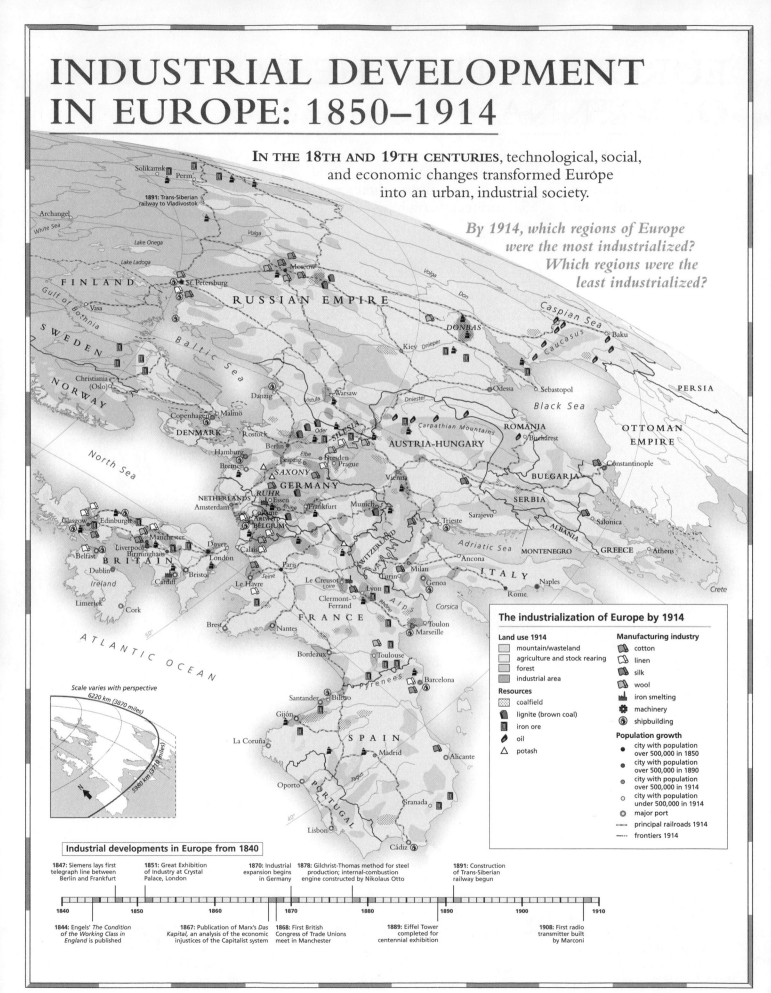

The industrialization of Europe by 1914

Land use 1914
- mountain/wasteland
- agriculture and stock rearing
- forest
- industrial area

Resources
- coalfield
- lignite (brown coal)
- iron ore
- oil
- potash

Manufacturing industry
- cotton
- linen
- silk
- wool
- iron smelting
- machinery
- shipbuilding

Population growth
- city with population over 500,000 in 1850
- city with population over 500,000 in 1890
- city with population over 500,000 in 1914
- city with population under 500,000 in 1914
- major port
- principal railroads 1914
- frontiers 1914

Industrial developments in Europe from 1840

1847: Siemens lays first telegraph line between Berlin and Frankfurt

1851: Great Exhibition of Industry at Crystal Palace, London

1870: Industrial expansion begins in Germany

1878: Gilchrist-Thomas method for steel production; internal-combustion engine constructed by Nikolaus Otto

1891: Construction of Trans-Siberian railway begun

| 1840 | 1850 | 1860 | 1870 | 1880 | 1890 | 1900 | 1910 |

1844: Engels' *The Condition of the Working Class in England* is published

1867: Publication of Marx's *Das Kapital*, an analysis of the economic injustices of the Capitalist system

1868: First British Congress of Trade Unions meet in Manchester

1889: Eiffel Tower completed for centennial exhibition

1908: First radio transmitter built by Marconi

FOREIGN IMPERIALISM IN EAST ASIA

THE RAPIDLY EXPANDING Qing economy of the 18th century made it prey to foreign ambitions. The dynasty's failure in the Opium War of 1839–42 revealed its weaknesses. Hong Kong was the first of many territorial and trading concessions which gave not only the Europeans but the Japanese valuable toeholds.

In what ways did foreign influence in Qing China weaken its stability?

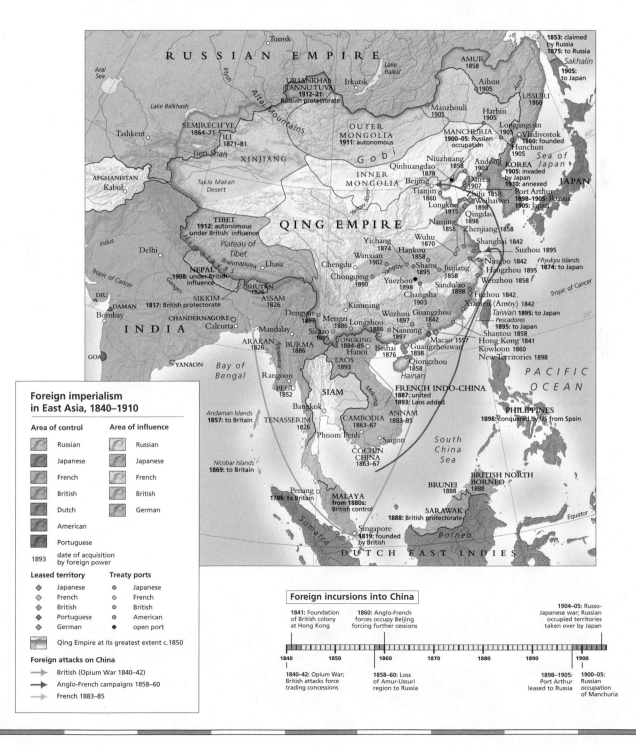

Foreign imperialism in East Asia, 1840–1910

Area of control
- Russian
- Japanese
- French
- British
- Dutch
- American
- Portuguese

Area of influence
- Russian
- Japanese
- French
- British
- German

1893 date of acquisition by foreign power

Leased territory
- Japanese
- French
- British
- Portuguese
- German

Treaty ports
- Japanese
- French
- British
- American
- open port

Qing Empire at its greatest extent c.1850

Foreign attacks on China
- British (Opium War 1840–42)
- Anglo-French campaigns 1858–60
- French 1883–85

Foreign incursions into China

1841: Foundation of British colony at Hong Kong

1860: Anglo-French forces occupy Beijing forcing further cessions

1904–05: Russo-Japanese war; Russian occupied territories taken over by Japan

1840–42: Opium War; British attacks force trading concessions

1858–60: Loss of Amur-Ussuri region to Russia

1898–1905: Port Arthur leased to Russia

1900–05: Russian occupation of Manchuria

1840 1850 1860 1870 1880 1890 1900

IMPERIALISM IN THE PACIFIC

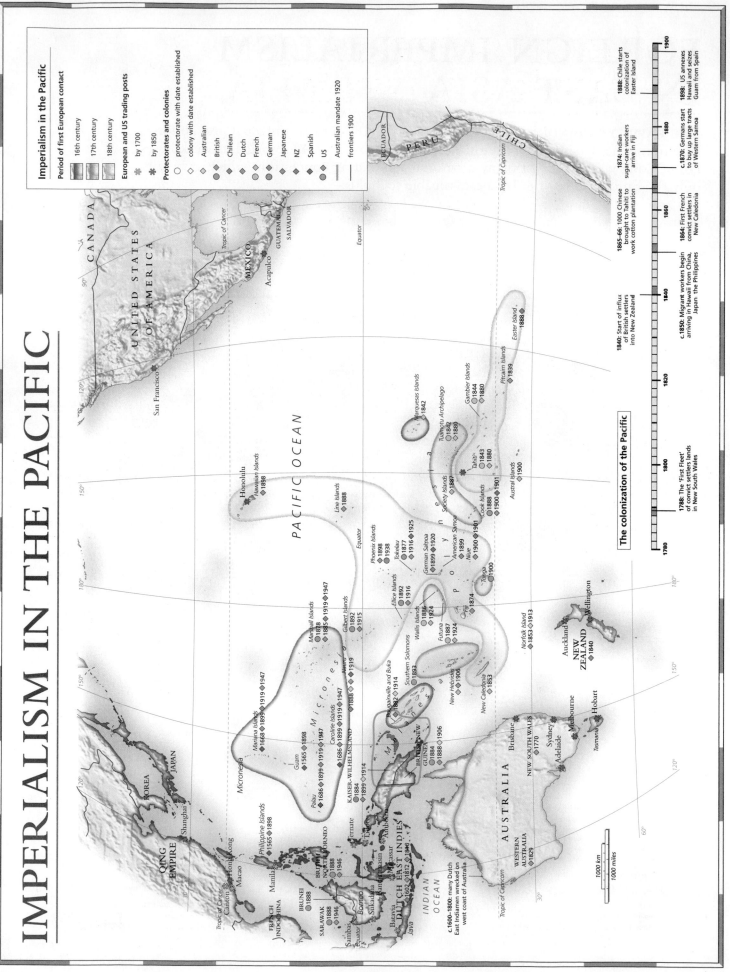

EARLY EUROPEAN IMPACT IN AUSTRALIA

THE 19TH CENTURY WITNESSED the near annihilation of many Pacific island societies, as European and American powers extended their rule. The British colonies of Australia and New Zealand rank with the US as the most successful transplantations of European culture to another continent; however in doing so, the Aborigines of Australia and the Maori of New Zealand were brutally subjugated.

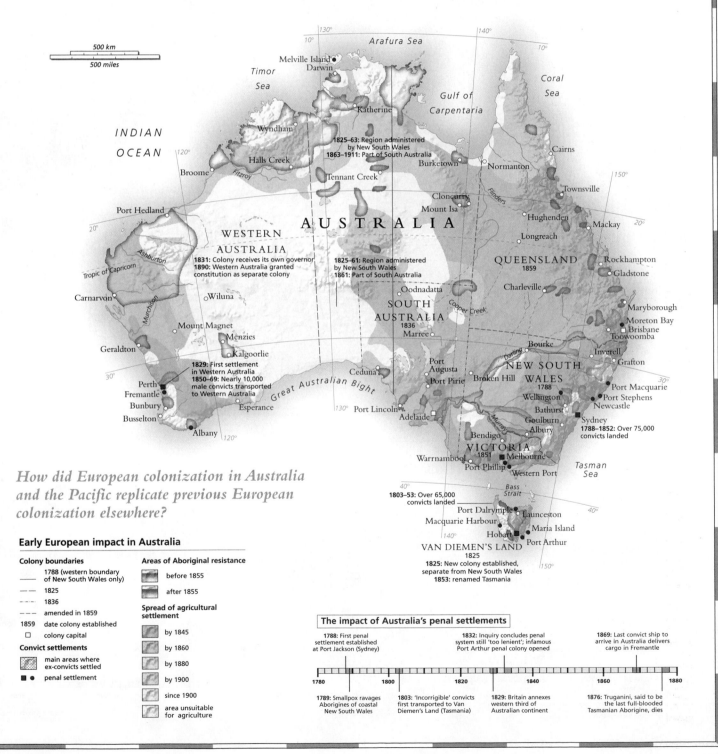

How did European colonization in Australia and the Pacific replicate previous European colonization elsewhere?

Early European impact in Australia

Colony boundaries

———	1788 (western boundary of New South Wales only)
– – –	1825
–·–·–	1836
– – – –	amended in 1859
1859	date colony established
▢	colony capital

Convict settlements

▨	main areas where ex-convicts settled
■ ●	penal settlement

Areas of Aboriginal resistance

▨	before 1855
▨	after 1855

Spread of agricultural settlement

▨	by 1845
▨	by 1860
▨	by 1880
▨	by 1900
▨	since 1900
▨	area unsuitable for agriculture

The impact of Australia's penal settlements

1788: First penal settlement established at Port Jackson (Sydney)

1832: Inquiry concludes penal system still 'too lenient'; infamous Port Arthur penal colony opened

1869: Last convict ship to arrive in Australia delivers cargo in Fremantle

1780 — 1800 — 1820 — 1840 — 1860 — 1880

1789: Smallpox ravages Aborigines of coastal New South Wales

1803: 'Incorrigible' convicts first transported to Van Diemen's Land (Tasmania)

1829: Britain annexes western third of Australian continent

1876: Truganini, said to be the last full-blooded Tasmanian Aborigine, dies

THE WORLD: 1800–1850

THE AFTERMATH of the French and American revolutions and the Napoleonic wars led to new nationalism and demands for democacy and freedom. There were mass movements of peoples to expanding cities or to new lives abroad. Hunger for raw materials to feed industry and the desire to dominate world markets soon led to unprecedented colonial expansion.

North America

1819: Parts of Spanish Florida conquered by US

1836: Texans rebel against Mexican rule and declare Republic of Texas

1849: Californian Gold Rush

1800 — 1810 — 1820 — 1830 — 1840 — 1850

1803: France sells territory between Mississippi and Rockies in Louisiana Purchase

1821: Mexico gains independence from Spanish colonists

1846–48: US victory in war with Mexico which cedes New Mexico and California to US

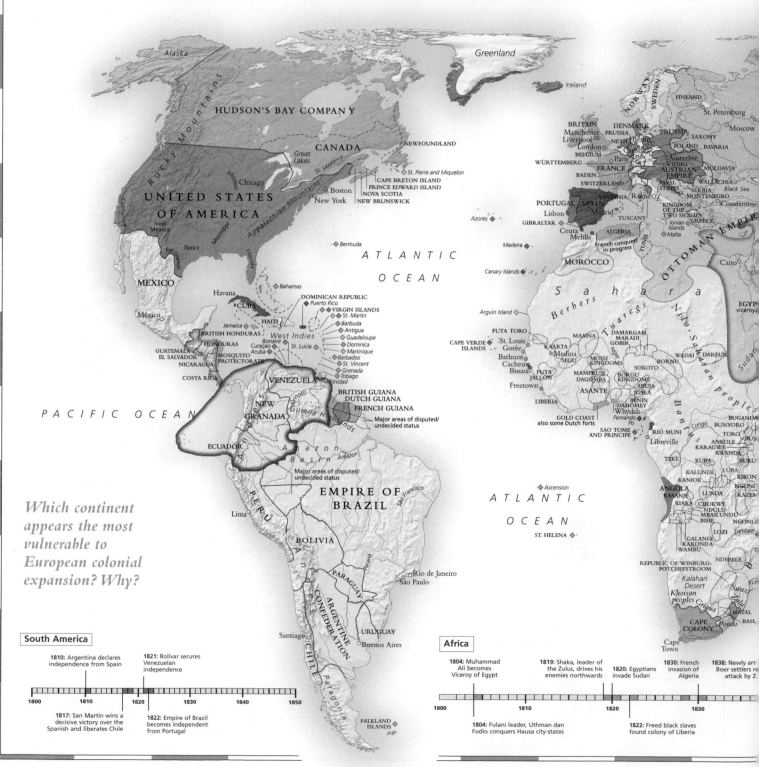

Which continent appears the most vulnerable to European colonial expansion? Why?

South America

1810: Argentina declares independence from Spain

1821: Bolivar secures Venezuelan independence

1800 — 1810 — 1820 — 1830 — 1840 — 1850

1817: San Martín wins a decisive victory over the Spanish and liberates Chile

1822: Empire of Brazil becomes independent from Portugal

Africa

1804: Muhammad Ali becomes Viceroy of Egypt

1819: Shaka, leader of the Zulus, drives his enemies northwards

1820: Egyptians invade Sudan

1830: French invasion of Algeria

1838: Newly arr Boer settlers r attack by Z

1800 — 1810 — 1820 — 1830

1804: Fulani leader, Uthman dan Fodio conquers Hausa city-states

1822: Freed black slaves found colony of Liberia

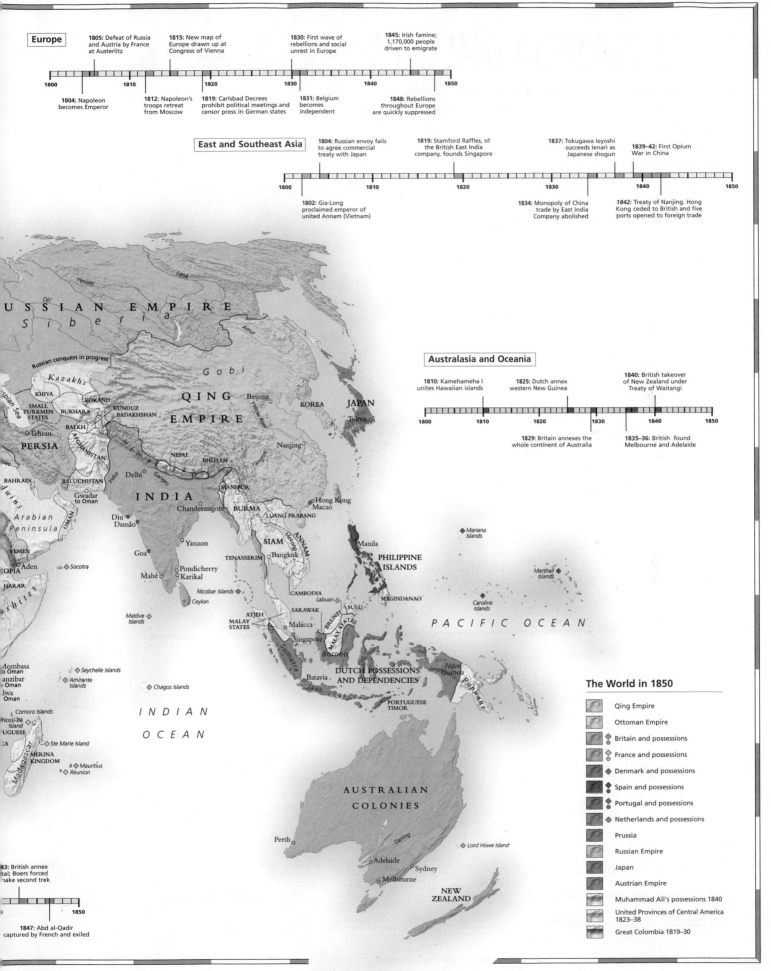

1805: Defeat of Russia and Austria by France at Austerlitz

1815: New map of Europe drawn up at Congress of Vienna

1830: First wave of rebellions and social unrest in Europe

1845: Irish famine; 1,170,000 people driven to emigrate

1800 1810 1820 1830 1840 1850

1804: Napoleon becomes Emperor

1812: Napoleon's troops retreat from Moscow

1819: Carlsbad Decrees prohibit political meetings and censor press in German states

1831: Belgium becomes independent

1848: Rebellions throughout Europe are quickly suppressed

East and Southeast Asia

1804: Russian envoy fails to agree commercial treaty with Japan

1819: Stamford Raffles, of the British East India company, founds Singapore

1837: Tokugawa Ieyoshi succeeds Ienari as Japanese shogun

1839–42: First Opium War in China

1800 1810 1820 1830 1840 1850

1802: Gia-Long proclaimed emperor of united Annam (Vietnam)

1834: Monopoly of China trade by East India Company abolished

1842: Treaty of Nanjing. Hong Kong ceded to British and five ports opened to foreign trade

Australasia and Oceania

1810: Kamehameha I unites Hawaiian islands

1825: Dutch annex western New Guinea

1840: British takeover of New Zealand under Treaty of Waitangi

1800 1810 1820 1830 1840 1850

1829: Britain annexes the whole continent of Australia

1835–36: British found Melbourne and Adelaide

43: British annex tal; Boers forced nake second trek

1850

1847: Abd al-Qadir captured by French and exiled

The World in 1850

- Qing Empire
- Ottoman Empire
- Britain and possessions
- France and possessions
- Denmark and possessions
- Spain and possessions
- Portugal and possessions
- Netherlands and possessions
- Prussia
- Russian Empire
- Japan
- Austrian Empire
- Muhammad Ali's possessions 1840
- United Provinces of Central America 1823–38
- Great Colombia 1819–30

103

NORTH AMERICA: 1783–1905

THE LOUISIANA PURCHASE of 1803 added to the US a huge swath of western lands formerly controlled by France. Settlers poured into the Great Plains, the Pacific Northwest, and the periphery of the Republic of Mexico, including California and Texas. The settlement of the West was met with serious armed resistance from Native Americans. Elsewhere, the nations of central America achieved independence beginning in the 1820s, though greatly weakened from their former colonial status.

What effect did US expansion have on the native peoples and ecosystems of the American West?

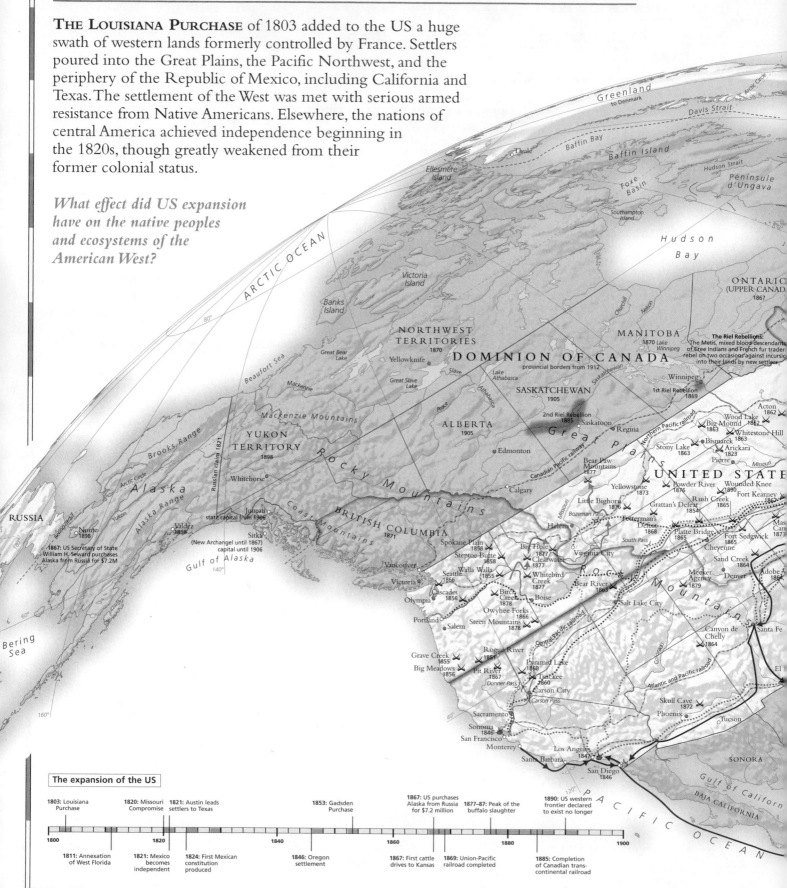

The Riel Rebellions:
The Metis, mixed blood descendants of Cree Indians and French fur trader rebel on two occasions against incursions into their lands by new settlers

The expansion of the US

1803: Louisiana Purchase

1820: Missouri Compromise

1821: Austin leads settlers to Texas

1853: Gadsden Purchase

1867: US purchases Alaska from Russia for $7.2 million

1877–87: Peak of the buffalo slaughter

1890: US western frontier declared to exist no longer

1800 | 1820 | 1840 | 1860 | 1880 | 1900

1811: Annexation of West Florida

1821: Mexico becomes independent

1824: First Mexican constitution produced

1846: Oregon settlement

1867: First cattle drives to Kansas

1869: Union-Pacific railroad completed

1885: Completion of Canadian transcontinental railroad

North America 1783–1905: struggles for nationhood and the seizing of the West

European settlement in the US and Canada

- extent of Russian claim 1821–24
- northern frontier of Mexico 1821
- Mexican territory 1821–23, United Provinces of Central America 1823–38
- Mexico after 1854
- Alaska Purchase 1867
- Canada at the creation of the Dominion, 1867
- Canadian territory 1880 with dates of provincial incorporation
- Canadian territory added in 1905

Conflicts between natives and settlers

- "Trail of Tears" removal of the southern tribes
- flight of the Nez Percé
- local wars 1783–1850
- Creek War 1813–14
- Seminole Wars 1816–58
- battles for the West 1850–1890

International conflicts

- War of 1812
- Texas Revolution 1835–36
- US victory: US-Mexican War 1846–48
- Mexican victory: US-Mexican War 1846–48
- Riel rebellions 1869–1885

Texas Revolution 1835–36

- routes of Santa Ana

The US-Mexican War 1846–48

- movement of US forces
- movement of Mexican forces

Wagon trails

- Oregon Trail
- Mormon Trail
- Central Overland Trail
- Southern Overland Trail
- Santa Fe Trail
- Old Spanish Trail
- California Trail
- Chisholm Trail
- Bozeman Trail

- □ country capital
- ● state/province capital
- 1804 date of independence
- railroad
- Pony Express route

Scale varies with perspective

8770 km (5450 miles)

12,230 km (7600 miles)

Texas Revolution 1835–36:
US settlers in Mexican province of Texas rebel, declaring independence from Mexico and driving out troops – led by General Santa Ana – sent in to quell the uprising

The US-Mexican War 1846–48:
Admission of Texas to the US in 1845 leads to war with Mexico. US quickly wins California and by 1848, Mexico has ceded 33% of its US territory for a fee of $15M

Labrador Sea

NEWFOUNDLAND
Newfoundland to France
ST PIERRE AND MIQUELON
Gulf of St Lawrence
PRINCE EDWARD ISLAND 1873
Charlottetown
NOVA SCOTIA 1867
NEW BRUNSWICK 1867
Fredericton
Halifax

QUEBEC (LOWER CANADA) 1867
Quebec
Montreal
Fort William
Ottawa
Sudbury
ault Ste Marie
Lake Superior
Battle of the Thames 1813
Toronto
Fort Niagara 1812
Buffalo 1812
Lake Huron
Lake Erie 1813
Detroit
Fallen Timbers 1794
Lansing
Lake Michigan
Chicago
Fort Dearborn 1812
Columbus
St. Clair's Defeat 1791
Cincinnati
Madison
Indianapolis
Frankfort
Stillman's Defeat 1812
Tippecanoe 1811
Louisville
Knoxville
Nauvoo
Springfield
St. Louis
Nashville
Jefferson City
AMERICA
Independence
Topeka
Chustenahlah 1861
Memphis
Little Rock
Vicksburg
Jackson
Bird Creek 1861
oked Creek 1861
Washita 1868
Wichita Village 1858
Shreveport
Soldier Spring 1868
McClellan Creek 1872
Duro yon
REPUBLIC OF TEXAS
1836: independent
1845: annexed by US
Houston
Dove Creek 1865
The Alamo 1836
Austin
San Antonio 1835: Capture of Correo Mexicano
(San Antonio de Béxar)
Coleto Creek 1836
Goliad Massacre 1836
Corpus Christi
Invincible disables Montezuma
Camargo
Matamoros
COAHUILA
NUEVO LEÓN
Monterrey
IHUAHUA
Chihuahua 1847
MEXICO
1821: monarchy
1822: empire
1824: federal republic
1863–67: empire
from 1824: federal republic
DURANGO
SINALOA
Mazatlán
US Navy via Cape Horn

Montpelier
Concord
Boston
Plattsburg 1813
Albany
Providence
Hartford
New York City
Trenton
Philadelphia
Harrisburg
Dover
Baltimore 1814
Annapolis 1814
Washington (DC from 1878) 1814
Richmond
Cleveland
Raleigh
Charleston
Columbia
Atlanta
Etowah 1793
Savannah
Tallasahatchee 1813
Enotachopco Creek 1814
Emuckfaw 1814
Fowltown 1817
Montgomery
Tallahassee
Burnt Corn Creek 1813
Gaine's Battle 1836
St. Marks 1818
Fort Minas 1813
Pensacola 1818
Osceola's Capture 1837
Fort Mellon 1837
Taylor's Battle
Dade's Battle 1835
Colee Hammock 1842
Big Cypress Swamp 1855–58
New Orleans 1814
Baton Rouge
Mobile
Jacksonville

ATLANTIC OCEAN

Tropic of Cancer

BAHAMAS *to Britain*
1783: recognised by Spain

PUERTO RICO 1898: to US from Spain
GUADELOUPE *to France*
DOMINICAN REPUBLIC 1844
Santo Domingo
DOMINICA *to Britain*
MARTINIQUE *to France*

CUBA
until 1898: to Spain
1898–1903: US occupation
Havana
HAITI 1804

JAMAICA *to Britain*
Kingston

Gulf of Mexico

Caribbean Sea

YUCATÁN
1841–43, 1846–48: independent
BRITISH HONDURAS
1859: to Britain
MOSQUITO COAST *to Britain*
1860: to Honduras
1860: to Nicaragua
HONDURAS 1838
Tegucigalpa
NICARAGUA 1838
Managua
GUATEMALA 1838
Guatemala City
EL SALVADOR 1838
San Salvador
COSTA RICA 1838
San José
PANAMA 1903

Buena Vista 1847
Saltillo
TAMAULIPAS
Tampico 1835
SAN LUIS POTOSÍ
San Luis Potosí
Zacatecas 1835
ZACATECAS
QUERÉTARO
GUANAJUATO
Cerro Gordo
VERACRUZ
Veracruz 1847
TABASCO
CHIAPAS
SOCONUSCO
TLAXCALA
Mexico City 1847
OAXACA
MICHOACÁN
PUEBLA
JALISCO
COLIMA

PACIFIC OCEAN

THE SCRAMBLE FOR AFRICA

THE RACE FOR EUROPEAN political control of Africa began in the early 1880s. In most cases, control was directly imposed by conquest. By 1914, Africa was fully partitioned along lines that bore little relations to cultural or linguistic traditions.

Why did European imperialism in Africa intensify in the late 19th century?

Imperialism in Africa, 1880–1920

Territory controlled by European nations by 1914

- Belgium
- Britain
- France
- Germany
- Italy
- Portugal
- Spain
- nominally Ottoman, under British control
- 1882 date of taking control
- — borders in 1914

Important mineral deposits

- coal
- copper
- diamonds
- gold

Scale varies with perspective

8200 km (5100 miles)

7000 km (4350 miles)

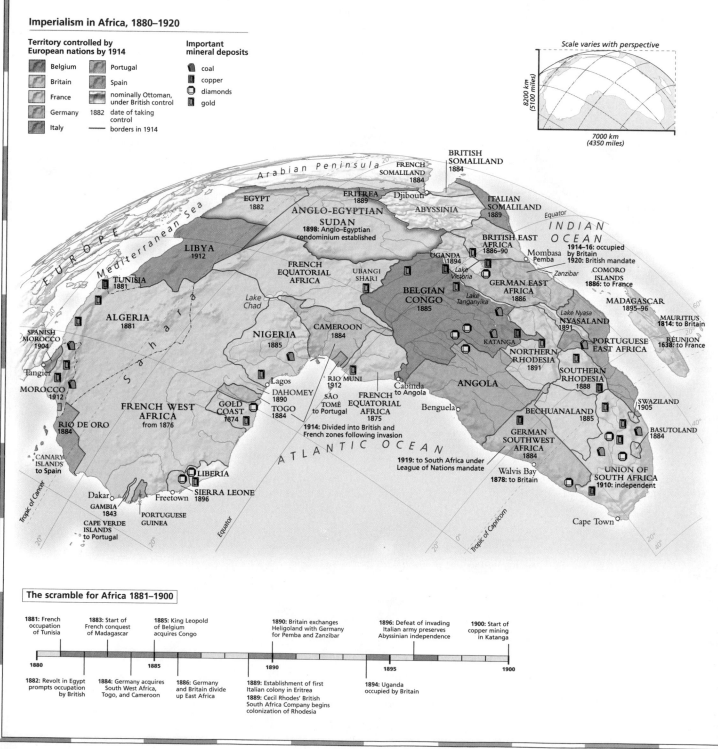

BRITISH SOMALILAND 1884
FRENCH SOMALILAND 1884
Arabian Peninsula
EGYPT 1882
ERITREA 1889
Djibouti
ITALIAN SOMALILAND 1889
ABYSSINIA
INDIAN OCEAN
Mediterranean Sea
ANGLO-EGYPTIAN SUDAN
1898: Anglo–Egyptian condominium established
LIBYA 1912
BRITISH EAST AFRICA 1886–90
1914–16: occupied by Britain
1920: British mandate
Mombasa
Pemba
UGANDA 1894
Lake Victoria
Zanzibar
COMORO ISLANDS 1886: to France
FRENCH EQUATORIAL AFRICA
UBANGI SHARI
BELGIAN CONGO 1885
GERMAN EAST AFRICA 1886
Lake Tanganyika
TUNISIA 1881
MADAGASCAR 1895–96
MAURITIUS 1814: to Britain
Lake Chad
Lake Nyasa
NYASALAND 1891
RÉUNION 1638: to France
ALGERIA 1881
CAMEROON 1884
NIGERIA 1885
KATANGA
NORTHERN RHODESIA 1891
PORTUGUESE EAST AFRICA
SPANISH MOROCCO 1904
Tangier
RIO MUNI 1912
Cabinda to Angola
ANGOLA
SOUTHERN RHODESIA 1888
MOROCCO 1912
Lagos
DAHOMEY 1890
SÃO TOMÉ to Portugal
FRENCH EQUATORIAL AFRICA 1875
Benguela
SWAZILAND 1905
FRENCH WEST AFRICA from 1876
GOLD COAST 1874
TOGO 1884
1914: Divided into British and French zones following invasion
BECHUANALAND 1885
BASUTOLAND 1884
RIO DE ORO 1884
GERMAN SOUTHWEST AFRICA 1884
1919: to South Africa under League of Nations mandate
CANARY ISLANDS to Spain
ATLANTIC OCEAN
Walvis Bay **1878:** to Britain
UNION OF SOUTH AFRICA **1910:** independent
Dakar
LIBERIA
SIERRA LEONE 1896
Freetown
GAMBIA 1843
PORTUGUESE GUINEA
CAPE VERDE ISLANDS to Portugal
Cape Town

The scramble for Africa 1881–1900

1881: French occupation of Tunisia

1883: Start of French conquest of Madagascar

1885: King Leopold of Belgium acquires Congo

1890: Britain exchanges Heligoland with Germany for Pemba and Zanzibar

1896: Defeat of invading Italian army preserves Abyssinian independence

1900: Start of copper mining in Katanga

1880 — 1885 — 1890 — 1895 — 1900

1882: Revolt in Egypt prompts occupation by British

1884: Germany acquires South West Africa, Togo, and Cameroon

1886: Germany and Britain divide up East Africa

1889: Establishment of first Italian colony in Eritrea

1889: Cecil Rhodes' British South Africa Company begins colonization of Rhodesia

1894: Uganda occupied by Britain

SOUTH AMERICA: 1830–1920

IN THE AFTERMATH OF LIBERATION, many South American countries saw power seized by *caudillos*, military dictators. Economies depended on raw materials such as coffee, rubber, and beef for export.

How did economic dependency inhibit South American attempts at nation-building?

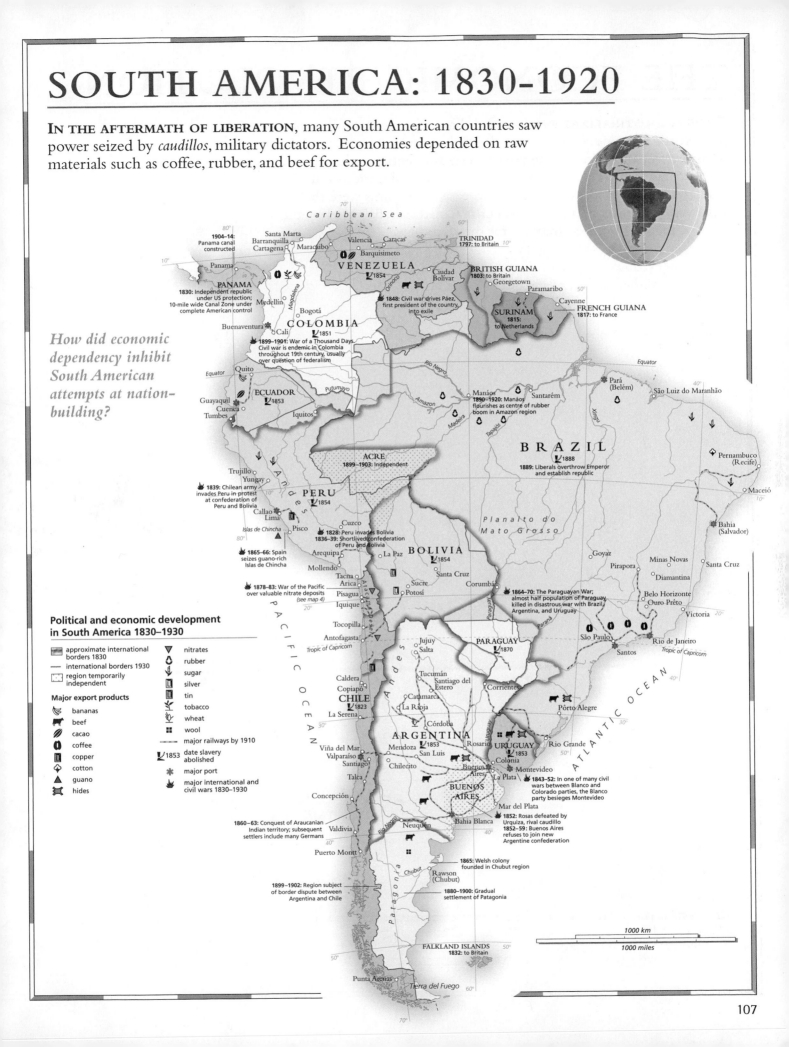

1904–14: Panama canal constructed

PANAMA
1830: Independent republic under US protection; 10-mile wide Canal Zone under complete American control

TRINIDAD 1797: to Britain

BRITISH GUIANA 1803: to Britain
Georgetown
Paramaribo

SURINAM 1815: to Netherlands

Cayenne — **FRENCH GUIANA 1817:** to France

VENEZUELA
Santa Marta
Barranquilla
Cartagena — Maracaibo
Valencia — Caracas
Barquisimeto
Ciudad Bolívar

1848: Civil war drives Páez, first president of the country, into exile

COLOMBIA
Medellín
Bogotá
Buenaventura — Cali

1851

1899–1901: War of a Thousand Days. Civil war is endemic in Colombia throughout 19th century, usually over question of federalism

ECUADOR 1853
Quito
Guayaquil
Cuenca
Tumbes
Iquitos

1890–1920: Manáos flourishes as centre of rubber boom in Amazon region
Manáos — Santarém
Pará (Belém)
São Luiz do Maranhão

B R A Z I L
1888
1889: Liberals overthrow Emperor and establish republic

Pernambuco (Recife)
Maceió

ACRE 1899–1903: Independent

PERU 1854
Trujillo
Yungay

1839: Chilean army invades Peru in protest at confederation of Peru and Bolivia

Callao — Lima
Cuzco
1828: Peru invades Bolivia
1836–39: Shortlived confederation of Peru and Bolivia
Pisco
Islas de Chincha

1865–66: Spain seizes guano-rich Islas de Chincha

Arequipa
La Paz
BOLIVIA 1854
Santa Cruz

Planalto do Mato Grosso

Goyaz
Minas Novas
Diamantina
Santa Cruz

Mollendo
Tacna
Arica
Sucre
Potosí
Corumbá
1864–70: The Paraguayan War; almost half population of Paraguay killed in disastrous war with Brazil, Argentina, and Uruguay

1878–83: War of the Pacific over valuable nitrate deposits (see map 4)
Pisagua
Iquique
Tocopilla

Belo Horizonte
Ouro Prêto
Victoria

Antofagasta
Jujuy
Salta
PARAGUAY 1870
São Paulo
Rio de Janeiro
Santos

Caldera
Copiapó
Tucumán
Santiago del Estero
Corrientes
Pôrto Alegre
Rio Grande

CHILE 1823
La Serena
Catamarca
La Rioja
Córdoba
ARGENTINA
Viña del Mar
Valparaíso
Santiago
Mendoza
San Luis
Chilecito
Rosario
URUGUAY 1853
Colonia
Montevideo

Talca
Buenos Aires
La Plata

BUENOS AIRES

1843–52: In one of many civil wars between Blanco and Colorado parties, the Blanco party besieges Montevideo

Concepción
Mar del Plata

1860–63: Conquest of Araucanian Indian territory; subsequent settlers include many Germans

Valdivia
Neuquén
Bahia Blanca

1852: Rosas defeated by Urquiza, rival caudillo
1852–59: Buenos Aires refuses to join new Argentine confederation

Puerto Montt

1865: Welsh colony founded in Chubut region

1899–1902: Region subject of border dispute between Argentina and Chile

Rawson (Chubut)

1880–1900: Gradual settlement of Patagonia

FALKLAND ISLANDS 1832: to Britain

Punta Arenas
Tierra del Fuego

Political and economic development in South America 1830–1930

- approximate international borders 1830
- international borders 1930
- region temporarily independent

Major export products

- bananas
- beef
- cacao
- coffee
- copper
- cotton
- guano
- hides

- nitrates
- rubber
- sugar
- silver
- tin
- tobacco
- wheat
- wool
- major railways by 1910
- **1853** date slavery abolished
- major port
- major international and civil wars 1830–1930

1000 km
1000 miles

THE ECONOMIC REVOLUTION

RAPID INDUSTRIALIZATION occurred throughout most of Europe and North America by the end of the 19th century. A stable currency and an effective banking system were seen as essential to the growth and success of every industrializing nation. The major industrial nations also began to invest heavily overseas. Their aims were the discovery and exploitation of cheaper raw materials, balanced by the development of overseas markets for their products.

What connections does this map reveal between industrialization and imperialism?

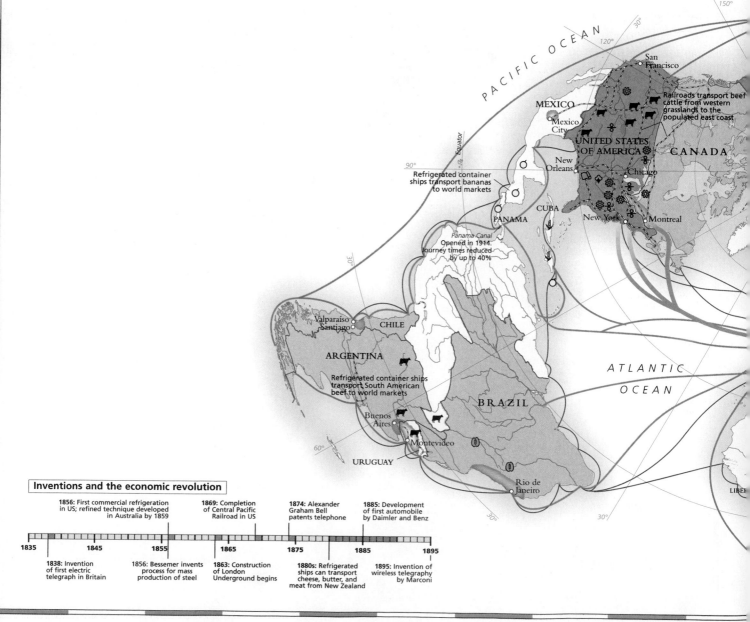

Railroads transport beef cattle from western grasslands to the populated east coast

Refrigerated container ships transport bananas to world markets

Panama Canal opened in 1914. Journey times reduced by up to 40%

Refrigerated container ships transport South American beef to world markets

PACIFIC OCEAN

ATLANTIC OCEAN

San Francisco

MEXICO
Mexico City
New Orleans
UNITED STATES OF AMERICA
CANADA
Chicago
New York
Montreal
CUBA
PANAMA

Valparaíso
Santiago
CHILE
ARGENTINA
Buenos Aires
BRAZIL
Montevideo
URUGUAY
Rio de Janeiro

LIBE

Inventions and the economic revolution

1856: First commercial refrigeration in US; refined technique developed in Australia by 1859

1869: Completion of Central Pacific Railroad in US

1874: Alexander Graham Bell patents telephone

1885: Development of first automobile by Daimler and Benz

| 1835 | 1845 | 1855 | 1865 | 1875 | 1885 | 1895 |

1838: Invention of first electric telegraph in Britain

1856: Bessemer invents process for mass production of steel

1863: Construction of London Underground begins

1880s: Refrigerated ships can transport cheese, butter, and meat from New Zealand

1895: Invention of wireless telegraphy by Marconi

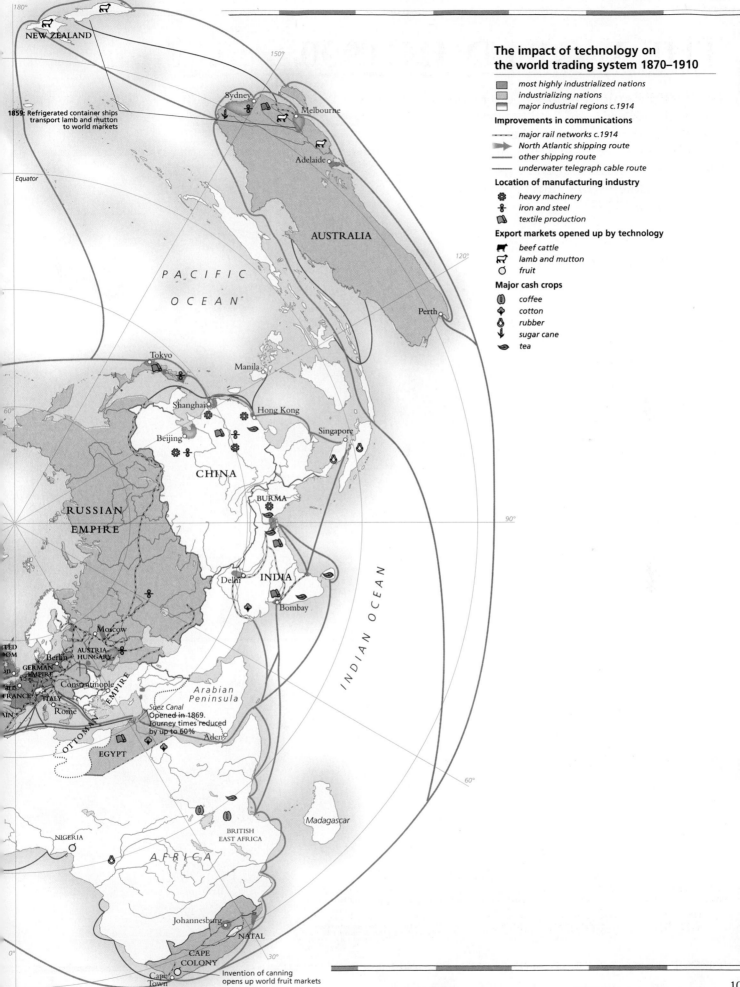

NEW ZEALAND

1859: Refrigerated container ships transport lamb and mutton to world markets

Equator

PACIFIC OCEAN

Sydney
Melbourne

Adelaide

AUSTRALIA

Perth

Tokyo

Manila

Shanghai
Beijing

Hong Kong

Singapore

CHINA

BURMA

Delhi
INDIA
Bombay

RUSSIAN EMPIRE

Moscow

INDIAN OCEAN

AUSTRIA-HUNGARY
Berlin
GERMAN EMPIRE
FRANCE
Constantinople
ITALY
Rome

TED OM
IN
ATES
AIN

OTTOMAN EMPIRE

Arabian Peninsula

Suez Canal
Opened in 1869.
Journey times reduced by up to 60%

Aden

EGYPT

Madagascar

NIGERIA

BRITISH EAST AFRICA

AFRICA

Johannesburg
NATAL

CAPE COLONY
Cape Town

Invention of canning opens up world fruit markets

The impact of technology on the world trading system 1870–1910

- *most highly industrialized nations*
- *industrializing nations*
- *major industrial regions c.1914*

Improvements in communications

- *major rail networks c.1914*
- *North Atlantic shipping route*
- *other shipping route*
- *underwater telegraph cable route*

Location of manufacturing industry

- ✿ *heavy machinery*
- ⚒ *iron and steel*
- ▨ *textile production*

Export markets opened up by technology

- 🐂 *beef cattle*
- 🐑 *lamb and mutton*
- ○ *fruit*

Major cash crops

- *coffee*
- *cotton*
- *rubber*
- *sugar cane*
- *tea*

THE WORLD IN 1900

By 1900, the major European powers had extended their economic and political influence to the very ends of the globe, colonizing virtually all of Africa, most of South and Southeast Asia, and exploiting the fatal weaknesses of China's crumbling Qing dynasty.

Compare this map with the map on pages 102–103. What has changed?

Compare this map with the map on pages 102–103.

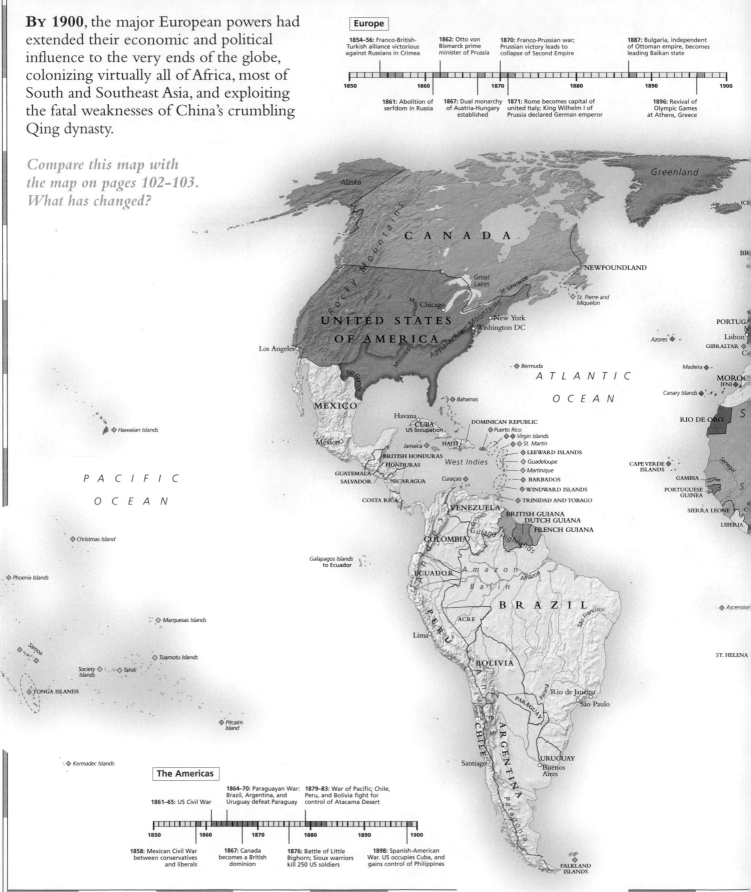

Europe

1854–56: Franco-British-Turkish alliance victorious against Russians in Crimea

1862: Otto von Bismarck prime minister of Prussia

1870: Franco-Prussian war; Prussian victory leads to collapse of Second Empire

1887: Bulgaria, independent of Ottoman empire, becomes leading Balkan state

1861: Abolition of serfdom in Russia

1867: Dual monarchy of Austria-Hungary established

1871: Rome becomes capital of united Italy; King Wilhelm I of Prussia declared German emperor

1896: Revival of Olympic Games at Athens, Greece

1850 1860 1870 1880 1890 1900

The Americas

1861–65: US Civil War

1864–70: Paraguayan War; Brazil, Argentina, and Uruguay defeat Paraguay

1879–83: War of Pacific; Chile, Peru, and Bolivia fight for control of Atacama Desert

1858: Mexican Civil War between conservatives and liberals

1867: Canada becomes a British dominion

1876: Battle of Little Bighorn; Sioux warriors kill 250 US soldiers

1898: Spanish-American War. US occupies Cuba, and gains control of Philippines

1850 1860 1870 1880 1890 1900

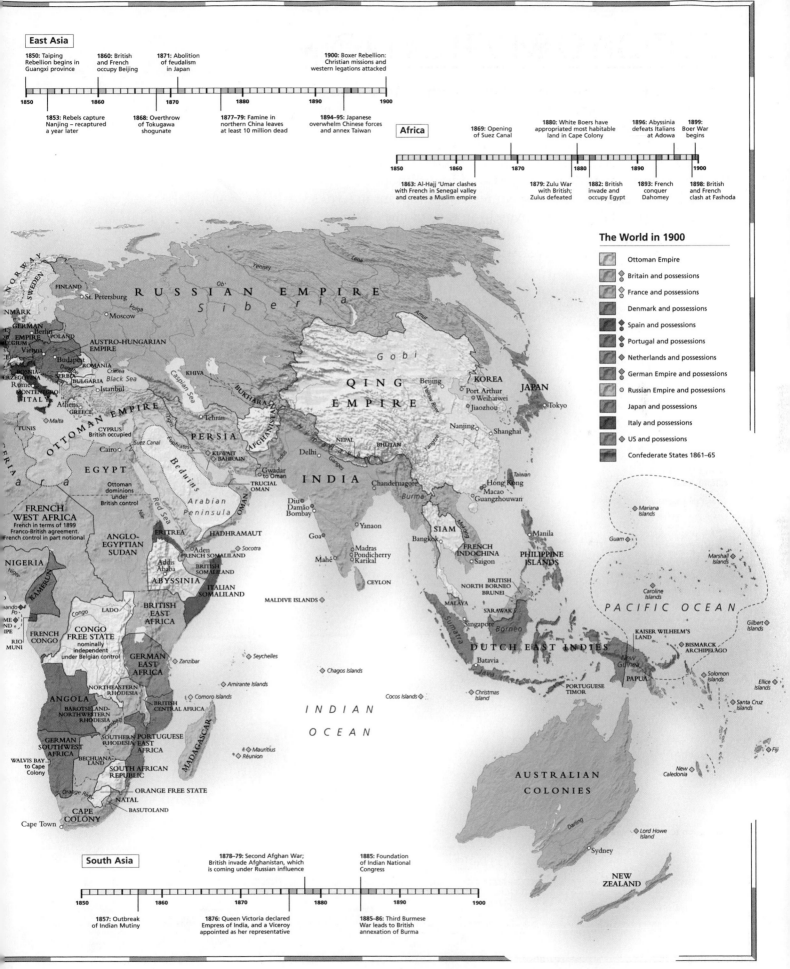

1850: Taiping Rebellion begins in Guangxi province

1860: British and French occupy Beijing

1871: Abolition of feudalism in Japan

1900: Boxer Rebellion: Christian missions and western legations attacked

1850   1860   1870   1880   1890   1900

1853: Rebels capture Nanjing – recaptured a year later

1868: Overthrow of Tokugawa shogunate

1877–79: Famine in northern China leaves at least 10 million dead

1894–95: Japanese overwhelm Chinese forces and annex Taiwan

Africa

1869: Opening of Suez Canal

1880: White Boers have appropriated most habitable land in Cape Colony

1896: Abyssinia defeats Italians at Adowa

1899: Boer War begins

1850   1860   1870   1880   1890   1900

1863: Al-Hajj 'Umar clashes with French in Senegal valley and creates a Muslim empire

1879: Zulu War with British; Zulus defeated

1882: British invade and occupy Egypt

1893: French conquer Dahomey

1898: British and French clash at Fashoda

The World in 1900

- Ottoman Empire
- Britain and possessions
- France and possessions
- Denmark and possessions
- Spain and possessions
- Portugal and possessions
- Netherlands and possessions
- German Empire and possessions
- Russian Empire and possessions
- Japan and possessions
- Italy and possessions
- US and possessions
- Confederate States 1861–65

Map labels

NORWAY, SWEDEN, FINLAND, St. Petersburg, Moscow, Volga, RUSSIAN EMPIRE, Siberia, Ob', Yenisey, Lena, Amur

NMARK, GERMAN EMPIRE, BELGIUM, Berlin, POLAND, Vienna, AUSTRO-HUNGARIAN EMPIRE, Budapest, Danube, ROMANIA, BOSNIA-ERZEGOVINA, SERBIA, BULGARIA, Crimea, Black Sea, MONTENEGRO, Rome, ITALY, Athens, GREECE, Malta, TUNIS

OTTOMAN EMPIRE, Istanbul, CYPRUS British occupied, Caspian Sea, Tehran, PERSIA, KHIVA, BUKHARA, AFGHANISTAN, Tigris, Euphrates, Suez Canal, Cairo, EGYPT, Ottoman dominions under British control, KUWAIT, BAHRAIN, Gwadar to Oman, TRUCIAL OMAN, OMAN, Arabian Peninsula, Beduins, Red Sea, Nile

Gobi, QING EMPIRE, Beijing, Yellow River, KOREA, Port Arthur, Weihaiwei, Jiaozhou, JAPAN, Tokyo, Nanjing, Shanghai, Yangtze, Taiwan, Hong Kong, Macao, Guangzhouwan

NEPAL, BHUTAN, Delhi, Ganges, Indus, INDIA, Chandernagore, Burma, Diu, Damão, Bombay, Goa, Yanaon, Madras, Pondicherry, Karikal, Mahé, CEYLON, MALDIVE ISLANDS

FRENCH WEST AFRICA French in terms of 1899 Franco-British agreement. French control in part notional, ANGLO-EGYPTIAN SUDAN, NIGERIA, Niger, KAMERUN, ERITREA, Addis Ababa, Socotra, Aden, FRENCH SOMALILAND, BRITISH SOMALILAND, ABYSSINIA, ITALIAN SOMALILAND, HADHRAMAUT

ando Po, ME ND IPE, RIO MUNI, FRENCH CONGO, Congo, LADO, CONGO FREE STATE nominally independent under Belgian control, BRITISH EAST AFRICA, GERMAN EAST AFRICA, Zanzibar, Seychelles, Amirante Islands, Comoro Islands, BRITISH CENTRAL AFRICA, ANGOLA, NORTHEASTERN RHODESIA, BAROTSELAND-NORTHWESTERN RHODESIA, Zambezi, SOUTHERN RHODESIA, PORTUGUESE EAST AFRICA, MADAGASCAR, GERMAN SOUTHWEST AFRICA, WALVIS BAY to Cape Colony, BECHUANA-LAND, SOUTH AFRICAN REPUBLIC, Orange River, ORANGE FREE STATE, NATAL, BASUTOLAND, CAPE COLONY, Cape Town, Mauritius, Réunion

SIAM, Bangkok, FRENCH INDOCHINA, Saigon, PHILIPPINE ISLANDS, Manila, BRITISH NORTH BORNEO, BRUNEI, SARAWAK, MALAYA, Singapore, Borneo, Sumatra, DUTCH EAST INDIES, Batavia, Java, Christmas Island, Cocos Islands, Chagos Islands, PORTUGUESE TIMOR

Mariana Islands, Guam, Caroline Islands, PACIFIC OCEAN, Marshall Islands, Gilbert Islands, KAISER WILHELM'S LAND, BISMARCK ARCHIPELAGO, New Guinea, PAPUA, Solomon Islands, Ellice Islands, Santa Cruz Islands, New Caledonia, Fiji

INDIAN OCEAN, AUSTRALIAN COLONIES, Darling, Lord Howe Island, Sydney, NEW ZEALAND

South Asia

1878–79: Second Afghan War; British invade Afghanistan, which is coming under Russian influence

1885: Foundation of Indian National Congress

1850   1860   1870   1880   1890   1900

1857: Outbreak of Indian Mutiny

1876: Queen Victoria declared Empress of India, and a Viceroy appointed as her representative

1885–86: Third Burmese War leads to British annexation of Burma

GLOBAL MIGRATION

THE TECHNICAL INNOVATIONS of the Industrial Revolution made the 19th-century world a much smaller place. More than 80 million people emigrated from their country of origin during the 19th and early 20th centuries. Over half of them moved across the Atlantic to North and South America. In the Russian Empire, movement was eastward from European Russia into Siberia and the Caspian region. Europeans moved south and east to take up employment in the colonies, while indentured laborers from China and India traveled to the Americas, Africa, and Southeast Asia.

What were the factors that led so many people to migrate during the 19th and early 20th centuries?

World migration c.1860–1920

Transatlantic migration
- to North America
- to South America and the Caribbean
- to Europe from the Americas

Other European migration
- to Australia and New Zealand
- to North Africa

Asian migration
- to the Americas and Australia
- Russian migration into Siberia
- Indian inter-colonial migration

- transcontinental railroad
- major exporters of people
- major importers of people

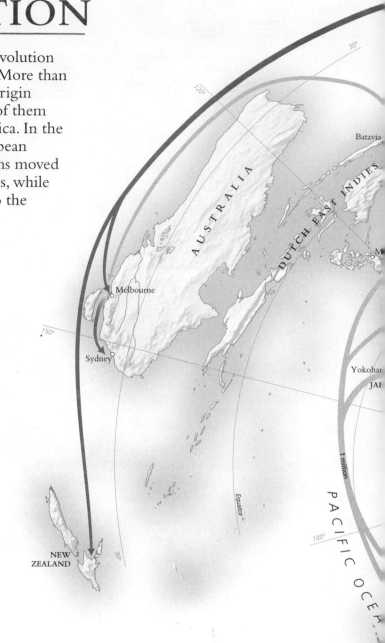

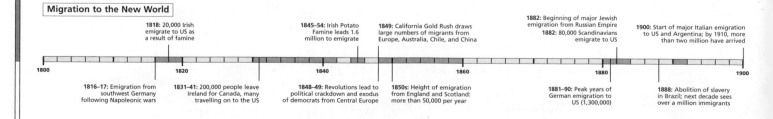

Migration to the New World

- **1816–17:** Emigration from southwest Germany following Napoleonic wars
- **1818:** 20,000 Irish emigrate to US as a result of famine
- **1831–41:** 200,000 people leave Ireland for Canada, many travelling on to the US
- **1845–54:** Irish Potato Famine leads 1.6 million to emigrate
- **1848–49:** Revolutions lead to political crackdown and exodus of democrats from Central Europe
- **1849:** California Gold Rush draws large numbers of migrants from Europe, Australia, Chile, and China
- **1850s:** Height of emigration from England and Scotland: more than 50,000 per year
- **1881–90:** Peak years of German emigration to US (1,300,000)
- **1882:** Beginning of major Jewish emigration from Russian Empire
- **1882:** 80,000 Scandinavians emigrate to US
- **1888:** Abolition of slavery in Brazil; next decade sees over a million immigrants
- **1900:** Start of major Italian emigration to US and Argentina; by 1910, more than two million have arrived

1800 | 1820 | 1840 | 1860 | 1880 | 1900

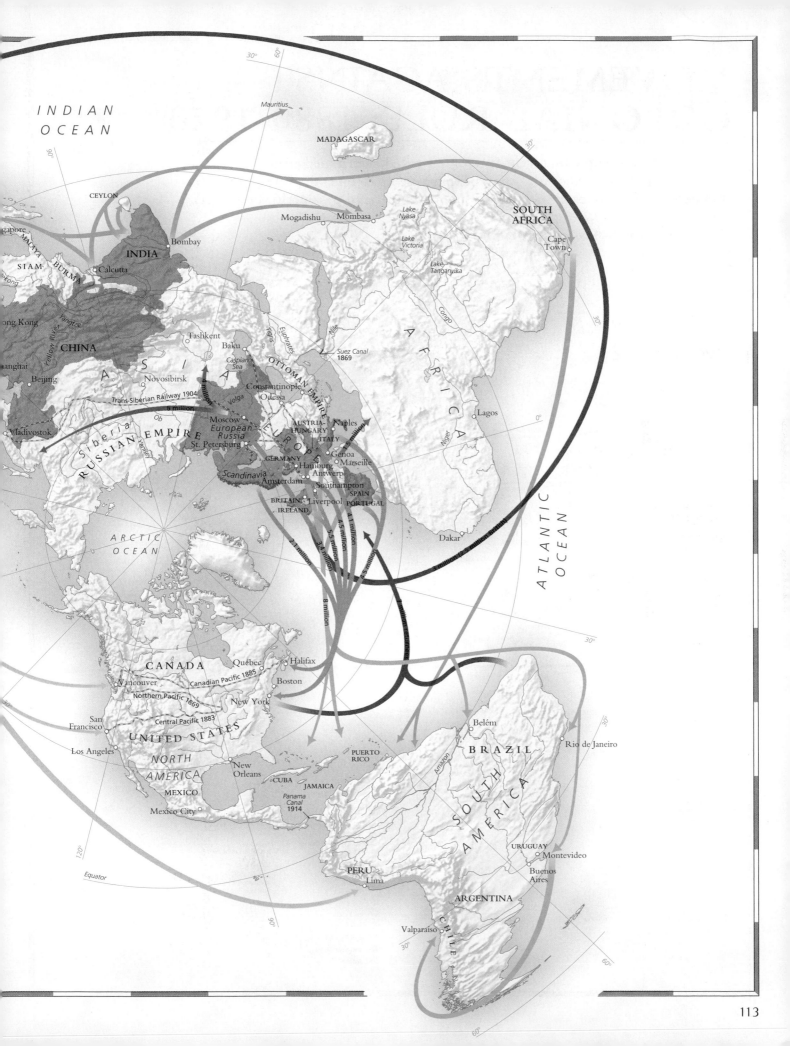

INDIAN
OCEAN

Mauritius

MADAGASCAR

CEYLON

Mogadishu
Mombasa

*Lake
Nyasa*

SOUTH
AFRICA

Bombay

*Lake
Victoria*

Cape
Town

INDIA

*Lake
Tanganyika*

apore

MALAYA

BURMA

Calcutta

SIAM

ong Kong

Yangtze

Tashkent

Baku

*Caspian
Sea*

Tigris

Euphrates

Nile

Suez Canal
1869

A F R I C A

CHINA

Congo

anghai

Yellow River

Beijing

A S I A

Novosibirsk

Ob

Trans-Siberian Railway 1904

6 million

Volga

Moscow
*European
Russia*

Constantinople

OTTOMAN EMPIRE

Odessa

AUSTRIA-
HUNGARY

Naples

Lagos

Vladivostok

Siberia

RUSSIAN EMPIRE

St. Petersburg

ITALY

0°

E U R O P E

Genoa
Marseille

Niger

Scandinavia

GERMANY

Hamburg
Antwerp

Amsterdam

Southampton

BRITAIN:
IRELAND

Liverpool

SPAIN
PORTUGAL

4.1 million

ARCTIC
OCEAN

4.5 million

2.1 million

3.4 million

5.5 million

Dakar

ATLANTIC
OCEAN

CANADA

Québec

Halifax

8 million

30°

Vancouver

Canadian Pacific 1885

Boston

Northern Pacific 1869

New York

San
Francisco

Central Pacific 1883

UNITED STATES

Belém

BRAZIL

Rio de Janeiro

Los Angeles

NORTH
AMERICA

New
Orleans

PUERTO
RICO

MEXICO

CUBA

JAMAICA

Amazon

S
O
U
T
H

Panama
Canal
1914

Mexico City

A
M
E
R
I
C
A

URUGUAY

Montevideo

Equator

PERU

Lima

Buenos
Aires

ARGENTINA

Valparaíso

CHILE

113

MOVEMENTS AGAINST COLONIAL RULE: 1880-1920

THE AGGRESSIVE SCRAMBLE FOR EMPIRE provoked determined armed resistance across Africa and Asia. Local peoples rose up to repel the European intruders, but in most cases they had to submit when faced by superior firepower.

How does this map show the connection between nationalism and resistance to foreign rule?

1916: Easter Rising — BRITAIN

NETHERLANDS
GERMANY
FRANCE
ITALY
PORTUGAL
SPAIN

RUSSIAN EMPIRE

1916: Large-scale revolt in Central Asia

QING EMPIRE

1899–1900: Boxer rebellion

1919–26: Rif war between Spain and Rif and Jibala tribes
1911: Jellaz incident
MOROCCO
1915–16: Rebellion against French
TUNISIA
OTTOMAN EMPIRE
1881–82: Arabi Pasha leads nationalist uprising
1906: Dinshaway incident
PERSIA
1905–09: Persian revolution
KUWAIT

1891: Anti-western riots in Wuchang
1911–12: Chinese revolution

PACIFIC OCEAN

Tropic of Cancer

SPANISH SAHARA
ALGERIA
1912–13: Sanusi war
LIBYA
EGYPT
NEJD

INDIA
BURMA
Tropic of Cancer

1883–88, 1883–1913: Guerrilla warfare against French
FRENCH INDO-CHINA

1881–98: Mahdiyya *jihad* against British and Egyptian rule

1905–09: Terrorist campaigns in Maharashtra and Bengal
1886–91: War against British rule

SIAM
ANNAM
1898–1902: Aguinaldo leads nationalist revolt

1897–1900: Rabih leads resistance against French
FRENCH WEST AFRICA

ANGLO-EGYPTIAN SUDAN
BRITISH SOMALILAND
1896: Italian defeat at Adowa
ABYSSINIA
1891–1920: Sayyid Muhammad resists British and Italian rule

1885–87, 1916: Rebellions against French rule
1885–86: Revolts against French rule
PHILIPPINE ISLANDS
1898–1913: Moro resistance

1884–98: Manda resistance
NIGERIA
1904: Anyang rebellion
FRENCH EQUATORIAL AFRICA
1900: Ashanti rebellion
GOLD COAST
Equator
CAMEROON

1890–98: Bunyoro resistance
UGANDA
1895–1905: Nandi resistance

INDIAN OCEAN

1881–1908: Jihad against Dutch

Sumatra

ATLANTIC OCEAN

FRENCH CONGO
BELGIAN CONGO
1911–17: Tutsi and Hutu resistance
GERMAN EAST AFRICA
BRITISH EAST AFRICA
1888–89: Abushiri resistance
1891–98: Hehe resistance
1905–07: Maji-Maji resistance

Equator

DUTCH EAST INDIES
Java

ANGOLA
NORTHERN RHODESIA
BRITISH CENTRAL AFRICA (NYASALAND)
1913: Risings against Portuguese rule

1890, 1914–17: Uprising by Saminist peasant movements
1881–94: Rebellions against Dutch

1896: Revolts by Matabele and Mashona
GERMAN SOUTHWEST AFRICA
BECHUANALAND
PORTUGUESE EAST AFRICA
MADAGASCAR
1898–1904: Anti-French risings

SOUTHERN RHODESIA

Tropic of Capricorn

Tropic of Capricorn

1904–06: Risings by Herero and Hottentots
1906: Zulu revolt
UNION OF SOUTH AFRICA
1899–1902: Boer war between Britain and two Boer republics

1000 km
1000 miles

Movements against colonial rule, 1880-1920

Anti-colonial uprisings and incidents

- anti-British
- anti-Dutch
- anti-French
- anti-German
- anti-Italian
- anti-Portugal
- anti-Russian
- anti-Spanish
- anti-US

Other partly anti-western rebellions

- Persia
- area of Chinese revolution 1911–12
- — boundary at 1914

JAPANESE MODERNIZATION

By 1900, Japan was a prosperous, sophisticated society
– socially developed, universally literate, ready for
modernization – and keen to dominate East Asian affairs.

*What is the relationship between modernization
and militarization?*

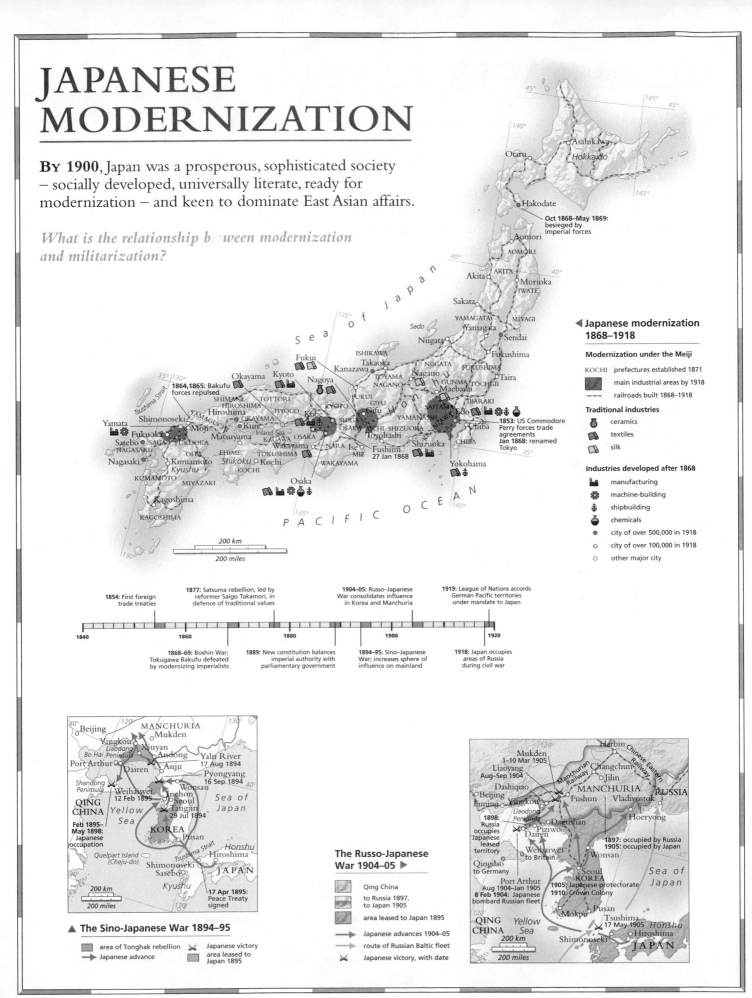

Oct 1868–May 1869: besieged by imperial forces

1864, 1865: Bakufu forces repulsed

1853: US Commodore Perry forces trade agreements
Jan 1868: renamed Tokyo

Japanese modernization 1868–1918

Modernization under the Meiji

KOCHI prefectures established 1871

▢ main industrial areas by 1918

- - - railroads built 1868–1918

Traditional industries

🏺 ceramics

🧵 textiles

🧶 silk

Industries developed after 1868

🏭 manufacturing

⚙ machine-building

⚓ shipbuilding

⚗ chemicals

● city of over 500,000 in 1918

◉ city of over 100,000 in 1918

○ other major city

1854: First foreign trade treaties

1877: Satsuma rebellion, led by reformer Saigo Takamori, in defence of traditional values

1904–05: Russo–Japanese War consolidates influence in Korea and Manchuria

1919: League of Nations accords German Pacific territories under mandate to Japan

1868–69: Boshin War; Tokugawa Bakufu defeated by modernizing imperialists

1889: New constitution balances imperial authority with parliamentary government

1894–95: Sino-Japanese War; increases sphere of influence on mainland

1918: Japan occupies areas of Russia during civil war

| 1840 | 1860 | 1880 | 1900 | 1920 |

The Sino-Japanese War 1894–95

17 Aug 1894

16 Sep 1894

12 Feb 1895

29 Jul 1894

Feb 1895–May 1898: Japanese occupation

17 Apr 1895: Peace Treaty signed

▲ **The Sino-Japanese War 1894–95**

▢ area of Tonghak rebellion

➤ Japanese advance

✕ Japanese victory

▢ area leased to Japan 1895

The Russo-Japanese War 1904–05 ▶

▢ Qing China

▢ to Russia 1897, to Japan 1905

▢ area leased to Japan 1895

➡ Japanese advances 1904–05

➡ route of Russian Baltic fleet

✕ Japanese victory, with date

Mukden 1–10 Mar 1905

Liaoyang Aug–Sep 1904

1898: Russia occupies Japanese leased territory

1897: occupied by Russia
1905: occupied by Japan

1905: Japanese protectorate
1910: Crown Colony

Port Arthur Aug 1904–Jan 1905
8 Feb 1904: Japanese bombard Russian fleet

17 May 1905

WORLD WAR I

WORLD WAR I is one of history's watersheds. The conflict mobilized 65 million troops, of whom nine million died and over one-third were wounded. The war was won by the Allied Powers, but at great cost. The German, Austro-Hungarian, Ottoman, and Russian empires were destroyed; European political and financial supremacy ended; and by 1918 the US had emerged as the greatest power in the world. The disillusionment that followed paved the way for the extremist forces of the left and right that emerged in the 1920s and 1930s.

*Why were the peace settlements after World War I
not as long lasting as those of the Congress of Vienna?*

The Western Front 1914–1918

➤	German invasion of France and Belgium, 1914
▲▲	furthest extent of German advance, 1914
➤	German retreat
▬	line from end of 1914–Jul 1916
– – –	Hindenburg line
▒	gains by Allied powers 1916–17
➤	Kaiserschlacht ('the Kaiser's battles') 1918
▲▲	German offensive Mar–Jul 1918
➤	Allied counter-attacks, 1918
▬	line at the Armistice 11 Nov 1918

Major battles

✶	1914
✶	1915
✶	1916
✶	1917
✶	1918

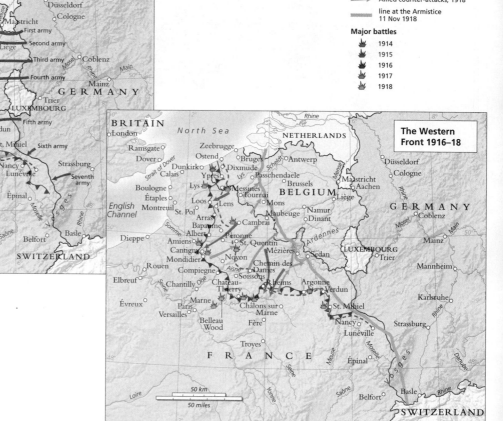

The Western Front 1914–16

The Western Front 1916–18

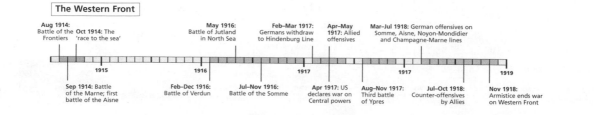

The Western Front

Aug 1914: Battle of the Frontiers

Oct 1914: The 'race to the sea'

May 1916: Battle of Jutland in North Sea

Feb–Mar 1917: Germans withdraw to Hindenburg Line

Apr–May 1917: Allied offensives

Mar–Jul 1918: German offensives on Somme, Aisne, Noyon-Mondidier and Champagne-Marne lines

Sep 1914: Battle of the Marne; first battle of the Aisne

Feb–Dec 1916: Battle of Verdun

Jul–Nov 1916: Battle of the Somme

Apr 1917: US declares war on Central powers

Aug–Nov 1917: Third battle of Ypres

Jul–Oct 1918: Counter-offensives by Allies

Nov 1918: Armistice ends war on Western Front

1915 1916 1917 1917 1919

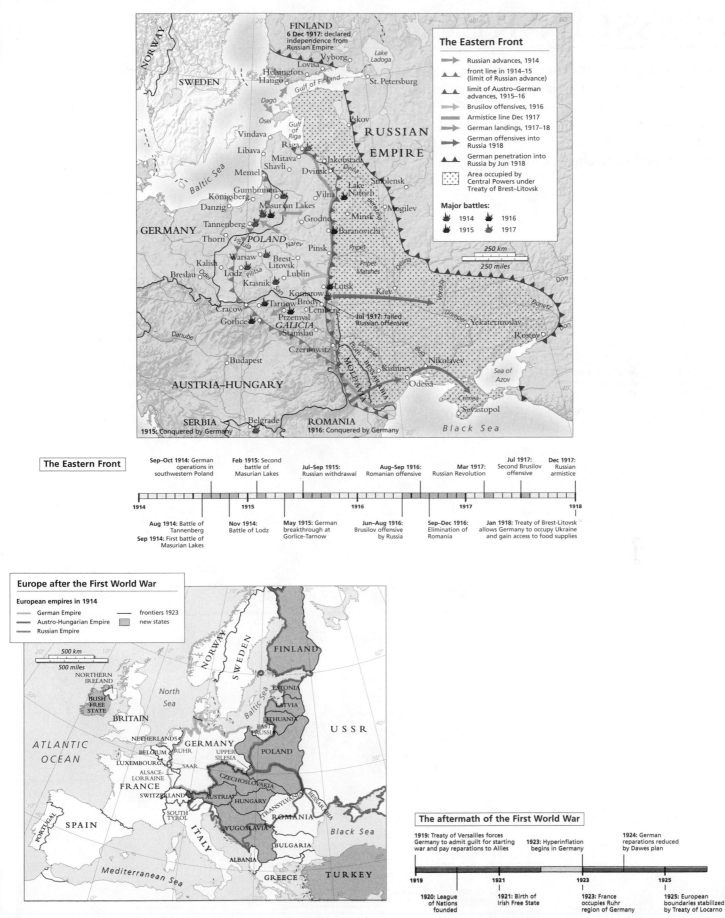

RUSSIAN REVOLUTION

IN 1917, RUSSIA'S TSARIST REGIME, ravaged by war and a failing economy, collapsed. The provisional government that replaced it failed to improve the economy, and in October 1917, the socialist Bolsheviks, led by V.I. Lenin, seized control. Civil War broke out, but by 1924 the Bolsheviks were firmly in control and the communist Soviet Union came into being.

Why did the Russian Revolution have such a profound impact on European politics?

Scale varies with perspective

The Russian Revolution, the Russian Civil War, and the formation of the Soviet Union 1917–24

- the Russian Empire in 1914
- countries/republics which declared independence from Russia in 1917–18

The Bolshevik revolution

- ● towns where Bolsheviks gained control 1917
- ● towns where Bolsheviks gained control 1918

The Russian Civil War

- Russian boundary after Treaty of Brest-Litovsk Mar 1918
- → Bolshevik forces
- → White Russian forces
- → Entente forces

The formation of the Soviet Union

- ★ republics temporarily independent from Russia 1917/18–21
- occupied by Japan 1918–22
- extent of Bolshevik territory in mid-1919
- Soviet Union by 1924
- — frontiers 1924
- --- Trans-Siberian railway

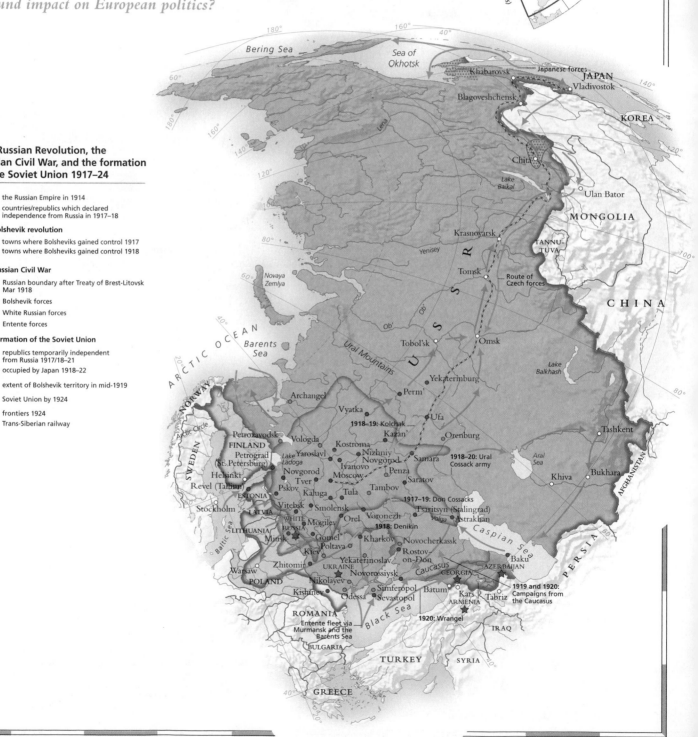

EUROPE DURING THE GREAT DEPRESSION

THE GREAT DEPRESSION, which began in the US in 1929, hit a Europe suffering from the aftermath of wartime dislocation. Industrial output and agricultural production fell sharply, unemployment increased dramatically, and poverty became widespread. The economic and social problems of the 1930s encouraged the growth of extreme political movements, especially in Germany and Italy.

How did the Great Depression in Europe pave the way for future instability?

500 km

500 miles

NORWAY
Oslo

FINLAND
1930, 1932: Lapcia attempt coups

SWEDEN

ESTONIA

North Sea

LATVIA

LITHUANIA

IRELAND
Belfast
Dublin
Jarrow
1931: Formation of the fascist 'Blueshirts'
Manchester
Liverpool
Birmingham
BRITAIN
1932: Oswald Mosley founds fascist 'Blackshirts'
89%
London

DENMARK

Danzig free port
EAST PRUSSIA to Germany

NETHERLANDS
Hamburg
Bremen

POLAND
63%
Cracow

USSR

ATLANTIC OCEAN

Lille
Brussels
BELGIUM
1934: Fascist activity
Le Havre
SAAR
GERMANY
1933: Nazi leader Adolf Hitler becomes German chancellor
60%

Paris
LUXEMBOURG
FRANCE
73%

CZECHOSLOVAKIA

SWITZERLAND
Geneva

AUSTRIA
1934: Failed coup by Austrian Nazis

HUNGARY

ROMANIA
1930: King Carol finances fascist Iron Guard

Bilbao

PORTUGAL
1933: Right wing constitution adopted under Salazar
Lisbon

Madrid
Toledo
SPAIN
1939: Nationalists under General Franco win civil war

Toulouse

Zagreb
Belgrade
YUGOSLAVIA

Bucharest
Black Sea

BULGARIA

Adriatic Sea

ITALY
1922: 'March on Rome' Fascists under Mussolini seize power
61%

ALBANIA

GREECE
Athens

TURKEY

Mediterranean Sea

The Great Depression in Europe and the growth of political extremism

- Fascist regime
- Communist regime
- other dictatorship
- △ more than 20% unemployment by 1932
- ✤ right-wing activity
- ⚒ strikes and riots during the 1930s
- ⬛60% decrease in industrial output since 1929 (1932 figures as a percentage of 1929)

The Great Depression in Europe

	1929: Wall Street crash precipitates worldwide depression	**1931:** European central banks collapse leading to further economic downturn	**1933:** Almost 25% of British workforce unemployed

1925   1927   1929   1931   1933   1935

1923: France invades Ruhr to secure reparations, German inflation soars

1930: Almost 40% of German workforce unemployed

WORLD WAR II

World War II was a protracted struggle by a host of Allied nations to contain and eventually destroy the Axis, a small group of extreme nationalist (fascist) states led by Germany and Japan. Its human costs were enormous, and its conclusion – the detonation of two atomic bombs over Japan – heralded the Nuclear Age.

Why is World War II known as a "Total War"?

7 Dec 1941: Pearl Harbor bombed by Japan

▲ The Second World War, Sep 1939–Dec 1941

———	political boundaries in 1939
■	Axis and its allies in Mar 1940
■	Allies in May 1940
■	Allies by Dec 1941
———	Axis territorial expansion by Jun 1940
———	Axis territorial expansion by Dec 1941
◆	Axis satellites following the German invasion of France, May 1940
☐	neutral state

◄ The Second World War, Dec 1941–Jul 1943

———	extent of Axis powers Dec 1942
■	Allies Jul 1943
■	Axis powers Jul 1943
☐	neutral state
●	Allied base
●	Axis base
☆	major battle

120

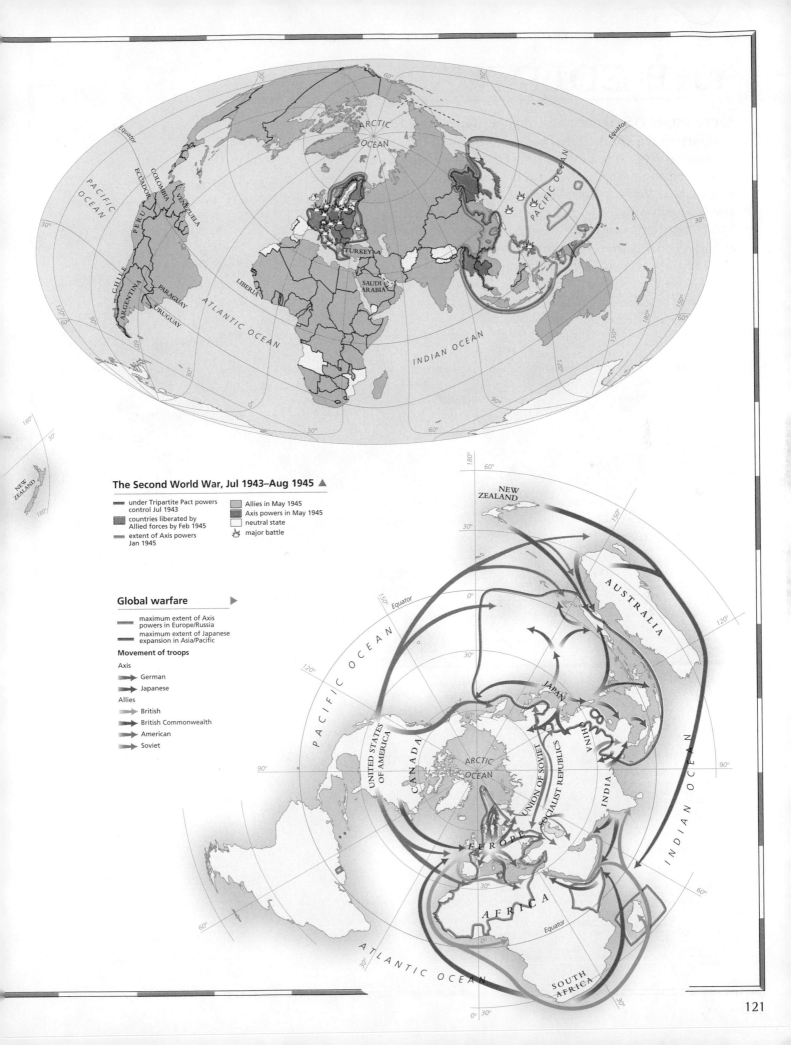

The Second World War, Jul 1943–Aug 1945 ▲

- under Tripartite Pact powers control Jul 1943
- countries liberated by Allied forces by Feb 1945
- extent of Axis powers Jan 1945
- Allies in May 1945
- Axis powers in May 1945
- neutral state
- major battle

Global warfare ▶

- maximum extent of Axis powers in Europe/Russia
- maximum extent of Japanese expansion in Asia/Pacific

Movement of troops

Axis

- German
- Japanese

Allies

- British
- British Commonwealth
- American
- Soviet

THE COLD WAR

DEEPENING US-SOVIET HOSTILITY, plus Western Europe's inability to defend itself, led to the creation of the North Atlantic Treaty Organization (NATO) in 1949; this in turn prompted the USSR and its satellite countries in Eastern Europe to form the Warsaw Pact. Thus the Cold War took shape, with the US committed to a policy of containment and the USSR intent on supporting anti-Western movements throughout the world. North Korea's invasion of the south in 1950 was immediately seen as a test of US credibility.

Why was the divide between Eastern and Western Europe known as an "Iron Curtain"?

The Cold War in Europe

- original NATO members in 1949
- later NATO members (with dates)
- Warsaw Pact members in 1955
- neutral states

1953: Widespread uprisings;
1961: Berlin Wall built

1944–47: Civil war;
1953: Strikes and riots

1968: Widespread demonstrations;
reformist government crushed

1956: Widespread uprising;
government withdraws from
Warsaw Pact, Russian invasion

1964: Nominal independence declared

1955: Allied occupied
partition ends

1948: Tito splits
from Soviet alliance;
1955: Détente

1968: Government
leaves Warsaw Pact

▲ The Korean War 1950–53

	area controlled by North Korean forces 15 Sep 1950
▲▲▲	front line 15 Sep 1950
➤	US forces 16 Sep–24 Oct 1950
➤	Chinese forces Oct 1950
▲▲▲	front line 24 Nov 1950
▲▲▲	front line 25 Jan 1951
·····	cease-fire line 27 Jul 1953

The Cold War in Europe 1947–68

1948: Berlin airlift following
Soviet blockade of Berlin

1948: Soviet-sponsored
regimes established in
Czechoslovakia and Hungary

1955: Formation
of Warsaw Pact

1957: Treaty of Rome;
basis of European
Economic Community

1968: Reforms in
Czechoslovakia
suppressed by Soviets

1950   1955   1960   1965

1947: Marshall Plan
for US economic
aid to Europe

1955: West Germany
admitted to NATO

1956: Uprisings in
Poland and Hungary
crushed by Soviets

1961: Berlin Wall built,
partition of Europe by
'Iron Curtain'

DECOLONIZATION OF AFRICA

MOST INDEPENDENT AFRICAN STATES were territorially identical to the colonies they replaced. The new leaders often became dictators; many governments were corrupt and a number of countries were devastated by war.

How has the legacy of colonialism affected African politics?

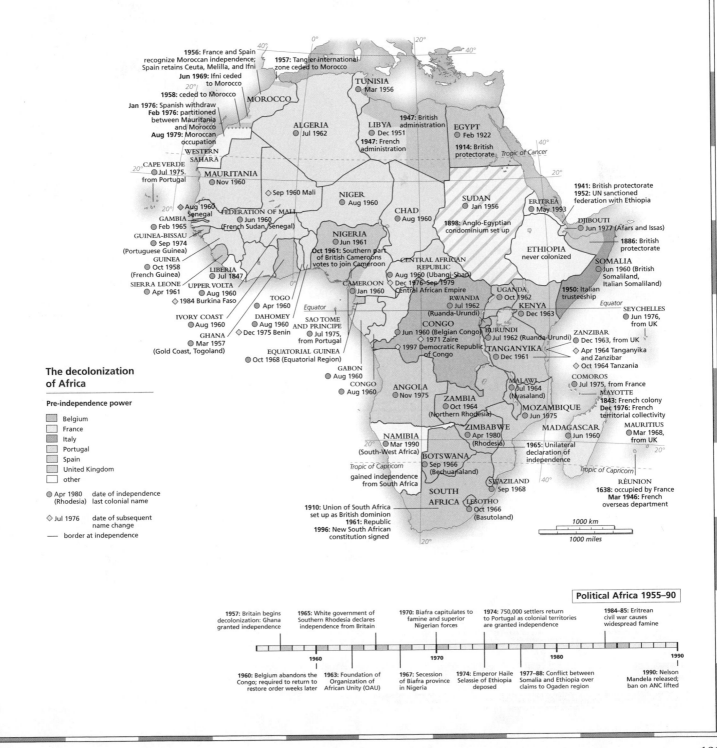

The decolonization of Africa

Pre-independence power

- Belgium
- France
- Italy
- Portugal
- Spain
- United Kingdom
- other

⊙ Apr 1980 (Rhodesia) date of independence / last colonial name

◇ Jul 1976 date of subsequent name change

— border at independence

1956: France and Spain recognize Moroccan independence; Spain retains Ceuta, Melilla, and Ifni
Jun 1969: Ifni ceded to Morocco
1958: ceded to Morocco
Jan 1976: Spanish withdraw
Feb 1976: partitioned between Mauritania and Morocco
Aug 1979: Moroccan occupation

1957: Tangier international zone ceded to Morocco

TUNISIA ⊙ Mar 1956

MOROCCO

WESTERN SAHARA

CAPE VERDE ⊙ Jul 1975, from Portugal

MAURITANIA ⊙ Nov 1960

ALGERIA ⊙ Jul 1962

LIBYA ⊙ Dec 1951
1947: French administration

1947: British administration

EGYPT ⊙ Feb 1922
1914: British protectorate

Tropic of Cancer

◇ Sep 1960 Mali

NIGER ⊙ Aug 1960

GAMBIA ⊙ Feb 1965

◇ Aug 1960 Senegal

FEDERATION OF MALI ⊙ Jun 1960 (French Sudan, Senegal)

CHAD ⊙ Aug 1960

SUDAN ⊙ Jan 1956
1898: Anglo-Egyptian condominium set up

ERITREA ⊙ May 1993
1941: British protectorate
1952: UN sanctioned federation with Ethiopia

DJIBOUTI ⊙ Jun 1977 (Afars and Issas)
1886: British protectorate

GUINEA-BISSAU ⊙ Sep 1974 (Portuguese Guinea)

NIGERIA ⊙ Jun 1961
Oct 1961: Southern part of British Cameroons votes to join Cameroon

GUINEA ⊙ Oct 1958 (French Guinea)

LIBERIA ⊙ Jul 1847

SIERRA LEONE ⊙ Apr 1961

UPPER VOLTA ⊙ Aug 1960
◇ 1984 Burkina Faso

CENTRAL AFRICAN REPUBLIC ⊙ Aug 1960 (Ubangi-Shari)
Dec 1976-Sep 1979 Central African Empire

ETHIOPIA never colonized

SOMALIA ⊙ Jun 1960 (British Somaliland, Italian Somaliland)
1950: Italian trusteeship

TOGO ⊙ Apr 1960

CAMEROON ⊙ Jan 1960

UGANDA ⊙ Oct 1962

RWANDA ⊙ Jul 1962 (Ruanda-Urundi)

KENYA ⊙ Dec 1963

Equator

SEYCHELLES ⊙ Jun 1976, from UK

IVORY COAST ⊙ Aug 1960

DAHOMEY ⊙ Aug 1960
◇ Dec 1975 Benin

GHANA ⊙ Mar 1957 (Gold Coast, Togoland)

SAO TOME AND PRINCIPE ⊙ Jul 1975, from Portugal

EQUATORIAL GUINEA ⊙ Oct 1968 (Equatorial Region)

CONGO ⊙ Jun 1960 (Belgian Congo)
◇ 1971 Zaire
◇ 1997 Democratic Republic of Congo

BURUNDI ⊙ Jul 1962 (Ruanda-Urundi)

TANGANYIKA ⊙ Dec 1961

ZANZIBAR ⊙ Dec 1963, from UK
◇ Apr 1964 Tanganyika and Zanzibar
◇ Oct 1964 Tanzania

GABON ⊙ Aug 1960

CONGO ⊙ Aug 1960

ANGOLA ⊙ Nov 1975

ZAMBIA ⊙ Oct 1964 (Northern Rhodesia)

MALAWI ⊙ Jul 1964 (Nyasaland)

MOZAMBIQUE ⊙ Jun 1975

COMOROS ⊙ Jul 1975, from France

MAYOTTE
1843: French colony
Dec 1976: French territorial collectivity

MADAGASCAR ⊙ Jun 1960

MAURITIUS ⊙ Mar 1968, from UK

ZIMBABWE ⊙ Apr 1980 (Rhodesia)
1965: Unilateral declaration of independence

RÉUNION
1638: occupied by France
Mar 1946: French overseas department

NAMIBIA ⊙ Mar 1990 (South-West Africa)

BOTSWANA ⊙ Sep 1966 (Bechuanaland)
gained independence from South Africa

Tropic of Capricorn

SWAZILAND ⊙ Sep 1968

SOUTH AFRICA

LESOTHO ⊙ Oct 1966 (Basutoland)

1910: Union of South Africa set up as British dominion
1961: Republic
1996: New South African constitution signed

1000 km
1000 miles

Political Africa 1955–90

1957: Britain begins decolonization: Ghana granted independence

1965: White government of Southern Rhodesia declares independence from Britain

1970: Biafra capitulates to famine and superior Nigerian forces

1974: 750,000 settlers return to Portugal as colonial territories are granted independence

1984–85: Eritrean civil war causes widespread famine

1960 — 1970 — 1980 — 1990

1960: Belgium abandons the Congo; required to return to restore order weeks later

1963: Foundation of Organization of African Unity (OAU)

1967: Secession of Biafra province in Nigeria

1974: Emperor Haile Selassie of Ethiopia deposed

1977–88: Conflict between Somalia and Ethiopia over claims to Ogaden region

1990: Nelson Mandela released; ban on ANC lifted

DECOLONIZATION OF SOUTH AND SOUTHEAST ASIA

THE GLOBAL WAVE of decolonization swept over the region with remarkable speed. Independence, however, did not always mean freedom from foreign presence, as Britain, France, and the US all sought to retain control, both commercially and through the maintenance of military bases.

How did the end of colonial rule affect South and Southeast Asia?

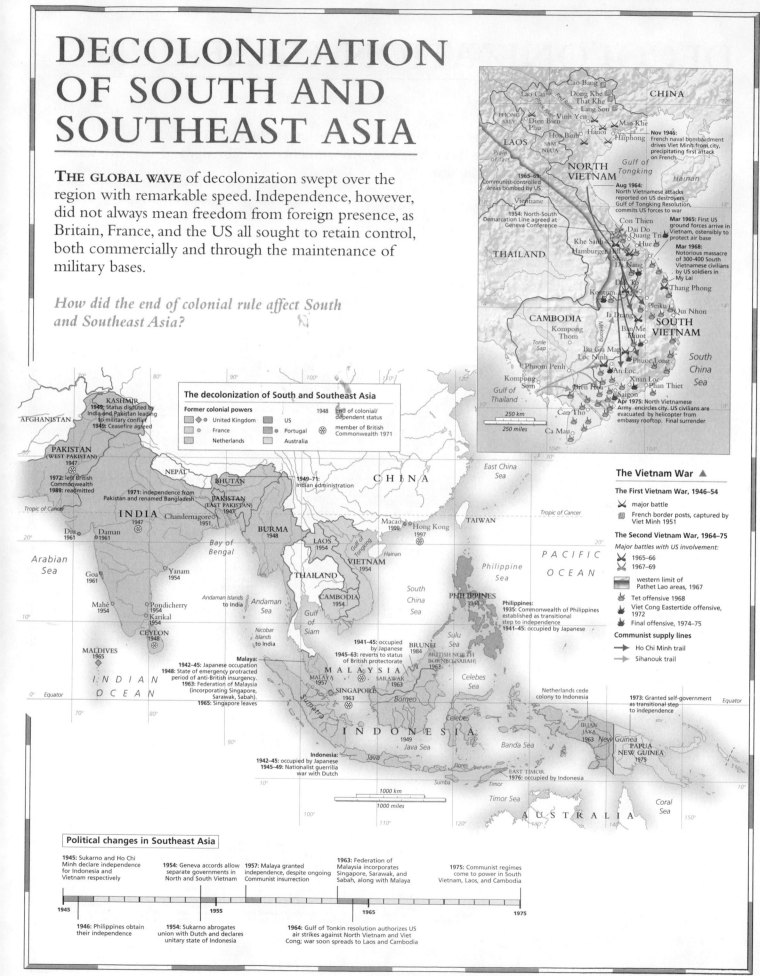

Nov 1946: French naval bombardment drives Viet Minh from city, precipitating first attack on French

Aug 1964: North Vietnamese attacks reported on US destroyers. Gulf of Tongking Resolution, commits US forces to war

Mar 1965: First US ground forces arrive in Vietnam, ostensibly to protect air base

Mar 1968: Notorious massacre of 300–400 South Vietnamese civilians by US soldiers in My Lai

1965–69: Communist-controlled areas bombed by US

1954: North-South Demarcation Line agreed at Geneva Conference

Apr 1975: North Vietnamese Army encircles city. US civilians are evacuated by helicopter from embassy rooftop. Final surrender

The decolonization of South and Southeast Asia

Former colonial powers

◇ ● United Kingdom	■ US	1948	end of colonial/dependent status
● France	● Portugal	⊛	member of British Commonwealth 1971
Netherlands	Australia		

The Vietnam War ▲

The First Vietnam War, 1946–54

⚔ major battle

▨ French border posts, captured by Viet Minh 1951

The Second Vietnam War, 1964–75

Major battles with US involvement:

⚔ 1965–66

⚔ 1967–69

☐ western limit of Pathet Lao areas, 1967

⚔ Tet offensive 1968

⚔ Viet Cong Eastertide offensive, 1972

⚔ Final offensive, 1974–75

Communist supply lines

➤ Ho Chi Minh trail

➤ Sihanouk trail

KASHMIR
1949: Status disputed by India and Pakistan leading to military conflict
1949: Ceasefire agreed

PAKISTAN (WEST PAKISTAN) 1947
1972: left British Commonwealth
1989: readmitted

1971: independence from Pakistan and renamed Bangladesh

1949–71: Indian administration

PAKISTAN (EAST PAKISTAN) 1947

INDIA 1947

Chandernagore 1951

Diu 1961
Daman 1961
Goa 1961
Yanam 1954
Mahé 1954
Pondicherry 1954
Karikal 1954

CEYLON 1948

MALDIVES 1965

BURMA 1948

Andaman Islands to India

Nicobar Islands to India

Macao 1999
Hong Kong 1997

LAOS 1954
VIETNAM 1954
THAILAND
CAMBODIA 1954

Malaya:
1942–45: Japanese occupation
1948: State of emergency protracted period of anti-British insurgency.
1963: Federation of Malaysia (incorporating Singapore, Sarawak, Sabah).
1965: Singapore leaves

1941–45: occupied by Japanese
1945–63: reverts to status of British protectorate

BRUNEI 1984

BRITISH NORTH BORNEO (SABAH) 1963

MALAYSIA
MALAYA 1957
SARAWAK 1963
SINGAPORE 1963

PHILIPPINES 1948

Philippines:
1935: Commonwealth of Philippines established as transitional step to independence
1941–45: occupied by Japanese

INDONESIA
Indonesia:
1942–45: occupied by Japanese
1945–49: Nationalist guerrilla war with Dutch

Netherlands cede colony to Indonesia

IRIAN JAYA 1963

1973: Granted self-government as transitional step to independence

EAST TIMOR 1976: occupied by Indonesia

PAPUA NEW GUINEA 1975

Political changes in Southeast Asia

1945: Sukarno and Ho Chi Minh declare independence for Indonesia and Vietnam respectively

1946: Philippines obtain their independence

1954: Geneva accords allow separate governments in North and South Vietnam

1954: Sukarno abrogates union with Dutch and declares unitary state of Indonesia

1957: Malaya granted independence, despite ongoing Communist insurrection

1963: Federation of Malaysia incorporates Singapore, Sarawak, and Sabah, along with Malaya

1964: Gulf of Tonkin resolution authorizes US air strikes against North Vietnam and Viet Cong; war soon spreads to Laos and Cambodia

1975: Communist regimes come to power in South Vietnam, Laos, and Cambodia

1945 — 1955 — 1965 — 1975

PALESTINE AND ISRAEL: 1947–2007

THE DECISION by the United Nations in 1947 to partition Palestine (which formerly had been under British control) to form the Jewish state of Israel sparked the Arab-Israeli conflict that continues to this day. Since 1948 Israel has absorbed millions of immigrants from Europe and the Middle East, particularly from the former Soviet Union, while tens of thousands of Palestinians have fled their homes.

Arab-Israeli Wars

1947: United Nations partition of Palestine

1956: Suez crisis; Israel, France, and Britain invade Egypt

1967: Six Day War; Israel takes Sinai, Gaza, Golan Heights, West Bank, and Jerusalem

1979: Egypt and Israel sign peace treaty based on Camp David accords

1993: Israel attacks Hizbollah in Lebanon

2006: Israel invades Lebanon

1945 1950 1960 1970 1980 1990 2000 2010

1948: Invading Arab armies repulsed; some 725,000 Arabs flee Palestine

1973: Yom Kippur War

1982: Israel invades Lebanon

1992: First Gulf War, Iraq launches missiles at Israel

2003: Israel evacuates from Gaza

Why is the Arab-Israeli conflict of special concern to Europe and the United States?

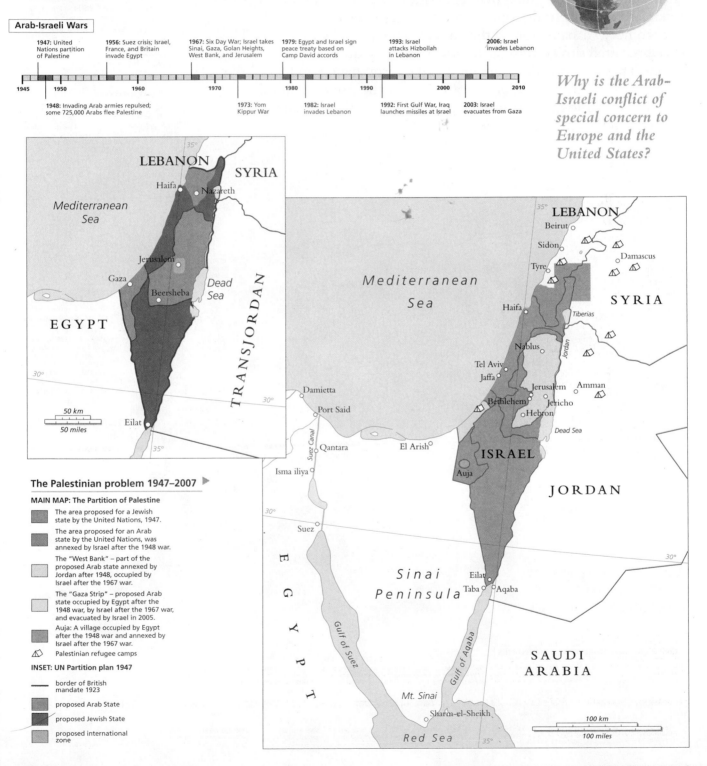

The Palestinian problem 1947–2007 ▶

MAIN MAP: The Partition of Palestine

- The area proposed for a Jewish state by the United Nations, 1947.
- The area proposed for an Arab state by the United Nations, was annexed by Israel after the 1948 war.
- The "West Bank" – part of the proposed Arab state annexed by Jordan after 1948, occupied by Israel after the 1967 war.
- The "Gaza Strip" – proposed Arab state occupied by Egypt after the 1948 war, by Israel after the 1967 war, and evacuated by Israel in 2005.
- Auja: A village occupied by Egypt after the 1948 war and annexed by Israel after the 1967 war.
- ⌂ Palestinian refugee camps

INSET: UN Partition plan 1947

- —— border of British mandate 1923
- proposed Arab State
- proposed Jewish State
- proposed international zone

THE UNITED STATES IN THE 1960s: PROTESTS AND URBAN UNREST

Inspired by decolonization movements abroad, and aided by a 1954 Supreme Court ruling that segregation was unconstitutional, black Americans challenged discrimination. In 1955, a bus boycott in Montgomery, Alabama forced the bus company to end segregation. The success inspired similar protests throughout the South. In 1964 and 1965 Congress passed legislation banning racial discrimination and protecting the rights of all Americans. The 1960s also saw the rise of political consciousness among other groups; protests against the Vietnam War grew in number throughout the decade.

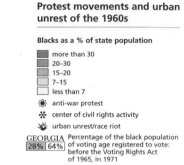

Protest movements and urban unrest of the 1960s

Blacks as a % of state population

- more than 30
- 20–30
- 15–20
- 7–15
- less than 7
- ✳ anti-war protest
- ✻ center of civil rights activity
- 🌾 urban unrest/race riot

GEORGIA | 28% | 64% | Percentage of the black population of voting age registered to vote: before the Voting Rights Act of 1965, in 1971

How is the legacy of the 1960s still a force in American politics today?

Civil Rights and other protest movements

1955: Bus boycott against segregation in Montgomery, Alabama

1961: Student freedom riders go into South to protest against segregation

1963: March on Washington led by Martin Luther King, Jr.

1965: Voting Rights Act increases number of black voters; Watts Riots in Los Angeles

1968: Assassination of Martin Luther King, Jr. sparks riots in 124 US cities

1970: Four students killed at Kent State University, Ohio in protest over US involvement in Cambodia

1955   1960   1965   1970   1975

1957: Martin Luther King, Jr. heads coordinated resistance movement

1964: Civil Rights Act forbids segregation in public places

1966: Race riots in Atlanta

1968: Riots and protests follow Democratic rally in Chicago

1969: 250,000 people march on Washington in protest against war in Vietnam

1974: High Court gives go-ahead to busing for integration of US schools

POLITICAL CHANGE IN SOUTH AMERICA FROM 1930

POLITICAL AND ECONOMIC INSTABILITY have plagued South America since the 1930s. Various factors, including a sharp rise in population and rapid urbanization and industrialization, exerted great pressures on the weak democratic institutions of most nations.

Why has South America been more unstable than North America?

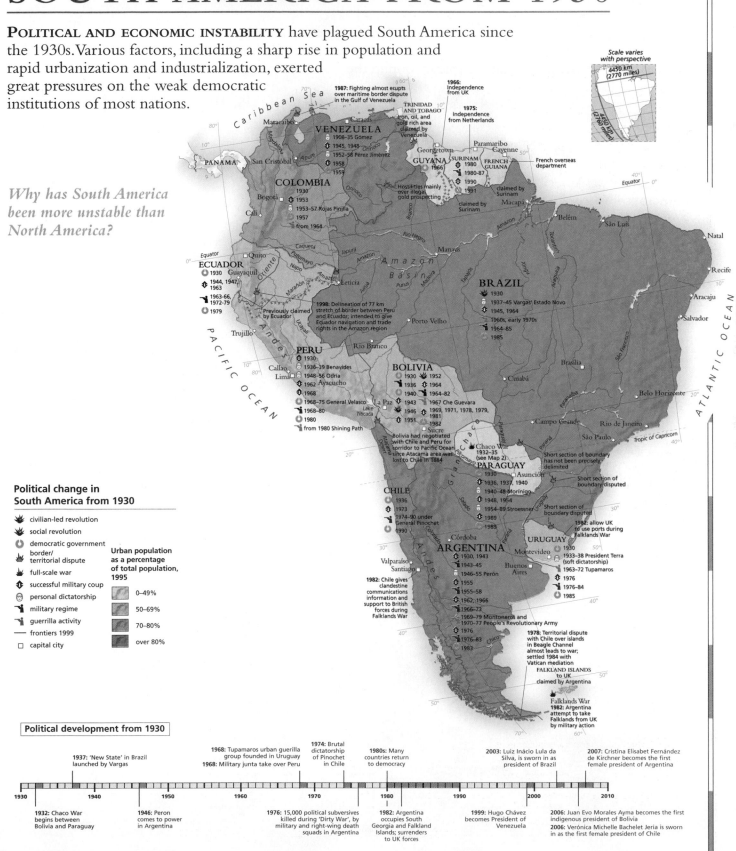

Scale varies with perspective

4450 km (2770 miles)

1987: Fighting almost erupts over maritime border dispute in the Gulf of Venezuela

1966: Independence from UK

1975: Independence from Netherlands

TRINIDAD AND TOBAGO Iron, oil, and gold rich area claimed by Venezuela

VENEZUELA
- 1908–35 Gómez
- 1945, 1948
- 1952–58 Pérez Jiménez
- 1958
- 1959

French overseas department

GUYANA 1966 **SURINAM** 1980 / 1980–87 / 1990 / 1991

FRENCH GUIANA

Hostilities mainly over illegal gold prospecting

claimed by Surinam

claimed by Surinam

COLOMBIA
- 1930
- 1953
- 1953–57 Rojas Pinilla
- 1957
- from 1964

ECUADOR
- 1930
- 1944, 1947, 1963
- 1963–66, 1972–79
- 1979

Previously claimed by Ecuador

1998: Delineation of 77 km stretch of border between Peru and Ecuador; intended to give Ecuador navigation and trade rights in the Amazon region

BRAZIL
- 1930
- 1937–45 Vargas' Estado Novo
- 1945, 1964
- 1960s, early 1970s
- 1964–85
- 1985

PERU
- 1930
- 1936–39 Benavides
- 1948–56 Odría
- 1962 Ayacucho
- 1968
- 1968–75 General Velasco
- 1968–80
- 1980
- from 1980 Shining Path

BOLIVIA
- 1930 / 1952
- 1936 / 1964
- 1940 / 1964–82
- 1943 / 1967 Che Guevara
- 1946 / 1969, 1971, 1978, 1979, 1981
- 1951 / 1982

Bolivia had negotiated with Chile and Peru for corridor to Pacific Ocean since Atacama area was lost to Chile in 1884

Chaco War 1932–35 (see Map 2)

Short section of boundary has not been precisely delimited

Short section of boundary disputed

PARAGUAY
- 1930
- 1936, 1937, 1940
- 1940–48 Morínigo
- 1948, 1954
- 1954–89 Stroessner
- 1989
- 1989

CHILE
- 1936
- 1973
- 1974–90 under General Pinochet
- 1990

1982: Chile gives clandestine communications information and support to British forces during Falklands War

Short section of boundary disputed

1982: allow UK to use ports during Falklands War

URUGUAY
- 1930
- 1933–38 President Terra (soft dictatorship)
- 1963–72 Tupamaros
- 1976
- 1976–84
- 1985

ARGENTINA
- 1930, 1943
- 1943–45
- 1946–55 Perón
- 1955
- 1955–58
- 1962, 1966
- 1966–73
- 1969–79 Montoneros and 1970–77 People's Revolutionary Army
- 1976
- 1976–83
- 1983

1978: Territorial dispute with Chile over islands in Beagle Channel almost leads to war; settled 1984 with Vatican mediation

FALKLAND ISLANDS to UK claimed by Argentina

Falklands War **1982:** Argentina attempt to take Falklands from UK by military action

Political change in South America from 1930

- civilian-led revolution
- social revolution
- democratic government
- border/territorial dispute
- full-scale war
- successful military coup
- personal dictatorship
- military regime
- guerrilla activity
- — frontiers 1999
- ☐ capital city

Urban population as a percentage of total population, 1995
- 0–49%
- 50–69%
- 70–80%
- over 80%

Political development from 1930

1937: 'New State' in Brazil launched by Vargas

1968: Tupamaros urban guerilla group founded in Uruguay
1968: Military junta take over Peru

1974: Brutal dictatorship of Pinochet in Chile

1980s: Many countries return to democracy

2003: Luiz Inácio Lula da Silva, is sworn in as president of Brazil

2007: Cristina Elisabet Fernández de Kirchner becomes the first female president of Argentina

1932: Chaco War begins between Bolivia and Paraguay

1946: Peron comes to power in Argentina

1976: 15,000 political subversives killed during 'Dirty War', by military and right-wing death squads in Argentina

1982: Argentina occupies South Georgia and Falkland Islands; surrenders to UK forces

1999: Hugo Chávez becomes President of Venezuela

2006: Juan Evo Morales Ayma becomes the first indigenous president of Bolivia
2006: Verónica Michelle Bachelet Jeria is sworn in as the first female president of Chile

1930 1940 1950 1960 1970 1980 1990 2000 2010

TIGER ECONOMIES AND CHINESE DEVELOPMENT

WHILE CHINA TOOK THE PATH of centralization and collectivization, between 1960 and 1998 Japan rebuilt and enjoyed an unprecedented economic boom. Spurred by the Japanese example, this success spread around the Pacific Rim, including China.

What factors account for East Asia's economic growth since World War II?

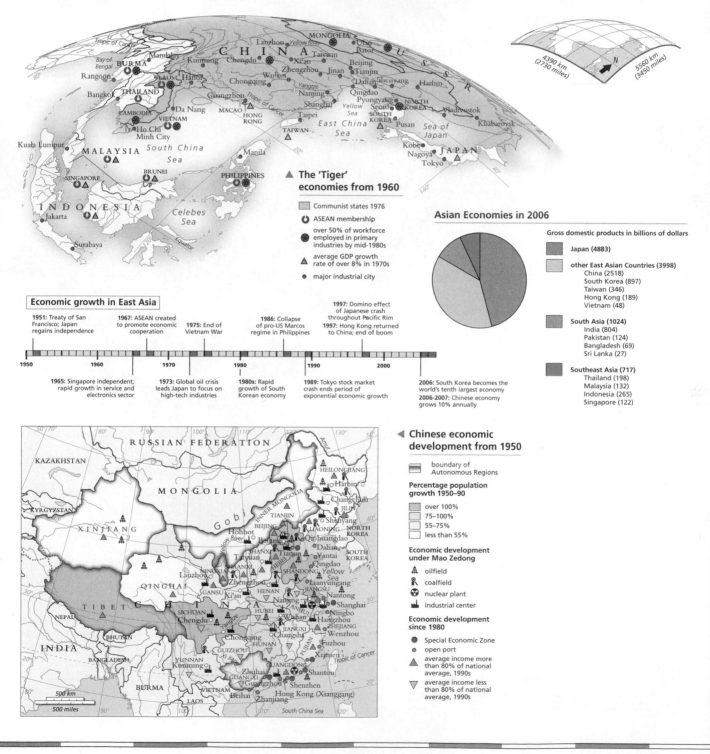

▲ The 'Tiger' economies from 1960

- ▢ Communist states 1976
- ☿ ASEAN membership
- ⊕ over 50% of workforce employed in primary industries by mid-1980s
- △ average GDP growth rate of over 8% in 1970s
- ● major industrial city

Asian Economies in 2006

Gross domestic products in billions of dollars

- **Japan (4883)**
- **other East Asian Countries (3998)**
  - China (2518)
  - South Korea (897)
  - Taiwan (346)
  - Hong Kong (189)
  - Vietnam (48)
- **South Asia (1024)**
  - India (804)
  - Pakistan (124)
  - Bangladesh (69)
  - Sri Lanka (27)
- **Southeast Asia (717)**
  - Thailand (198)
  - Malaysia (132)
  - Indonesia (265)
  - Singapore (122)

Economic growth in East Asia

1951: Treaty of San Francisco; Japan regains independence
1967: ASEAN created to promote economic cooperation
1975: End of Vietnam War
1986: Collapse of pro-US Marcos regime in Philippines
1997: Domino effect of Japanese crash throughout Pacific Rim
1997: Hong Kong returned to China; end of boom

1950 — 1960 — 1970 — 1980 — 1990 — 2000

1965: Singapore independent; rapid growth in service and electronics sector
1973: Global oil crisis leads Japan to focus on high-tech industries
1980s: Rapid growth of South Korean economy
1989: Tokyo stock market crash ends period of exponential economic growth
2006: South Korea becomes the world's tenth largest economy
2006–2007: Chinese economy grows 10% annually

◀ Chinese economic development from 1950

- ▭ boundary of Autonomous Regions

Percentage population growth 1950–90
- ▢ over 100%
- ▢ 75–100%
- ▢ 55–75%
- ▢ less than 55%

Economic development under Mao Zedong
- ⚒ oilfield
- ⚒ coalfield
- ☢ nuclear plant
- 🏭 industrial center

Economic development since 1980
- ● Special Economic Zone
- • open port
- △ average income more than 80% of national average, 1990s
- ▽ average income less than 80% of national average, 1990s

CHINESE EXPANSION AND ASIAN NATIONALISM

Expansionism has characterized Chinese foreign policy since 1949, evidenced most notably by the invasion of Tibet in 1950. In Central Asia, Islam has survived suppression and political change to reemerge as a vital force, accompanied by a resurgence of traditional ethnic rivalries.

How does the revitalization of Islam affect Asian politics?

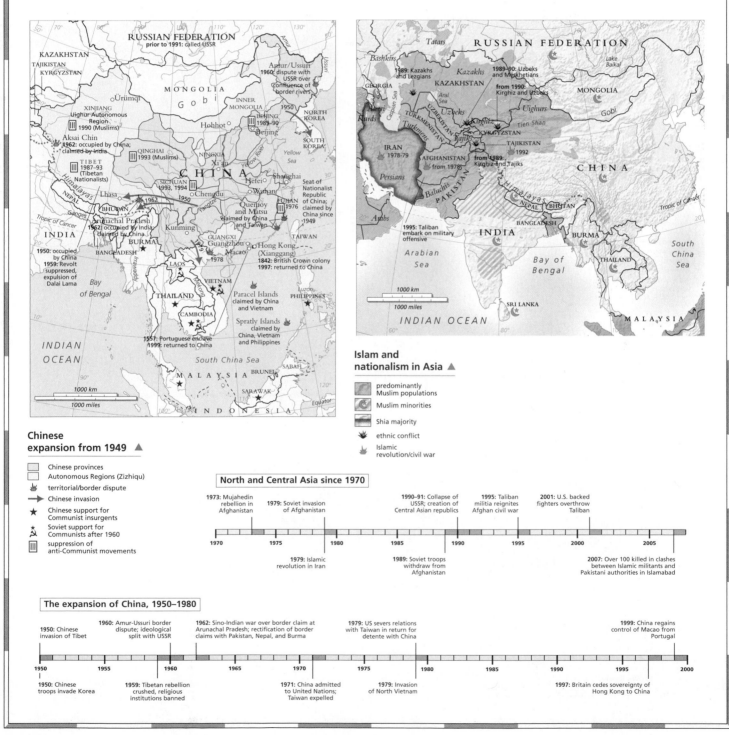

Chinese expansion from 1949 ▲

- ☐ Chinese provinces
- ☐ Autonomous Regions (Zizhiqu)
- ☙ territorial/border dispute
- → Chinese invasion
- ★ Chinese support for Communist insurgents
- ★ Soviet support for Communists after 1960
- ▥ suppression of anti-Communist movements

Islam and nationalism in Asia ▲

- ▨ predominantly Muslim populations
- ▨ Muslim minorities
- ▨ Shia majority
- ☙ ethnic conflict
- ☙ Islamic revolution/civil war

North and Central Asia since 1970

- **1973:** Mujahedin rebellion in Afghanistan
- **1979:** Soviet invasion of Afghanistan
- **1990–91:** Collapse of USSR; creation of Central Asian republics
- **1995:** Taliban militia reignites Afghan civil war
- **2001:** U.S. backed fighters overthrow Taliban
- **1979:** Islamic revolution in Iran
- **1989:** Soviet troops withdraw from Afghanistan
- **2007:** Over 100 killed in clashes between Islamic militants and Pakistani authorities in Islamabad

(timeline: 1970 1975 1980 1985 1990 1995 2000 2005)

The expansion of China, 1950–1980

- **1950:** Chinese invasion of Tibet
- **1960:** Amur-Ussuri border dispute; ideological split with USSR
- **1962:** Sino-Indian war over border claim at Arunachal Pradesh; rectification of border claims with Pakistan, Nepal, and Burma
- **1979:** US severs relations with Taiwan in return for detente with China
- **1999:** China regains control of Macao from Portugal
- **1950:** Chinese troops invade Korea
- **1959:** Tibetan rebellion crushed, religious institutions banned
- **1971:** China admitted to United Nations; Taiwan expelled
- **1979:** Invasion of North Vietnam
- **1997:** Britain cedes sovereignty of Hong Kong to China

(timeline: 1950 1955 1960 1965 1970 1975 1980 1985 1990 1995 2000)

COMMUNISM AND THE EU

THE EUROPEAN ECONOMIC COMMUNITY was established in 1957 to guarantee the economic success of its members, and to develop a political union of states in an attempt to alleviate the risk of war. In December 1991 the European Union (EU) was created, which committed the members to a single currency. From an initial six members in 1957, by 2004 the EU had 25 member states. In 1989, the fall of the Berlin Wall signaled the end of the Cold War and the collapse of communism in Eastern Europe and Russia.

What geopolitical factors are involved in the growth of the European Union?

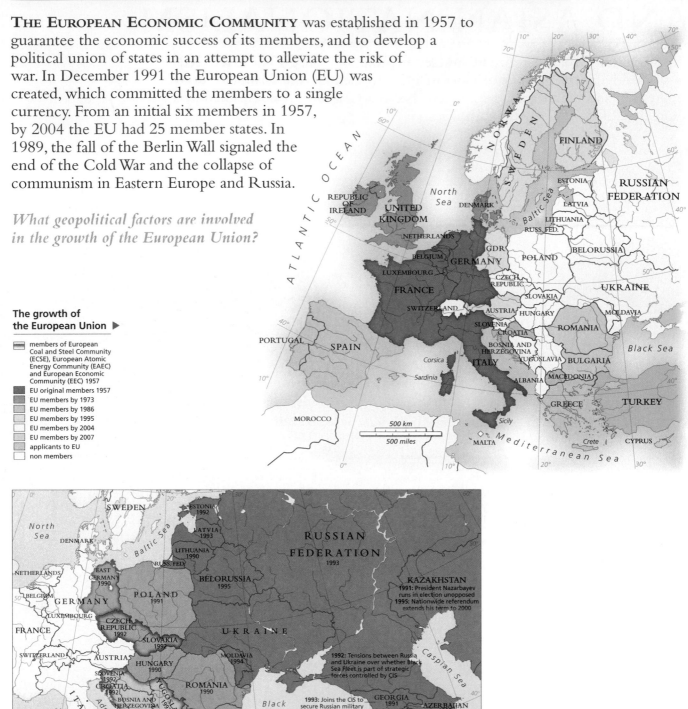

The growth of the European Union ▶

- members of European Coal and Steel Community (ECSE), European Atomic Energy Community (EAEC) and European Economic Community (EEC) 1957
- EU original members 1957
- EU members by 1973
- EU members by 1986
- EU members by 1995
- EU members by 2004
- EU members by 2007
- applicants to EU
- non members

▲ The collapse of Communism in Eastern Europe

- Soviet Union to 1991
- Soviet-dominated Eastern Europe to 1989
- German Democratic Republic (GDR), united with Federal Republic of Germany 1990
- Czechoslovakia to Dec 1992
- Yugoslavia to 1991
- other Communist state before 1991
- 1990 date of first free election

THE PANISLAMIC WORLD

THE WORLD AT THE END of the 20th century was increasingly globalized, reinforced by digital technology and the spread of telecommunications. At the same time, links of ethnic origin, cultural affinity, or religious identity defined many communities, such as Islam, that transcended national boundaries.

The pan–Islamic World

Percentage of Muslims in population

- 91–100%
- 51–90%
- 21–50%
- 6–20%
- 1–5%
- less than 1%

Official status of Islam

- ☾ formally designated Islamic republic
- ● secular state where population is more then 50% Muslim
- ▥ established religion is Islam
- ❋ membership of Organization of the Islamic Conference (OIC)
- active conflict involving militant Islam

Is globalization incompatible with cultural and religious identity?

GLOBAL WARMING: 1976–2006

THE WARMING EARTH. The scientific evidence is clear: surface temperatures are warming at a pace that signals a decisive shift in the global climate. Previous epochal changes of climate, such as the Ice Age that ended 12,000 years ago, were set in motion by natural causes. Global warming today is the result of human intervention, which has affected the average global temperature in the past century, especially in the past 30 years. The Arctic is experiencing the fastest rate of warming as its reflective covering of ice and snow shrinks. In the mid-latitudes there are now fewer cold nights; heat waves are more common. The Indian Ocean and the western Pacific Ocean are warmer than at any point in the past 12,000 years. Unless carbon emissions are slashed, the planet will likely heat up even faster, fundamentally changing the world we live in.

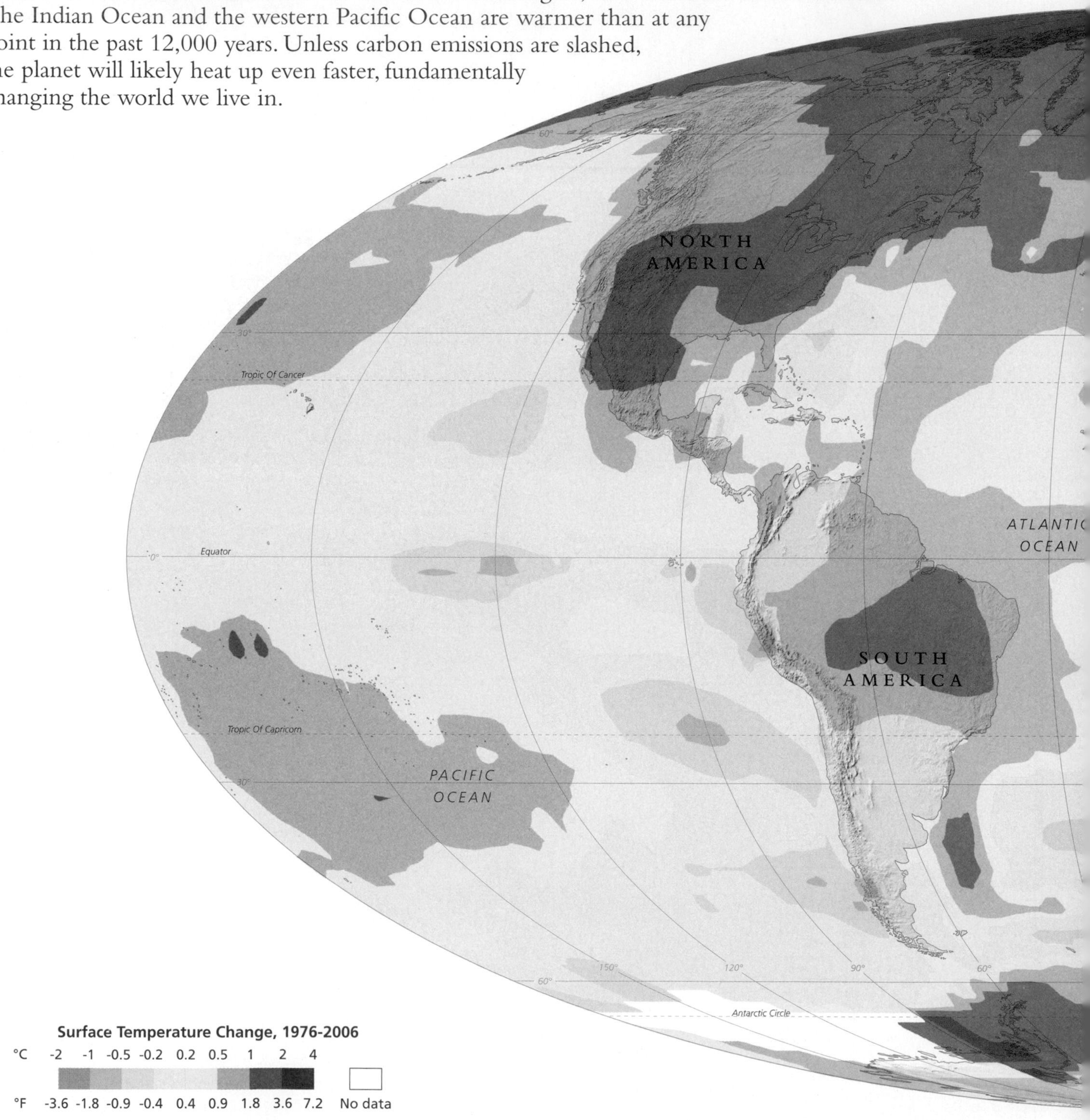

NORTH AMERICA

SOUTH AMERICA

ATLANTIC OCEAN

PACIFIC OCEAN

Tropic Of Cancer

Equator

Tropic Of Capricorn

Antarctic Circle

Surface Temperature Change, 1976-2006

°C	-2	-1	-0.5	-0.2	0.2	0.5	1	2	4	
°F	-3.6	-1.8	-0.9	-0.4	0.4	0.9	1.8	3.6	7.2	No data

What events from the past presented challenges similar to the ones posed by global warming today?

Are there any lessons from these past events that can be applied to today's crisis?

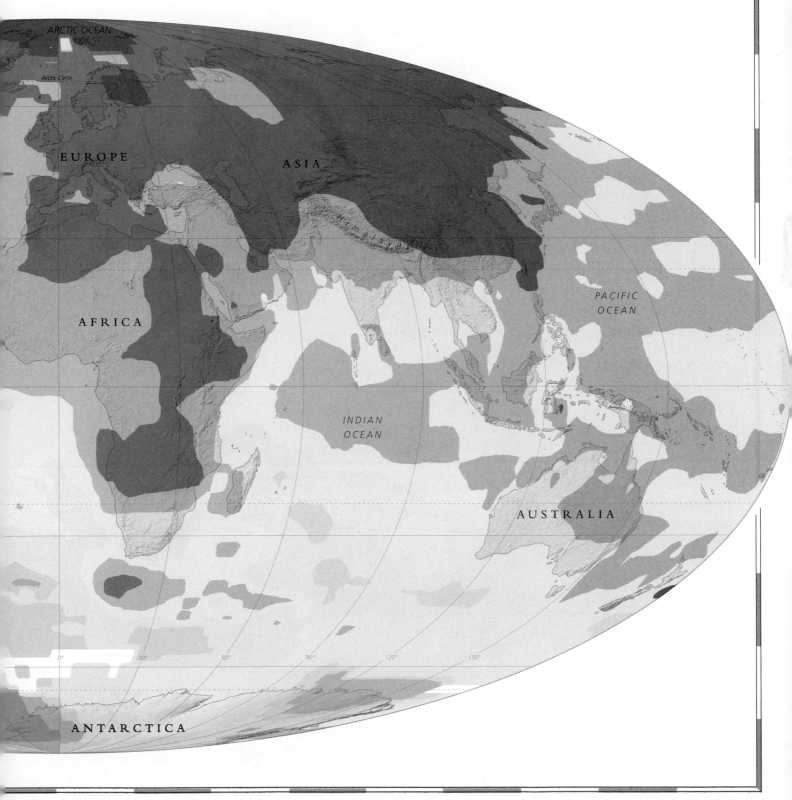

ARCTIC OCEAN

Arctic Circle

EUROPE

ASIA

Himalaya

AFRICA

PACIFIC
OCEAN

INDIAN
OCEAN

AUSTRALIA

0°   30°   60°   90°   120°   150°

ANTARCTICA

THE MODERN WORLD

RAPID POPULATION GROWTH, environmental degradation, ethnic conflicts, global terrorism, and nuclear proliferation mark the beginning of the 21st century.

How is humanity responding to the challenges that confront the world today?

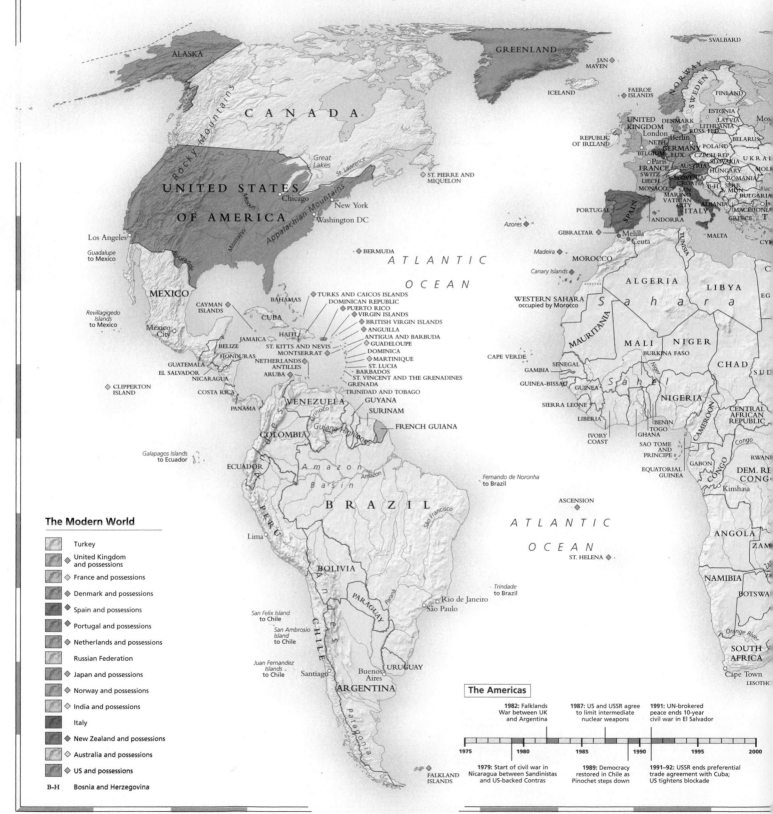

The Modern World

- Turkey
- United Kingdom and possessions
- France and possessions
- Denmark and possessions
- Spain and possessions
- Portugal and possessions
- Netherlands and possessions
- Russian Federation
- Japan and possessions
- Norway and possessions
- India and possessions
- Italy
- New Zealand and possessions
- Australia and possessions
- US and possessions

B-H   Bosnia and Herzegovina

The Americas

1982: Falklands War between UK and Argentina

1987: US and USSR agree to limit intermediate nuclear weapons

1991: UN-brokered peace ends 10-year civil war in El Salvador

1975   1980   1985   1990   1995   2000

1979: Start of civil war in Nicaragua between Sandinistas and US-backed Contras

1989: Democracy restored in Chile as Pinochet steps down

1991–92: USSR ends preferential trade agreement with Cuba; US tightens blockade

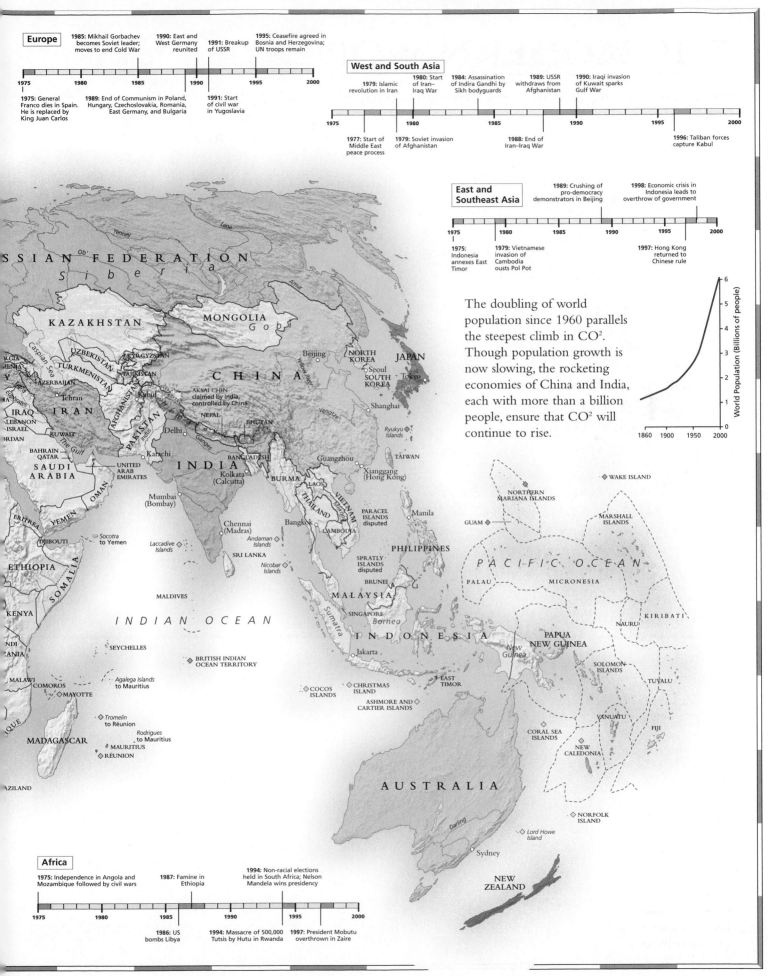

Europe

1975 — 1980 — 1985 — 1990 — 1995 — 2000

1985: Mikhail Gorbachev becomes Soviet leader; moves to end Cold War

1990: East and West Germany reunited

1991: Breakup of USSR

1995: Ceasefire agreed in Bosnia and Herzegovina; UN troops remain

1975: General Franco dies in Spain. He is replaced by King Juan Carlos

1989: End of Communism in Poland, Hungary, Czechoslovakia, Romania, East Germany, and Bulgaria

1991: Start of civil war in Yugoslavia

West and South Asia

1975 — 1980 — 1985 — 1990 — 1995 — 2000

1979: Islamic revolution in Iran

1980: Start of Iran–Iraq War

1984: Assassination of Indira Gandhi by Sikh bodyguards

1989: USSR withdraws from Afghanistan

1990: Iraqi invasion of Kuwait sparks Gulf War

1977: Start of Middle East peace process

1979: Soviet invasion of Afghanistan

1988: End of Iran–Iraq War

1996: Taliban forces capture Kabul

East and Southeast Asia

1975 — 1980 — 1985 — 1990 — 1995 — 2000

1989: Crushing of pro-democracy demonstrators in Beijing

1998: Economic crisis in Indonesia leads to overthrow of government

1975: Indonesia annexes East Timor

1979: Vietnamese invasion of Cambodia ousts Pol Pot

1997: Hong Kong returned to Chinese rule

The doubling of world population since 1960 parallels the steepest climb in CO_2. Though population growth is now slowing, the rocketing economies of China and India, each with more than a billion people, ensure that CO_2 will continue to rise.

Africa

1975 — 1980 — 1985 — 1990 — 1995 — 2000

1975: Independence in Angola and Mozambique followed by civil wars

1987: Famine in Ethiopia

1994: Non-racial elections held in South Africa; Nelson Mandela wins presidency

1986: US bombs Libya

1994: Massacre of 500,000 Tutsis by Hutu in Rwanda

1997: President Mobutu overthrown in Zaire

INDEX

REGION

TOPIC

Agriculture: 12-13, 14-15, 16-17, 18-19, 20-21, 22-23, 24, 25, 50-51, 52-53, 71, 72-73, 101

Biological Exchanges: 66-67, 75

Culture: 8-9, 9-10, 16-17, 20-21, 22-23, 32-33, 34-35, 38-39, 42-43, 44-45, 46-47, 48-49, 50-51, 52-53, 54, 57, 58-59, 64-65, 68-69, 70, 71, 72-73, 76-77, 80, 88-89, 92, 98, 102-103, 108-109, 110-111, 115, 126, 127, 129, 131, 134-135

Empire/Colonization: 24, 28-29, 32-33, 34-35, 36-37, 38-39, 40-41, 42-43, 44-45, 48-49, 52-53, 54, 57, 58-59, 62-63, 68-69, 70, 71, 74-75, 76-77, 78, 79, 81, 82, 83, 84-85, 86, 87, 91, 93, 94-95, 96, 97, 99, 100, 101, 102-103, 106, 108-109, 110-111, 114, 115, 118, 123, 124, 125

Environment: 6-7, 8-9, 10-11, 12-13, 14-15, 16-17, 22-23, 25, 52-53, 56, 57, 66-67, 70, 71, 72-73 75, 98, 101, 104-105, 106, 107, 108-109, 112-113, 132-133

Human Evolution: 6-7, 8-9

Migration: 8-9, 10-11, 12-13, 14-15, 24, 33, 48, 50-51, 52-53, 56, 91, 100, 104-105, 112-113, 125

Religion: 38, 46, 48, 51, 54, 55, 56, 60-61, 68-69, 76-77, 80, 123, 125, 131

Revolutions/Revolts: 42-43, 44-45, 55, 58-59, 68-69, 76-77, 86, 88-89, 94-95, 97, 101, 102-103, 104-105, 107, 110-111, 114, 118, 119, 122, 123, 124, 126, 127, 129, 130, 134-135

Slavery: 88-89, 90, 102-103

Trade/Industry: 26, 34-35, 40-41, 50-51, 56, 64-65, 66-67, 72-73, 78, 79, 84-85, 88-89, 91, 98, 100, 102-103, 106, 107, 108-109, 115, 119, 128, 130

Urbanization: 20-21, 22, 25, 26, 27, 30-31, 50-51, 52-53, 55, 64-65, 90, 98, 127, 128

War: 28-29, 32-33, 34-35, 36-37, 38-39, 40-41, 42-43, 44-45, 48-49, 52-53, 54, 55, 56, 58-59, 60-61, 62-63, 68-69, 71, 72-73, 76-77, 79, 81, 82, 83, 84-85, 86, 87, 91, 94-95, 96, 97, 99, 102-103, 104-105, 110-111, 112-113, 114, 116-117, 118, 120-121, 122, 123, 124, 125, 127, 129, 131, 134-135

ABOUT THE MAPS ON THE FRONT AND BACK COVERS

FRONT COVER

Jaina World View (bottom center)

Jainism, an Indian religion distinct from Hinduism and Buddhism, was founded by VardhamÇna MahÇvira, called "the Jina" (conqueror), who lived in the sixth century B. C. Among other variations from Hindu culture, Jainism has its own version of geography and cosmology. This chart from the nineteenth century shows the world of human habitation as a central continent with mountain ranges and rivers, surrounded by a series of concentric oceans (with swimmers and fish) and ring-shaped continents.

Source: Manusyaloka (The Human World). Western Rajasthan: late nineteenth century. Southern Asian Section, Asian Division, Library of Congress.

Islamic World Map (top left)

At the center of the map are the two holiest cities of Islam: Mecca and Medina. The map shows China and India in the north and the "Christian sects and the states of Byzantium" in the south. The outer circles represent the seas. The manuscript is a cosmology, not meant to be accurate geographically, but only to present the reader with a systematic overview of the existing knowledge about the world at the time.

Source: 'Umar bin Muzaffar Ibn al-Wardi. *Kharidat al-'Aja'ib wa Faridat al-Ghara'ib* (The Pearl of Wonders and the Uniqueness of Things Strange). Late seventeenth century. Near East Section, African and Middle Eastern Division, Library of Congress

Map of Africa from the Cedid Atlas (top center)

In 1803 the Turkish Military Engineering School published a world map that was the first Ottoman map to use Mercator's projection, in an atlas using European geographical knowledge and map-making techniques. Shown here is Africa.

Source: Africa Division, Library of Congress

Polynesian Reed Map (top right)

Traditional Polynesian maps of the Pacific show routes across the ocean in the form of linked reeds between islands symbolized by small shells. The patterns of the reeds enable navigators to identify changes in the ocean swell.

Source: Geography Division, Library of Congress

BACK COVER

Measuring the Yellow River

This pictorial map of the Yellow River is both an artistic masterpiece and scientific source of information. The work was completed by ten famous painters representing China's northern and southern schools. Ordered by Taizu, the first emperor of the Ming Dynasty (1368-1644), the work, executed in true proportions, was an invaluable tool to assess the impact of the frequently flooded Yellow River. The houses on the map indicate the population of the cities, each house representing one hundred families.

Source: Huang He Wan Li Tu (Pictorial Map of Yellow River). China, facsimile of 1368–1378 original. Chinese Rare Book Collection, Asian Division, Library of Congress

NOTES

NOTES

NOTES